THEOLOGY OF
THE LUTHERAN CONFESSIONS

Friedrich Mildenberger

THEOLOGY OF
THE LUTHERAN CONFESSIONS

Translated by Erwin L. Lueker

Edited by Robert C. Schultz

Fortress Press   Philadelphia

Translated from the German *Theologie der Lutherischen Bekenntnisschriften* by Friedrich Mildenberger, copyright © 1983, Verlag W. Kohlhammer GmbH, Stuttgart, Berlin, Köln, Mainz, West Germany.

Library of Congress Cataloging-in-Publication Data

Mildenberger, Friedrich.
  Theology of the Lutheran confessions.

  Translation of: Theologie der Lutherischen
Bekenntnisschriften.
  Includes bibliographies.
  1. Lutheran Church—Creeds. 2. Lutheran Church—
Doctrines. I. Schultz, Robert C. (Robert Charles),
1928–   . II. Title.
BX8068.A1M5413 1986   238'.41   85-47727
ISBN 0–8006–0749–X

1709D86   Printed in the United States of America   0–749

Contents

CONTENTS

CONTENTS

vii

CONTENTS

CONTENTS

Preface

This study of the theology of the Lutheran confessions is designed to fill a need in the teaching of theology. First, it introduces the reader to the basic concepts of the Lutheran confessions. Second, it attempts to describe the relationships of these basic concepts to one another and to indicate their significance for current theological discussions. It is my hope that this will show students preparing for the ministry of the gospel how their confessional subscription will be a help and not a burden to their ministry.

In addition, this book should help the reader to study the traditional Lutheran confessions in a theologically responsible way. These Lutheran confessions are often cited in controversies in the church in a way that reveals an ignorance of their actual meaning. This is especially likely to happen when the person making such a misinterpretation claims to represent the confessional position. I am, of course, not able to teach those who are unteachable. Still, I hope that some others will become aware of the fact that we may, at one and the same time, agree with the confession and disagree with the confessional writings. Indeed, we need to be free to disagree with these historical writings, especially when we seek help from our confessional traditions in responding to the questions that currently confront us.

I dedicate this theology of the Lutheran confessions to Karl Steinbauer. His name represents all those many others who knew what the situation demanded of them in 1933 and the following years and remained faithful to the confessions of their church.

Erlangen
August 1983   FRIEDRICH MILDENBERGER

Translator's Note

Although this book can be read independently of the confessional writings, reading the Lutheran confessional writings alongside this text will greatly increase its usefulness.

The standard English translation of the writings is the Tappert edition of the Book of Concord.[1] It is the only English translation based on the standard critical edition of the Lutheran confessional writings.[2]

Although the use of one of these two texts is recommended, the references to the text of the confessional writings give the standard article and marginal paragraph numbers so that the reader may use any modern edition of the Book of Concord. The endnotes also supply the page references to the Tappert edition (BC).

With the exception of the Augsburg Confession (AC)[3] and the Apology of the Augsburg Confession (Ap.), the Lutheran confessional writings were written in German. The Apology was written in Latin. The Augsburg Confession was presented simultaneously in a Latin and a German version, and in the Tappert edition the translation of the German appears in the upper part of the page and the Latin translation below it. The notes specify if the reference is to one version or the other.

In the introduction to the German edition, the author points out:

The literature dealing with the Lutheran confessions is so extensive that I could not explicitly come to terms with the great number of publications dealing with the topics of this book. This book is intended for the use of students, pastors, and teachers of religion. For that reason, no attempt was made to provide a complete scholarly apparatus and bibliography. Such an apparatus would have conflicted with the basic purpose of the book. I have, of course, identified direct quotations. I take this opportunity to thank all the authors whose work has stimulated my own—even when I have disagreed with them.[4]

In this translation, an effort has been made to provide references to direct quotations and specific references to the literature and to provide a reference to an English translation, if available. The author's extensive bibliographical lists at the beginning of each chapter have been omitted, however[5].

Technical theological expressions have been explained as they appear. The German edition provided a combined glossary and index.[6] When this glossary seemed relevant to the English terms, the material has been incorporated at the first appearance of the text. The index of this book combined with the index of the Book of Concord will direct the reader to additional material in the confessions themselves.

Two terms require special mention. The German word *evangelisch* was the descriptor that the Lutheran Reformers preferred. It is preserved in the English "evangelical" as a modifier of other terms, such as Evangelical Lutheran. In modern English, however, evangelical is frequently used to describe a particular movement in the church. To avoid confusion with that usage, the term "Protestant" has been used except in organizational names.

In addition, an effort has been made to differentiate the German terms: *Bekenntnis* ("confession"), *Bekenntnisschrift* ("confessional writing"), and *Konfession* ("confessional church"). In English all three meanings are often expressed by the term "confession." In this translation, I have attempted to avoid that ambiguity by rendering each German term in a different way. Mildenberger differentiates between *Bekenntnis* as the church's *confession* which may at a given time have been more or less adequately expressed by a specific *confessional writing*. In this book, when it is used in the singular and not capitalized, it should never be understood as referring to the text or even the content of any one or more confessional writings. This usage of the term "confession" must be carefully noted, especially because this differentiation is not frequently made in the English-language literature. The Lutheran confessional writings, that is, the Lutheran confessions, may or may not be valid expressions of the Lutheran confession which is defined independently of those writings. ("Lutheran confessions" always refers to the confessional writings.) The term "confessional church" became popular in the nineteenth century as a designation of an ecclesiastical body distinguished by its adherence to a specific confessional tradition. It is always translated as "confessional church," never as "confession."

Introduction:
Goal and Method

The Binding Character of the Confession

This book seeks to introduce its readers to the collected Lutheran confessions and to give them guidance in their own study of these texts. It does not provide a historical introduction, although it regularly takes the historical context into consideration. Rather, this book starts from the fact that the Lutheran church ascribes binding character to the texts of these documents. This binding character is defined by the constitutions of the various Lutheran churches. I will not analyze this assertion of the binding character of the confession in terms of ecclesiastical law. Rather this character is presupposed in the unde-fined way in which it is asserted in these churches' constitutions.

[In order to signal this distinction, the singular "confession" denotes that which the confessional documents witness. The "Lutheran confessions," or "the confessions," denotes the texts of historically defined docu-ments.—Trans.]

Here are two examples of church constitutions that ascribe binding charac-ter to the confession:

The constitution of the United Evangelical Lutheran Church of Germany says:

Article 1. (1) The United Evangelical Lutheran Church is founded on the gospel of Jesus Christ. This gospel has been given to us in the Holy Scriptures of the Old and New Testaments. The confessional writings of the Evangelical-Lutheran Church, especially the Unaltered Augsburg Confession of 1530 and the Small Catechism of Martin Luther are witnesses to this gospel. (2) The United Church is a federation of Evangelical-Lutheran Churches (the member churches) that

1

understand themselves as being bound to the confession in proclamation and administration of the sacraments, in regulations, leadership, and administration, and all activities. . . . The United Church, together with its member churches, is associated with the other Evangelical [Protestant] Churches in Germany in an association of confessional churches. The members of this association preserve and develop the fellowship that has been given to them in their common struggle to defend their confession. This fellowship was attested by the confessional statement adopted by the Synod of Barmen in 1934. The positions rejected in that confessional document, interpreted in conformity to the Lutheran confession, remain determinative for the work of the member churches and of this United Church.

The basic article of the constitution of the Evangelical-Lutheran Church in Bavaria asserts:

The Evangelical-Lutheran Church in Bavaria is the fellowship of the one, holy, catholic church. As part of this church, it lives from the Word of God that became man in Jesus Christ and is witnessed to by the Holy Scriptures of the Old and New Testaments. Together with the Christian churches in this world, it confesses its faith in the triune God in terms of the ecumenical creeds of the early church. In its teaching and life, it conforms itself to the Evangelical-Lutheran confession, particularly as expressed in the Augsburg Confession of 1530 and the Small Catechism of Dr. Martin Luther. This confession bears witness to the justification of the sinner through faith for Christ's sake as the center of the Gospel.

These formulations assert that the confession or, the Evangelical-Lutheran confession is binding for the churches concerned. This confession is never simply identified with the confessional writings, however. Rather the significance of the confession depends on its relationship to the gospel of Jesus Christ, that gospel to which the Holy Scriptures of the Old and New Testaments bear witness. As a result, these church constitutions refer only to this confession as binding. At the same time however, this confession, including its specific formulations, is the presupposition of the church's life and never subject to its disposal. "The confession is not subject to the regulations of the church."[1] Because this obligation to the confession is the constitutive element of the Lutheran church, the church can only acknowledge its confessional position. It can never enact any ecclesiastical law that will change this obligation to the confession.

The same is true of the pledge that the candidate for ordination in the Evangelical-Lutheran Church in Bavaria makes during the rite of ordination. The ordinand pledges "to preach purely and clearly the gospel as it is given in the Holy Scripture and witnessed to by the confession of our Evangelical-Lutheran church." At this point, we must seriously ask what this "confession of our Evangelical-Lutheran church" which witnesses to the gospel really is. Surely, it is not to be identified with the text of documents that are named in the church constitutions. Rather, we need to ask whether the contents of those documents themselves conform to that confession which the church constitutions define as binding on the whole life of the church. It is this confession that teaches us how to understand the gospel which the ordinand pledges to preach clearly and purely. This question indicates the goal of this theology of the Lutheran confessions. We are going to examine the confession of the church in the context of its relationship to the gospel and to the Scripture.

When we examine this relationship of the confession to the gospel and Scripture, we become aware that the confession cannot be understood as though it were expressed in the text of a definitive statement. This cannot be the case, because the confession is our witness to the gospel. As such it is always our answer to the gospel and, therefore, always bound together with the process in which this preached gospel meets with faith. Certainly, the confession has previously produced some specific formulations of the gospel, such as, "And the Gospel teaches that we have a gracious God, not by our own merits but by the merit of Christ, when we believe this."[2] Such formulations, however, only become meaningful as gospel when they are incorporated into proclamation in the here and now. Because the church only comes into being when the gospel meets with faith, the church's confession is, because it bears witness to this faith, binding on the preacher. This binding character, however, consists in the fact that the confession turns our attention back again to the process of proclamation.[3]

The purpose of this book, stated more precisely, is an attempt to understand what the confession means for this process that calls the church into being. In considering this, we must be careful not to define this process too narrowly. For example, it is not limited to the Sunday sermon. Rather it refers to all those expressions of faith that bear witness to God's gracious acceptance of us in Jesus Christ.

The Theology of the Lutheran Confessions and Dogmatics

The goal of this theology of the Lutheran confessions is thus to understand the confession in terms of its relationship to the gospel that works faith. Since this gospel is the gospel to which the Scripture bears witness, we need to understand the significance that the confession has for the interpretation and application of Scripture. To do this, we must first differentiate the method we shall follow in this study of the Lutheran confessions from the method followed in dogmatics. As I understand dogmatics, it is concerned with the whole proclamation of the church in the present. This may also be described as a concern for the way in which the consciousness of faith objectifies itself in and through such proclamation. Dogmatics then analyzes this material by asking whether and how it is based in the revelation of God through the Bible and whether or not it is meaningful in the context of the contemporary situation.[4]

Karl Barth has described a "regular dogmatics" as one that treats its entire content in a way appropriate to the special task of theological instruction.

By regular dogmatics we mean an enquiry into dogma which aims at the completeness appropriate to the special task of the school, of theological instruction. . . . Thus a regular or academic dogmatics must cover the whole field in respect of the range of concepts and themes that are significant for the Church proclamation, in respect of the biblical witness in which this proclamation has its concrete criterion, in respect of orientation to the history of dogmas and dogmatics, i.e., to the concrete forms of Church proclamation existing thus far, in respect of real and possible difficulties and contradictions that one will find in every individual question, and finally in respect of the implicit and explicit distinctness of the path of knowledge.[5]

This task of treating all possible elements of the church's proclamation, or of its consciousness of faith in a way appropriate to theological instruction is not the task of a theology of the confessions. Although it would be possible to assemble a group of statements from the extensive collection of writings that constitute the Lutheran confessions that would be related to almost all questions of dogmatics and ethics. These statements could even be arranged in such a way that we would have a kind of dogmatics derived from the confessions.

Leonhard Hutter's *Compendium Locorum Theologicorum*[6] actually was such a collection. Hutter, however, intended to provide a handbook that could be used in teaching and never claimed to have written a dogmatics of the Lutheran confessions. Whenever he could not find a suitable statement in the confessions themselves, Hutter quoted other texts, such as the later editions of Philip Melanchthon's *Loci Communes*.[7] This procedure, however, failed to evaluate the significance of each statement in terms of its context in the various confessions. In addition, it did not give adequate attention to the claims that the confessions made for themselves. The confessions never intended to define the normative teaching of the church but rather to provide norms that were based on the Scripture as the criterion by which the church's proclamation was to be evaluated. In presenting themselves as interpretations of the Scripture, they placed themselves under the authority of Scripture. They thus claimed the right to be heard by the interpreter of Scripture.

This distinction between the theology of the Lutheran confessions and dogmatics has—as we might have expected—been applied by various theologians with quite different results. Friedrich Brunstäd saw these two tasks as closely related. His theology of the confession was in some ways a handbook of dogmatics. He attempted to validate this by saying that there is a difference between what the confessions intended to teach and the form of this teaching. By testing the form as an adequate expression of the intention, Brunstäd felt that it was possible to develop a valid and useful knowledge of dogmatics by further developing the confessions.[8] It seems to me, however, that we can take for granted that anyone who understands the confessions will make this distinction between the teaching intended by the individual texts and of the con-

4

fessions and the form in which they present that teaching. We must make such a distinction whenever we, for ourselves and for our time, try to replicate the process of thinking by which the confessions reached their conclusions—even in those situations in which our critical evaluation of the confessions' own intention leads us to conclude that their intention is not appropriate to our dogmatic task.

Edmund Schlink more clearly differentiated his theology of the Lutheran confessions from a dogmatics. Schlink emphasized both the normative character of the confessions as the standard by which a dogmatics was to be measured and the contemporary relevance of a dogmatics.

> Two facts must here be considered: (a) The Confessions are the model of all church doctrine, including all dogmatic endeavor, which teachers of the church undertake. . . . As the voice of the church, the Confessions have more authority than the voice of an individual. (b) On the other hand, the norm for dogmatics is not the Confession, but solely the Holy Scriptures. Dogmatics, like the Confession, must teach the summary of Scripture. Thus, unlike a theology of the Confessions, dogmatics has the ever-new task of measuring the exegesis of the Confessions by the Scriptures through the process of retracing their exegesis, and of teaching the doctrine of the church in the act of expounding the Scripture.[9]

Holsten Fagerberg's study of the Lutheran confessions[10] was more historically oriented than those of Schlink and Brunstäd. This shows itself in the fact that he does not take the Formula of Concord into account.

In spite of these differences in approach, however, these three modern studies of the theology of the Lutheran confessions present the content of the confessions in a systematic form, the outline of which corresponds to the arrangement of the articles of the Augsburg Confession. They preserve the form of a dogmatics at least insofar as they begin by collecting the statements about Scripture and the confession. Then they describe statements about individual doctrines, beginning with the doctrine of God.

In writing this theology of the Lutheran confessions, I have attempted to so maintain the distinction between it and a dogmatics that I could clearly emphasize the actual content of the confessions. I have not attempted to arrange the material "systematically," that is, not in the order that I would follow if I were writing a dogmatics. Rather, I have attempted to focus on the decisions actually made in the confession and the results of these decisions. My presentation seeks to clarify these decisions and to indicate their implications.

In considering the implications of the decisions made in the confessions, we today must give special consideration to the increasingly important question about the unity of the church. It will certainly not be adequate simply to emphasize the claim of our own confession to be ecumenical and then to retreat behind the boundaries of our own confessional churches. Rather, we will need to consider the historically determined nature of such boundaries and take very seriously our own goals of increasing church fellowship. Obviously, we shall not be able to do that by simply ignoring the previously established boundaries. We must first understand and appropriate our own heritage and then offer it as a relevant contribution to the conciliar process of the ecumenical movement.

1

The Confession and
the Confessional Churches

The key words in the title of this chapter, "confession" (*Bekenntnis*) and "confessional churches" (*Konfession*), indicate the problem which now confronts us.[1] Because the confession is the Christian confession, it is always the confession of our faith in Christ (Rom. 10:9). This confession must be stated differently at different times—differently, for example, in the fourth, sixteenth, and twentieth centuries. Yet, because Jesus Christ, whom this confession acknowledges as Lord, is the one head of his one body, this confession must also be the unanimous answer of the one church to the one gospel that is always the same in every age. The problem is that this unquestionably valid conclusion that the confession is unanimous is contradicted by the real plurality of the confessional churches.

It might seem that the variety of these confessional churches simply corresponds to the differing forms in which each teaches the single truth. That easy solution is, however, disproved by the fact that the confessional churches explicitly contradict one another in their statements of what they confess and what they condemn. We must constantly come to terms with this self-contradiction of the church: Those who are united in a common confession are in actuality separated by the very real disagreements of their confessional statements.

For example, Lutheran pastors in Germany at the time of their ordination promise "to preach clearly and purely the gospel as it is given in the Holy Scripture and witnessed to by the confession of the Evangelical Lutheran church." Does this specific definition in terms of the confession of the Evangelical-Lutheran church mean that the other elements are also defined in

7

such a specific way—as though there were an Evangelical-Lutheran gospel that is preached on the basis of Luther's translation of the Bible. That it obviously not the meaning. For that reason, we need to be clear from the very beginning that our study of the gospel as witnessed to by the confession is a contradiction in terms. This contradiction lies in the effort to comprehend a universal claim in a particular tradition. Only by remaining aware of this underlying contradiction will we be able to escape the danger of prematurely ending our search for the Evangelical-Lutheran confessions' version of the confession, concluding that our own tradition is the one true expression of the confession.

THE BOOK OF CONCORD
IN ITS HISTORICAL CONTEXT

The Historical Necessity of the Development of a Lutheran Confessional Church

The term "confessional church" is obviously connected in some way to the confession. These are churches that developed as a result of the religious controversies of the sixteenth century—most obviously the Roman Catholic, the Lutheran, and the Reformed. Although the Eastern Orthodox Church was almost totally unaffected by the sixteenth-century religious controversies, we may describe it as a fourth confessional church. In any case, church historians who study the confessional churches usually include the Orthodox church in their studies. It is also certain that the publication of the Book of Concord in 1580—the fiftieth anniversary of the Augsburg Confession—was not the most significant factor in the development of a Lutheran confessional church. More likely, that distinction belongs to the Religious Peace of Augsburg of 1555.[2]

This development of the Lutheran confessional church was itself a reaction to the Roman Catholic reforms. As part of that reform movement, the Council of Trent (1545–63) established Tridentine Catholicism as the distinct form of the Roman Catholic confessional church, thereby differentiating itself from the Protestant Reformation. Against this background, the publication of the Book of Concord in 1580 can now be described as an important stage in the development of the Lutheran confessional church. Lutheranism thereby established its boundaries, separating itself not only from Roman Catholicism but also from Calvinism. Calvinism defined itself and absorbed the Zwinglian tradition by the formulation of the *Consensus Tigurinus* (Consensus of Zurich) in 1549.[3]

This development of confessional churches became unavoidable as soon as it was clear that there was no way of overcoming the schisms in the church. The attempt to find a political solution to the problem within the confines of the German Empire failed when the Smalcald War, an attempt to suppress the Protestant movement by military force, proved unsuccessful. The attempt to resolve the religious controversies through theological dialogues had also failed. When the council—which so many had so often demanded—was finally convened, it could introduce reforms of Roman Catholicism; however, it could not provide the context for reaching an equitable resolution of the conflicts that had resulted from the Protestant Reformation.

Thus the separate confessional churches developed between the poles of the Council of Trent on one hand and the Religious Peace of Augsburg on the other. Under these pressures, the Lutherans in the various territorial churches were each going their own way until the development of the Lutheran confessional church began to create a minimal unity. As a result, the formulation of the Lutheran confession in the Book of Concord and in the Formula of Concord, an explanation of the right interpretation of the Augsburg Confession, was from the very beginning burdened by the need of this developing confessional church to express its own individuality. The Lutheran confessional church was consequently not able to maintain the ecumenical claim to represent the position of the whole church. Given the fact that not even all the Lutheran territories could be convinced to accept the Book of Concord, Lutherans were particularly well aware of the limited significance of any doctrinal agreement. The only remnant of the original claim of the Augsburg Confession to represent the position of the whole church was the Lutherans' rejection of any doctrinal statements that differed from the Lutheran formulation and would therefore hinder the unification of the whole church on the basis of the Lutheran statement of doctrine.

The immediate purpose of the Formula of Concord and the Book of Concord was to resolve the doctrinal controversies within Lutheranism.[4] The development of the Formula of Concord was characterized by the effort to set limits to the mediating effects of the Melanchthonian tradition. A side effect was that the boundaries with Calvinism were even more sharply defined. The motivating factors in this whole process were as much political as religious. It was the fate of the Reformation in Germany to become increasingly a conflict among the estates of the empire. It had begun as a popular movement, but it was completed, or, as the case might be, politically suppressed by the Catholic Reformation, through the growing political power of the territorial princes.

As a result, the development of the Formula of Concord was primarily burdened by two political problems. First, the Religious Peace of Augsburg was valid only for the supporters of the Roman Church and those who subscribed to the Augsburg Confession. The Reformed territories, as a matter of political reality, also enjoyed the protection of this treaty of peace. Understandably, however, they sought to establish their legal right to its benefits by supporting those revisions of the Augsburg Confession, such as the altered text *(Variata)* of 1540.[5] They could do this because these revisions contained a compromise statement of the doctrine of the Lord's Supper. This, in turn, however, also justified the claims of the papal[6] theologians that there were hardly two theologians of the Reformation who taught the same way. In response, the Lutherans sought to define their position in terms of the Unaltered Augsburg Confession of 1530. This is still the Lutheran position.[7] This insistence on pure Lutheran teaching made it difficult to maintain the political solidarity of Protestantism.

These realities had implications not only for the German Empire, but also for all of Europe. The violent conflict over the Reformation, which had been temporarily ended by the Religious Peace of Augsburg, was only one part of the much larger conflicts of the time. These conflicts were basically power struggles, but the religious dimensions were also important. The wars against the Huguenots in France, the struggles of the Netherlands for freedom from Spain, and England's efforts to maintain its independence from Spanish influence by its ongoing conflicts with Spain made an alliance of the Protestants against the threats of the Roman Catholic powers seem attractive. The Formula of Concord's sharp rejection of Calvinism made it difficult for the Lutherans to participate in such an alliance. Anyone who was aware of these political implications—for example, the leaders of Hesse—had to be reluctant to participate in this effort to unite the German Lutherans.

The Formula of Concord's rejection of Calvinism had other effects beyond this frustration of the possible political benefits of a Protestant alliance. Its condemnation of the Melanchthonian wing of the Lutheran Reformation also required Lutherans to reject their own past. The theologians who supported the Formula of Concord, for example, Martin Chemnitz, had been trained in the Melanchthonian tradition. And the most distinguished signer of the Formula of Concord, Elector Ludwig of the Palatinate, had only begun the restoration of Lutheranism in the Palatinate in 1576. His father, Elector Friedrich, had supported the Calvinist Reformation in this territory and had supported the development of the Heidelberg Catechism.[8] Lutherans could not be united without clearly drawing the boundaries between Lutheranism and Calvinism. In drawing them as sharply as they did, Lutherans did not choose the easiest possible solution.

The explanation of the condemnations of other doctrines of the Lord's Supper found in the Introduction to the Formula of Concord reflects this pain.[9] Those persons who err because of weakness are distinguished from the false doctrines and teachers who are the real targets of the condemnations. And the authors emphasize that this "Christian agreement"—which also differentiated them from the Calvinists—"in no way . . . give occasion . . . for any molestation and persecution of poor, oppressed Christians." For these there is a "special sympathy with them . . . [and] a corresponding loathing for and a cordial disapproval of the raging of their persecutors."[10]

In spite of all this, concern for the purity of doctrine and clarity about the truth of the gospel made it impossible to avoid drawing these boundaries—

given the religious and theological presuppositions of that time. By defining the Lutheran confessional church in terms of its doctrine, Lutheranism was saved from disintegrating into a series of territorial churches, each with its own doctrinal statement. Thus the Formula of Concord made it possible for Lutheranism to define itself as a confessional church and this in turn guaranteed its existence as a historical entity. That was no small contribution. The price paid for this, however, was the drawing of a confessional boundary down the middle of Protestantism. That was a high price to pay. The dangers and difficulties resulting from this one confessional church's claim to be the exclusive representative of the truth should never be forgotten—no matter how understandable it is that Lutherans should be proud of their rich spiritual heritage.

The Lutheran Confessional Writings
as a *Corpus Doctrinae*

In our search for the Evangelical-Lutheran confession we encounter the Lutheran confessional church both as a historical and as a present reality. The Lutheran confession cannot be expressed in any single formula, however. We have approached this issue historically by asking how the Book of Concord— which has since become the definitive collection of Lutheran confessional writings—was originally understood. It was the successful culmination of the efforts to guarantee the doctrinal unity of Lutheranism.

These efforts resulted from the need to meet the conditions of the Religious Peace of Augsburg. That could not be done by creating a normative Lutheran dogmatics, however. For the teaching that was at stake was not a dogma that Lutherans could be required to believe—in the sense of being a defined formula of the kind described by the First Vatican Council as the official teaching of the Roman Catholic Church.[11] The Lutheran theologians consistently thought of teaching as a process that they sometimes referred to as the teaching of the gospel *(doctrina evangelii)* and, at other times, as the pure preaching of the gospel *(die reine Predigt des Evangeliums)*. The church is bound to this preaching. If it is missing, the church is not there and eschatological salvation is not available. Melanchthon said this very clearly in his examination of candidates for ordination: "God's church is certainly present wherever the pure Christian teaching is preached. For there God is working mightily through the gospel and there will always be some in that congregation who are saints and chosen to be saved.[12]

Melanchthon then drew the obvious conclusion:

Thus the first and most important thing which you should do is to sow the whole, pure Christian teaching, the self-revelation of God's nature and will as contained in the prophetic and apostolic Scriptures in the Apostles', Nicene, and Athanasian creeds. Luther's catechisms, his personal confession of faith, and the Augsburg Confession presented to the Emperor in 1530 all agree with the pure Christian

11

teaching and you should also teach these. Pastors themselves should know all this doctrine and its necessary parts and present it to the people in an accurate, orderly, and understandable manner. Then the people will be able to remember all the necessary parts accurately and will be able to tell the difference between the true doctrine and the false teachings of the sectarians.[13]

Melanchthon thereby not only began to define a *corpus doctrinae,* literally, a body of doctrine, referring sometimes to a collection of documents containing the doctrines that pastors are obligated to teach and at other times to the doctrines themselves. Melanchthon's statement, however, also indicated the problem that inevitably accompanied this concept. He emphasized the critical function of the theologian, who is required to think about doctrine in terms of which doctrines should be affirmed and which doctrines should be condemned. This then became a basic emphasis, even of preaching the gospel to the common people. In spite of all this, however, doctrine is still understood as a process.

At the same time, this process of teaching the gospel must itself be regulated. From the very beginning of the Reformation, this preaching of the gospel occurred alongside medieval Catholicism's false preaching of good works. And the theological development of the preaching of the gospel led on the one hand to more precision, but on the other hand to more variation in the ways in which it was preached. As a result, serious differences developed about the teaching of the gospel. The effort to find the way back to the pure doctrine made it necessary to define more exactly the boundaries of the *corpus doctrinae.* Characteristically, this was not done by redefining the teaching but rather by referring to the normative witnesses of the evangelical teaching. Future teaching was to conform to the standard of this witness.

In this way, the process of teaching was bound to the standard of the normative teaching of the tradition. The Holy Scripture, as the basic witness to the gospel, became the first and primary among the normative standards of doctrine. Yet it was well known that such a reference to Scripture did not by itself clearly define the normative contents of the *corpus doctrinae.* This was the function of the confession. It had demonstrated its usefulness as a defense against corruptions of the Scriptural gospel. For that reason, it could also be assigned additional functions. The confession was not established as an independent entity in relation to Scripture but rather as a reference to the sound doctrine found in Scripture. This Scripture was to be interpreted according to the analogy of faith. This meant that one passage of Scripture explained the other. The symbolic creeds were thought of as the distilled essence of the Scripture, and therefore as reliable guides to the gospel.

The Augsburg Confession could then be thought of as the corresponding symbolic statement of the confession of the churches of the Reformation. Because of the then-current controversies, however, such a reference was still not an adequate definition of the *corpus doctrinae*. Other writings were needed to reestablish the true interpretation of the Augsburg Confession.

The regulations governing the life of the church in Wolfenbüttel are a characteristic example of this process. Chemnitz and Jakob Andreä were members of the group that produced these regulations in 1569—they would later be two of the principal authors of the Formula of Concord. These regulations clearly state the concept of the *corpus doctrinae*.

This then is now the summary statement, the *corpus doctrinae*, the form and model of pure doctrine as it is from now on to be preached and taught in the churches of this principality: The holy, prophetic, and apostolic Scriptures, simply, truly, genuinely, and soundly understood according to their own self-interpretation; the brief summary of this same understanding, drawn from and in accordance to God's word, found in the old approved symbolic creeds, the Apostles', the Nicene, and the Athanasian, and in the articles of the Augsburg Confession.

In addition, it was necessary to make a statement about the then-current controversies. The pure understanding of the Augsburg Confession is to be guaranteed by the following assertion: "We accept the Augsburg Confession as it has been explained on the basis of God's word and as this understanding has been preserved, first, by the Apology later attached to this confession, then, by the Smalcald Articles, and finally, by the Catechism and other writings of Luther."[14]

These statements refer to the process of teaching. The content of this teaching cannot be simply defined in terms of prescribed statements. For this teaching takes place through the process of interpreting Scripture over and over again in new ways. The *corpus doctrinae* is the norm of such interpretation, however.

From now on then, no one will be allowed to teach anything else in the churches and schools of this principality. Whatever is taught must conform to and agree with the *corpus doctrinae* listed above. It must agree not merely in substance but also be expressed in these same sound words ('non tantum quod ad res ipsas attinet, verum etiam quod attinet ad formam sanorum verborum'). Any teaching that is different, contrary, or opposed to this standard shall not be tolerated; rather, it shall be prevented and abolished.[15]

This narrow limitation to the words themselves may alienate us today. It is important to note, however, that these statements make it very clear that the *corpus doctrinae* is a point of reference for teaching. It was never intended to take the place of the Scripture, or of the gospel that was to be preached on the basis of Scripture—never on the basis of the *corpus doctrinae*.

We may presuppose that the Formula of Concord was written on the basis of such an understanding of the *corpus doctrinae*. This is true even though the phrase does not appear in the Bergen Book, the final version of the Formula of Concord. It was still used in the Torgau Book of 1576, the earlier draft of the Formula of Concord that was circulated among the Lutheran estates of the empire in order to evoke their responses and suggestions. Thus the introductory article of the Formula of Concord has this long heading: "The Summary Formulation, Basis, Rule, and Norm, Indicating How All Doctrines Should Be Judged in Conformity with the Word of God and Errors Are to Be Explained and Decided in a Christian Way."[16] The heading of this section was shorter in the Torgau Book: "The Certain, Clear, Common, Public *Corpus Doctrinae.*"[17] The Formula of Concord eliminated the expression *corpus doctrinae* from the title and throughout the discussion by revising the text, because the expression itself had too many Melanchthonian associations. That, however, did not change their understanding of teaching in any way. The confessional writings are intended to preserve the process of teaching the gospel in its purity. The Scripture is the basic norm of that process and is the model of teaching. The confessions are subordinate to the Scripture and show how the Scripture is to be properly interpreted.[18]

The Formula of Concord accordingly defined the limits of the *corpus doctrinae* as the standard of teaching by referring to normative witnesses to the teaching. The process of teaching must definitely continue, but the *corpus doctrinae* gives it a point of orientation. This process is therefore understood as taking place within the tension between the Scripture, which is the basic teaching of the gospel, and the contemporary situation, which requires that the Scripture be interpreted in a new way in order to reveal the gospel. In this always-changing situation, new errors develop and new teachers of error constantly arise. The basic truth of the gospel must be defended against such falsification. Thus, at the time of the early church, "the true Christian doctrine as it was correctly and soundly understood was drawn together out of God's Word in brief articles or chapters against the aberrations of heretics."[19] The Augsburg Confession was then described as a similar summary of teaching against the aberrations of the papacy.

The Formula of Concord did not understand itself as such a confession—even though it has together with the whole Book of Concord in fact been treated in that way. The Formula of Concord intended only to resolve the controversial questions of its time on the basis of the Scripture and the then-available confessional writings. However, because it also solemnly condemned various doctrinal opinions—although never persons—it adds itself to the list of confessional writings.[20] Error and aberration in teaching require a new explanation of the basic truth of the scriptural gospel. Thus the Formula of Concord took the contemporary situation as well as the Scripture into account. Because our contemporary situation is different, we must go beyond the self-understanding of the confessional writings themselves when we use them for our own purposes.

In all of this, we still have not answered our basic question about the

Evangelical-Lutheran confession. We have determined that the Book of Concord was designed to be a Lutheran *corpus doctrinae,* a standard of teaching that provides a permanent point of orientation for the process of teaching the gospel. That is important for our use of the Book of Concord. The basic question that it seeks to answer is not the question about the confession and confessing. The question that it wants us to ask is the question about what the gospel is and how to preach the gospel in its purity.

THE AUGSBURG CONFESSION AS THE EVANGELICAL-LUTHERAN SYMBOLIC CREED

The Confession as Formula and as an Act of Proclamation

We are still dealing with the contradiction that is inherent in the effort to express the confession in the definite way that confessional documents are written. We shall now trace the manifestations of this problem as they have appeared in the later history of the church. The role of the Book of Concord in the history of the church was determined by its intention to serve as a systematic norm of teaching. This intention also generated the kinds of questions that developed.

In the course of time, the Book of Concord has succeeded in establishing itself as the Lutheran *corpus doctrinae.* Even though a number of Lutheran territories refused to recognize the Book of Concord as the basis of Lutheran unity at the time when it was published, it is the only defined collection of Lutheran confessions that is recognized today. This is true even though its original functions as a normative *corpus doctrinae* have now receded into the background. The two church constitutions quoted earlier[21] put two of the confessional documents contained in the Book of Concord, the Unaltered Augsburg Confession and Luther's Small Catechism, into a special category. At the very least this means that there is presently no felt need for a clearly defined and commonly accepted Lutheran *corpus doctrinae.* What has apparently happened is that the Lutheran confessional identity has been so well established during the past four hundred years that it no longer seems necessary to demand that pastors subscribe to a common doctrinal form that is as clearly stated as possible. It would be difficult to do that in any case, since the actual form of teaching has radically changed since 1580.

There are still problems at this point, however, as the heresy trial of Pastor Paul Schulz from Hamburg clearly demonstrated. Schulz asked the commission hearing his case to tell him what the official teaching of the Evangelical-Lutheran Church in Germany was on subjects such as prayer, the virgin birth, and Jesus' resurrection from the dead. The chairman of the commission could answer only that there was "widespread agreement [magnus consensus] in the preaching of the church" without being able to offer any more exact description of these doctrines. It would have been very helpful in answering Dr. Schulz's questions if a clearly defined Lutheran corpus doctrinae had been available. At the very least, it would have made it possible to evaluate the relative significance of the doctrines under discussion.[22]

The question that we have raised about the Evangelical-Lutheran confession is not really answered by reference to the fact that the concept of a corpus doctrinae appears to have become obsolescent. Can we then regard the Unaltered Augsburg Confession as this Lutheran confession? The Formula of Concord does indeed attempt to treat it as though it were on the level of the symbolic creeds of the early church. "This symbol distinguishes our reformed churches from the papacy and from other condemned sects and heresies. We appeal to it just as in the ancient church it was traditional and customary for later synods and Christian bishops and teachers to appeal and confess adherence to the Nicene Creed."[23] The basic meaning of symbol is that of a token that identifies the bearers as genuinely being what they claim to be. The Nicene Creed was such a symbol of genuine Christianity in the early church. The Augsburg Confession was proposed as a symbol by which Lutheran churches could be identified.

This inevitably leads to other theological questions. The description of the Augsburg Confession as the symbol of the Lutheran church presupposes that we think of the church as an organization, in this case the legally constituted territorial church that is still common in Germany. Lutheran churches in the United States are also organizations and are legally incorporated. These churches are commonly identified as Lutheran because of the confessional position specified in their constitutions. This situation is taken for granted. Such a corporation itself cannot believe or confess, however. Our discussion of the Evangelical-Lutheran confession requires that we be as careful to ask who is the subject of the confession as we are in asking whether there is a normative formulation of this confession or a way of defining this Evangelical-Lutheran confession in terms of its content.

In addition, we must ask whether there are any criteria for the confession and the corresponding act of confessing. Only then will we be able to return to the main question of whether the Augsburg Confession is only an identifying symbol or whether it can be described as a confession in the strict sense of the term.

(I shall defer any questions about the nature of the situation in which the confession of the church is explicitly and clearly required—the status confessionis. These questions will be raised later in other contexts.)[24]

The place where confession occurs is the same as the place in which the gospel is heard. This is the service of worship of the gathered congregation. In order to avoid possible misunderstanding, I need to add that this place expands to include the whole place in which the congregation carries out its mission, wherever life is lived in faith, hope, and love. This place of confession also defines the subject that is active in confessing. This subject is the gathered congregation. As Wilhelm Dantine has said, "Real, living confession is the living *eucharistia,* the people of God publicly giving thanks for the experience of grace."[25]

In order to express this confession of thanksgiving, the congregration needs to use a common formulation. Without spending time discussing the possibility of new formulations, I shall simply draw attention to the fact that symbolic creeds of the early church, the Nicene and the Apostles' Creeds, have proved very useful.[26] We still use these creeds in our Lutheran liturgy as expressions of our confession. To what extent, however, may we speak of an Evangelical-Lutheran confession? We must certainly distinguish the liturgical confessions used and the confessional statements of doctrine produced by the Reformation. At the same time, we should avoid rash statements such as "The confessional writings of the Reformation are not, like the ancient symbols, primary creeds for use in the worship service of the congregation, but secondary doctrinal norms which are to serve the interest of a scriptural understanding of the creed."[27] Regin Prenter, of course, conceded that these doctrinal confessions are closely related to the liturgy—he followed the usual practice of especially drawing attention to the Augsburg Confession and to Luther's Small Catechism. He still asserted "it is necessary that we see clearly the difference between the character of these doctrinal norms and the character of the creeds. The latter are primarily confessions of faith made directly to God in the context of worship. The former are secondary confessions of faith. They stand, we might say, both immediately before and after the worship service alongside the creeds, giving testimony concerning the creeds: 'Thus they are to be understood.' "[28]

In my opinion, Prenter too closely associated the formulations of the creeds of the early church with the process of liturgical confession. These are given preferential status in practice; however, they were never defined as the only real liturgical confessions—as though it were unthinkable that there might be others. In addition, they exercise the same function of serving as norms of the proclamation of the gospel that the Reformation's doctrinal confessions exercise.[29]

On the other hand, we should not be too quick to raise questions about the traditional formulations by separating them from their function in the context of the liturgical proclamation of the gospel. The Athanasian Creed describes itself as a dogmatic statement that is to be believed. We ought not describe the Apostles' and Nicene Creeds as being in the same category. Nor should we understand the doctrinal confessions as claiming to give us a statement of the truth that is valid for all times, as Dantine seems to have done. "Dogmas and doctrinal confessions are not able to keep their promises. They promise that they define theological truth. And they claim that such definitions enable them to clearly define the Christian life."[30] We are not here arguing whether or not that might be true of the dogma of the Eastern Orthodox Church. It is in any case quite clear that it is not true of the Lutheran *corpus doctrinae* which is aimed at the actual preaching of the gospel. Still, these clarifications leave open the questions about the identity of the confessing subject and the nature of the formulation of the Evangelical-Lutheran confession. In an attempt to resolve those questions, we shall again turn our attention to the Augsburg Confession.

The Historical Place of the Augsburg Confession

When the Latin text of the Augsburg Confession was first printed, it was given the motto: "I will also speak of thy testimonies before kings, and shall not be put to shame" (Ps. 119:46).[31] This indicates that the public reading and presentation of the Augsburg Confession at the Diet of Augsburg on June 25, 1530, was interpreted as an act of confession. Neither the intention of the authors in writing the Augsburg Confession nor the terminology they used corresponded to this interpretation, however. The text simply does not convey the feelings associated with confession. The text of the Augsburg Confession cannot be exempted from theological analysis because of the unusual circumstances under which it was publicly read. Nor can we on that basis argue that the formulations of the Augsburg Confession are particularly significant on the grounds that God's Spirit was obviously at work when this Lutheran testimony to the truth of the gospel was presented to the emperor and the empire. A brief description of the process by which this text was developed will make that clear.

The Reformers had first been condemned under imperial law at the Diet of Worms in 1520. During the following ten years, they were sometimes tolerated, sometimes condemned. They were again condemned by the majority of the Diet of Speyer in 1529. On April 19, 1529, the imperial estates who agreed with the Reformation "protested" the validity of their understanding of the gospel and disagreed with the majority opinion.[32] In so doing, they established themselves as the "Protestant" party. In that same year, they began a series of negotiations aimed at a political alliance.[33] After the Diet of Augsburg in 1530, the Smalcald League was established. During 1529 and 1530, the situation became quite critical. In 1529, Emperor Charles V concluded his wars with the pope and with France. The terms of both peace treaties were favorable to Charles. The Turkish attack on Vienna had also been repelled. The emperor was now free to give his full attention to settling the religious controversies within the empire. People could predict how he might go about that after he ungraciously responded to the minority's protest at the Diet of Speyer:

Rather than receiving the delegation that presented the Protest, he had them put into prison.

His letter summoning the estates to the Diet of Augsburg created the hope that he would deal fairly with both sides. It seemed that the Emperor was willing to accept both the papal party and the Lutherans as equals and to negotiate with them about a compromise solution. On this basis, Electoral Saxony decided that for political purposes, the differences should be played down as much as possible. This tactic was reflected in the final text of the Augsburg Confession. A paragraph concluding the doctrinal articles (I–XXI) says, "this teaching is grounded clearly on the Holy Scriptures and is not contrary or opposed to that of the universal Christian church, or even of the Roman church (in so far as the latter's teaching is reflected in the writings of the Fathers."[34] The conclusion is then drawn that the opponents cannot disagree with the position of the Lutheran estates as expressed in these doctrinal articles. "The dispute and dissension are concerned chiefly with various traditions and abuses."[35] That was clearly a political fiction, for the Lutheran reforms in particular were directly related to their basic decision about the doctrine of justification.[36]

The plan of Electoral Saxony was to limit the issues discussed at the Diet of Augsburg to reforms in the life of the church. It seemed that neither the papal theologians nor the emperor could deny that such reforms were needed. This plan could not be carried out at the diet. The polemical attacks of the papal theologians, especially Eck's list of 404 heresies attributed to the Reformers,[37] required the Reformers to refute the accusations that they were heretics. They also had to differentiate clearly their position from that of the Anabaptists and defend themselves against the suspicion of being revolutionaries. In addition, the emperor was not at all the neutral mediator that they had hoped he would be on the basis of the summons to the diet. If the religious controversies had been settled at this time, the costs to the Reformation would have been high. In this situation, the fact that the Lutheran imperial estates were able to read the Augsburg Confession publicly and then present it to the whole diet must be considered a major success. The public reading and the presentation had political as well as religious significance in that context. It was possible to interpret this as primarily a religious act of confession only from the perspective of a later time.

The Formulation of the Augsburg Confession and the Identity of the Confessors

The historical process that resulted in the development of the Augsburg Confession, its intention of establishing an agreement with the papal theologians, and the willingness of its author, Philip Melanchthon, to make concessions all point to the difficulty of now recognizing this text as the normative formulation of the Evangelical-Lutheran confession. The view that this text was really the confession of those who signed it also creates theological difficulties. That interpretation may be possible if we think of the Lutheran princes who signed the confession. However, the list of signers also includes the Senate and magistrate of Nuremberg and the Senate of Reutlingen.[38] This raises the very serious question as to whether such administrative entities can be the subjects of an act of confessing. If such a collective group were to be named, the Church of Nuremberg or of Reutlingen would be the only appropriate group. Certainly it can be said that a community like the city of Nuremberg could also be regarded as a Christian congregation, even when it was represented politically by its senate or city council. People at that time also recognized the distinction between these two entities, however—as Gregor Brück's "Preface" to the Augsburg Confession clearly shows.[39]

This preface begins with a reference to the emperor's summons to the diet and the request that each party submit its opinion in writing. "Wherefore, in dutiful obedience to Your Imperial Majesty, we offer and present a confession of our pastors' and preachers' teaching and of our own faith, setting forth how and in what manner, on the basis of the Holy Scriptures, these things are preached, taught, communicated, and embraced in our lands, principalities, dominions, cities, and territories."[40] The preface then expresses the Lutherans' readiness to negotiate with the other party after the others have submitted their confession in writing. "Thus the matters at issue between us may be presented in writing on both sides, they may be discussed amicably and charitably, our differences may be reconciled, and we may be united in one, true religion."[41]

In case the other side does not accede to this wish, does not recognize the Lutherans as a party to the negotiations, and refuses to submit its doctrine for discussion, the Lutherans appeal to a general council to be convened by the pope and the emperor. Because the diet is a political entity, it cannot decide the religious questions should the participants in the controversy not be able to reach agreement. Such a decision must be made by the council as an organ of the church. The preface had earlier made a distinction between the imperial estates and their preachers. Now it made a parallel distinction between a diet and a council of the church. There were, of course, valid political and tactical reasons for making this distinction. That does not lessen their reality and introduces a whole new level of complexity into our discussion of the dogmatic question about the identity of the confessing subject of the Augsburg Confession.

The Augsburg Confession is characterized by an inner conflict that results from its attempt to serve simultaneously as the basis of religious and political negotiations and as a confession of faith. We can see that from the way it speaks of the content of faith as though it were a neutral party making an objective report, without being directly involved. The German version reported what was taught by the Lutherans. The Latin version made such teaching or preaching of the congregations the subject of its report: "Our churches teach with great unanimity. . . . Our churches also teach. . . . Our churches also teach."[42] This neutral perspective really dominates the second part of the Augsburg Confession which reported on the reforms in the life of the church. Thus the Augsburg Confession was and is a statement of the Lutheran princes and city councils reporting on the way in which they dealt with the reform of the church in their respective territories and on the form of teaching that then prevailed in the congregations in these territories.

At best, then, the Augsburg Confession provides a basis for drawing an indirect conclusion about the subject of the act of confession. In addition, it is possible to draw some conclusions about the faith and confession of the congregations on the basis of their preaching as described in the Augsburg Confession.

It is of considerable importance that we clearly recognize the theological significance of these difficulties in the formulation of the Augsburg Confession: The Augsburg Confession does not claim to expressing the faith of the universal or "catholic" church as the confession of Christ does. Instead it was the offer of a religious party to negotiate its position. In addition, this analysis of the actual formulation of the Augsburg Confession means that it is not able to fulfill the role assigned it in the ordination oath. It simply can not serve as "the confession of our Evangelical-Lutheran church."[43] The Augsburg Confession does not present us with a clear and simple formulation of this confession.

The Religious-Political Significance of the Augsburg Confession

This difficult and complex problem becomes even clearer when we examine the political function of the Augsburg Confession. It was not accidental that the political authorities presented it and took responsibility for it. It is not necessary for us at this place to consider the role of territorial princes in the introduction of the Reformation. It is, however, important for our analysis of the religious-political significance of the Augsburg Confession that we understand the relationship of the imperial estates to the empire and to the emperor. Could the imperial states exempt themselves from religious-political decrees of the emperor and the empire? If so, how could they do so and on what basis? There was general agreement that we ought to obey God rather than people (Acts 5:29). But could such obedience take any other form than the endurance of suppression by superior force? If the gospel were threatened in such a situation, could the imperial states resist the emperor with military force without becoming guilty of rebelling against the divinely instituted authorities? Clearly, there was no unanimously accepted answer to this question. There wree many distinctly different theological and legal opinions. And the general respect in which the Lutheran estates held their theological advisors required them to pay careful attention to their opinions—especially if the unity of the Protestant camp were to be preserved.

After making their protest at the Diet of Speyer in 1529, the Protestants entered into long negotiations that eventually resulted in the formation of a Protestant alliance. This alliance was directed not only against the threat that came from the imperial estates that remained loyal to the pope but also against the threat that came from the emperor. It was a matter of considerable religious and legal importance that any military defense of the gospel against the emperor and empire could only be offered as protection of the pure gospel and not on behalf of dangerous and shameful errors. The so-called Schwabach Articles were written in order to make this very certain.[44] Representatives of the territories of Electoral Saxony and Brandenburg-Ansbach agreed to these at a meeting in Schleiz (October 3–7, 1529) and they were then presented to a larger meeting in Schwabach that included representatives of the Protestant cities (October 16–19, 1529). Without attempting to view the history of the negotiations leading to the alliance, it is important to note that the Southern German cities, who were under the leadership of Strassburg, were not permitted to sign the Augsburg Confession. This was because of differences in the doctrine of the Lord's Supper that were first resolved by the Wittenberg Concord of 1536.[45] While there was not complete agreement, it was sufficient to remove the religious obstacles to the admission of the Southern German cities to the Smalcald League.

Beginning in 1530, subscription to formulation of the gospel in the Augsburg Confession became the condition of admission to the Lutheran defensive alliance. This religious-political function of the Augsburg Confession and its resulting particularistic character must be considered in any study of the Lutheran Confession. There is no question that the text of the Augsburg Confession emphasized its catholicity. From the very beginning, however, there was an equally strong emphasis on its particularistic character. It is not completely accidental that the preface referred to above used the concept of "party." The Formula of Concord was obviously characterized by this design of the confession to meet the needs of a confessional church. This emphasis, however, was already present in the Lutheran confession from the very beginning. Both the formulation and the actual function of the Augsburg Confession made this very clear. Perhaps for this reason, all attempts that were made in both the sixteenth and the twentieth centuries to generate acceptance of the Augsburg Confession outside the Lutheran confessional church have not succeeded.

Up until this point, we have tried to answer our question about the Evangelical-Lutheran confession primarily on the basis of historical data. We have seen that there is a whole series of questions that cannot be satisfactorily answered on this basis. The basic questions about the formulation of the Evangelical-Lutheran confession, the subject of this act of confessing, and the place in which the confession takes place all remain unresolved. In addition, we have seen that although the Augsburg Confession claims to be universally valid, it is also characterized by its particularistic affirmation of religious-political boundaries. In order to deal with this reality, we have had to be very self-consciously aware and critical of such particularism. At the same time, we are aware that the necessary spirit of openness could easily be distorted into an indifferent attitude toward our own confessional heritage that would dissipate its substance. I do not think that this heritage is found in any one particular formulation or confessional writing; rather the concept of the *corpus doctrinae* is our point of reference for a witness to the gospel that is also faithful to the Scripture. Any study of the theology of the Lutheran confessions must fulfill this dual task of both preserving the Lutheran confessional identity and at the same time leaving the way open for the church of Jesus Christ to realize its oneness.

2

The Basic Decision of
the Reformation:
God Alone Works Our Salvation

The confession of the Evangelical-Lutheran church cannot be contained within the limits of a traditional document. Neither the Book of Concord, the normative collection of the Lutheran confessional writings, nor the Augsburg Confession, the most widely accepted and most highly valued individual document contained in this collection, can fulfill this function. This is not possible for a variety of reasons. First, these documents were—from the moment at which they were written—characterized by a confessional particularism that is not appropriate to the universal claim which the Christian confession must make for itself. Second, their content, the theological reflection and discussion, is too far removed from our present situation for these documents to serve as the basis for expressing our own personal confession. The third and most important reason is the fact that these confessional writings described themselves in terms of their dependence on the gospel and Scripture. The confessional writings intend to lead us to the kind of teaching or preaching of the gospel that is in agreement with Scripture. They ascribe an unconditional primacy to the Scripture over the confessional writings. Since the Scripture is the original witness to the gospel, it is also the sole norm of any other witnesses. Insofar as the confessional writings reject the aberrations in the teaching of the gospel that were characteristic of the time at which these confessions were written, they are meaningful only in the context of those times.

The confession is centered in a witness to the gospel that is in harmony with Scripture. The traditional confessional documents want to help us find our way to this center. The confession of the Evangelical-Lutheran church can then

24

be described in terms of the fact that this church clings to this process, derives its life from it, and confesses that its very nature as the church depends on God's ongoing activity through this gospel. Such a definition cannot permit the concept of the "gospel" to be used merely as a formal concept without defining its content. This gospel can also never be confined within any simple formulation. For it is the nature of this gospel that it encounters people where they are and addresses itself to their specific situations. At the same time, this gospel is enduring truth. This enduring truth is defined by the decisions that have been handed down to us in the various formulations of the confession. They show us how the gospel was previously heard in a way that was in harmony with Scripture as well as how it was not heard correctly. Both the affirmations and the rejections found in the confessional documents show us how the gospel in the Scripture has been rightly heard and witnessed to. The expectation is that the gospel can continue to be rightly preached and heard by those who accept these decisions. The confessions assert that this gospel cannot be rightly heard and witnessed to by those who ignore the availability of these decisions.

This means that the concept of the *corpus doctrinae* will be a useful tool in our study of the Lutheran confessions. I shall use it primarily to emphasize the confessions' basic decisions about the correct understanding of the Scripture. These decisions of the confessional documents will be defined and explained in the process of commenting on the texts of the confessional documents. This will involve a discussion of the historical situation as well as the real meaning of the decisions. Description of the content of the confessional documents will, therefore, be accompanied by reflections on their meaning.

THE NATURE OF CONFESSIONAL
FORMULATIONS AND THEIR ACCEPTANCE

Confessing as a Communal Act and the
Theological Defense of the Confession
and Its Decisions

Before we analyze the basic decision made by the Reformation in developing its understanding of the gospel in harmony with Scripture, we must first clarify the nature of the church's confession. The material to be discussed is quite complex. I shall, therefore, begin with a simple, commonly accepted insight: When we make our decisions, we at first usually do so automatically as members of the community to which we belong. Obviously, this happens in some very different ways. Whenever we think that we have consciously made a decision, however, we do so within the context of what has already been decided for us. Usually, many decisions have already been made for us. We already belong to a family, a national group, a historical age with its particular emphases, as well as to a religion and to a confessional church. All these are decisions that have been made for us, but we still must consciously make them our own. In that process, we may also revise these decisions. Such a revision is usually the exception, because the attraction of the group to which we belong and the practices to which we are accustomed is strong. It is never an easy task to disagree with the community to which we belong.

To a large extent, this is also true of our religious allegiances. We experience ourselves as members of a religious community long before we understand the nature of these experiences. Even if we consciously confirm this membership in a religious fellowship, we usually do so on the basis of these experiences of the community and because we have already been shaped by these experiences. Thus membership is more easily and strongly expressed in terms of belonging to a community and being familiar with its customs than in understanding its doctrinal teaching. As a result, we become familiar with the confession on the basis of having practiced it as part of the liturgical ritual. Through regular participation in the liturgy, we memorize the text of the liturgical confession, usually the Apostles' Creed. This does not necessarily mean that we understand this formula better than other parts of the liturgy—better, for example, than such foreign language words as "Amen," "Hallelujah," or "Kyrie eleison." Such an acceptance based on repetition may be described as a kind of implicit faith. The Protestant Church and Protestant theology have good reasons for not highly valuing this kind of faith. After all, it does not express our conscientious personal commitment to the gospel and the God of the gospel, but rather expresses our trust in the authority of the church, or of whatever religious group in which we have experienced community.

The question that is typically raised at this stage is usually not the question as to how such implicit faith can become understanding faith. Rather, we usually ask whether the theologian whose role in the teaching of the gospel is that of preacher personally understands what is being preached. The preacher's personal commitment to the community of the church can not long survive on the basis of previous experiences of community. Rather, the preacher needs to gain critical distance from the community and its liturgy. Without that critical distance, the preaching of the gospel will itself become an empty ritual. Having gained this critical distance, the preacher must personally come to understand the tradition and personally adopt it. For example, our practice of the historical-critical method requires us to study both the biblical texts and the liturgical confession with such critical objectivity. Anyone who tries to avoid this disciplined critical analysis of these texts because it might endanger "faith" will hardly ever achieve an independent understanding of the gospel and will, therefore, not be able to preach the gospel responsibly. For the only faith that could be endangered by such critical analysis is that implicit faith which is enough only if we merely wish to belong to a religious community, participate in its ritual, and say how much we appreciate it.

Critical objectivity creates its own problems for understanding. In terms of the liturgical confession, these problems are usually experienced in reference to those details that are difficult to understand, particularly the virgin birth. Controversies about the Apostles' Creed and the obligation to use it in the liturgy usually arise in connection with such details. How is theological analysis related to this question? I am assuming that this problem has proved to be especially troublesome for theologians—although I am also aware that many lay persons have also had difficulty with it. One way of dealing with it is by assuming critical distance. This can be done either by not using the Creed at all or by introducing it in a way that reveals this distance. Intellectual honesty requires such critical objectivity. If there is something that I cannot both believe and understand, I cannot use it as my confession. Then, however, the traditional formula for the confession and its personal appropriation with understanding are contradictory and mutually exclusive. I cannot make this text my own confession, precisely because I have gained a critical understanding of it. Expressing such critical disagreement publicly usually leads to a break with the community, which continues to use the challenged text as its own confession.

This critical attitude toward the literal meaning of the traditional confession does not seem to me to be the most appropriate response. It is much more useful to analyze the function of the liturgical Creed. It is really a symbol, a mark by which the community of faith identifies and recognizes itself. The Creed is understood to be part of the community ritual. The community really needs such a sign by which it can be recognized. As a member of the community, I also participate in its confession. This does not mean that I personally agree with everything that is done or said in the religious community of which I am a member. I have good theological reasons for my disagreement. I have a corresponding attitude toward the symbolic or confessional formulation used by this community. I both can and do accept it as a whole, even though I find some individual statements of the Creed to be questionable and in need of theological analysis. At the same time I am aware that it is difficult to find a contemporary formulation of the faith that can be used by a confirmation class or in family devotions. A statement acceptable to some people will not be acceptable to others. For this reason, none of them could take the place of the ancient Creed as the identifying symbol of the community of faith.

Still more needs to be said about the hermeneutics—the principles of interpretation—governing our understanding of the confession. The ancient symbolic Creed is acceptable not only because we do not have a suitable replacement for it in the liturgy. The Creed also must prove acceptable after critical theological analysis. To the extent that its content expresses a basic decision about the Christian faith, the Creed is irreplaceable. For the purposes of discussion, I shall now make a statement about this basic decision. This statement will be more thoroughly analyzed as the basic theme of the next chapter. "Biblical history teaches: The world and salvation have both been given to us by the one and the same God." The first thing that can be said about this statement is that it expresses my own personal thinking. It has, however, been formulated with the intention of being understood and agreed to by others. The hope is that others will agree that this statement summarizes what the Apostles' Creed says. As such a statement, it also helps us understand what it means that we are obligated to teach in harmony with the Creed. In order for an individual to make the Creed a personal confession of faith or for the community to identify itself with this symbolic Creed, we primarily need to identify clearly the Creed's decision of faith in response to hearing the gospel.

Agreement that this statement summarizes the basic decision expressed by the Apostles' Creed cannot be achieved only through theological discussion. Rather, such agreement is primarily reached on the basis of practicing the interpretation of the Scripture as gospel. The gospel to which the Scripture bears witness is rightly understood and this gospel rightly preached only when the world and salvation are described as gifts of the one and the same God. This is still only an intellectual formulation. It is a formulation, however, that assists us in the process of understanding the essential meaning of the Apostles' Creed as we recite it as part of the Sunday liturgy. Theological reflection is part of the process of reaching such agreement. It must, however, take place in the service of the preaching of the gospel to which the Scripture bears witness. And the credal formulation needs to demonstrate its validity by opening the meaning of the Scripture to us and permitting us to hear the Scripture as gospel. If the confession as we have understood it proves useful in this process, then, and not until then, the validity of a formula such as the one I have proposed is demonstrated. Then this formula can help us to make the traditional credal formulation our own confession, our response to the gospel we have heard. This confession in turn provides the basis for hearing more of the gospel than we heard before.

Affiliation, Understanding, and Agreement in the Confessional Churches

We have thought about a hermeneutics of the confession in terms of the liturgical Creed. Some changes need to be made in order to apply this hermeneutics to the process by which we personally appropriate the traditional confession of a confessional church. The three major stages of membership, critical theological analysis of the meaning of the confession, and agreement still apply. However, the special characteristics of confessional formulations in the form of more extensive theological presentations makes it almost impossible to express our membership in the Evangelical-Lutheran church by memorizing and reciting a particular confessional document. (The most we can do is to memorize a few catechetical slogans in confirmation instruction.) Membership is more likely to be experienced in terms of a rather general sense of confessional identity that expresses itself in familiarity with a specific liturgy. Differences between the confessional churches are only rarely experienced as differences in the confession. Thus Lutherans are aware that the Roman Catholic Church has a hierarchy under the leadership of the pope, of the unfamiliar reverence of Mary and the saints, of different kinds of ceremonies such as processions and pilgrimages. Church members are usually more consciously aware of such differences than of any contrasts in the doctrine of salvation. In addition, the more members of the confessional churches live together in the same towns and the more they take it for granted that they do so, their consciousness of membership loses its socially divisive and polemical character. Fortunately, "Lutheran" and "Roman Catholic" are less and less used as expressions of contempt.

This also means that whether one belongs to a church at all is more important than which confessional church one belongs to. Intentional membership in the Christian church, whether it is Roman Catholic or Protestant, primarily distinguishes church members from those who are religiously indifferent rather than identifying opposition to other confessional churches. Lutherans have begun to participate in religious ceremonies with Roman Catholics and even to worship with them. One's own confessional commitment is usually accepted as the presupposition of being a religious person. Conversions are the exception. It is then not possible, however, to regard confessional affiliation as a considered personal decision. In order to do that, Lutherans would have to disparage the Christianity of their Roman Catholic friends and thereby call their common experience of religious community into question. As a result, confessional differences are not taken very seriously in the present situation. That does have the effect of making it harder to get at the confession of the confessional churches.

This raises the question as to whether the confession of the confessional churches is available only to the critical theologian. There can be no doubt that this question challenges us not only to understand and personally appropriate the confession of our own tradition, but also on this basis to explain both to ourselves and others why we are Lutheran and not Roman Catholic. Any book about the theology of the Lutheran confessions must also take seriously the fact that the confessional documents were written to establish boundaries separating Lutherans from and protecting them against other confessional churches. We cannot do justice to the reality of such boundaries by explaining them on the basis of peripheral differences. On the other hand, neither Lutherans nor Roman Catholics can maintain these polemical boundaries by asserting that there is simply no way of reconciling traditional confessional statements. It is very easy to demonstrate such unresolvable disagreements in the traditional statements. That is not a good reason for us to maintain the confessional boundaries today, however. In order to continue to maintain these polemical boundaries, we would need to be able to demonstrate that there is a significant difference in the understanding of the gospel—so significant that it requires us to maintain the confessional boundaries in the life of the church.

In order to gain a critical understanding of the Lutheran confession and to show why it is still necessary to remain separate from Roman Catholicism, we must briefly summarize the basic decision of the Reformation in a way that also expresses the unique character of the Lutheran confessional church in contrast with the unique character of Roman Catholicism. The body of written material that we need to work is really quite large. This makes it all the more important that we begin with a clear statement of the most important issue that will guide us in making this our own confession. The confession of the Evangelical-Lutheran Church in Bavaria refers to the statement of the doctrine of justification in Article IV of the Augsburg Confession. The Evangelical-Lutheran Church in Bavaria "conforms itself to the Evangelical—Lutheran confession, particularly as expressed in the Augsburg Confession of 1530 and the Small Catechism of Dr. Martin Luther. This confession bears witness to the justification of the sinner through faith for Christ's sake as the center of the Gospel. . . ."[1] Critical theological understanding of the confession will have to come to terms with this assertion. For the distinction between the Lutheran and the Roman Catholic churches can be maintained only if the substance of the confession can be so clearly defined that such a separation is clearly necessary in order to preserve the Lutheran substance. This task can be undertaken primarily on the basis of a comparative analysis of the positions. It certainly cannot be done through polemical arguments.[2]

Given the present situation of the confessional churches, the process of reaching agreement also requires conscious reference to the existing separation. The necessary reasons for this separation must be clearly described as related to a presentation of the gospel that is in harmony with the Scripture. This must also be done in a way that leaves open the possibility of future reconciliation of the separated confessional churches. Once again, such reconciliation must be based on the substance of the gospel. Such agreement cannot be raised solely on the basis of theological dialogue. Agreement that is compatible with the right understanding of the basic Reformation decision about the gospel must demonstrate itself in the way in which the gospel is preached. Thus understandings arrived at on the basis of critical theological work must demonstrably affect the life of the church. Once again, confessional polemic is not needed. Rather, because it takes place in the context of the life and work of the church, critical analysis based on the Lutheran confession starts as an act of self-criticism which asks whether or not the gospel is still a dynamic force in the Lutheran church itself.

Our task at this point is to arrive at a critical theological understanding of the situation. Obviously, such a theological understanding must not only be compatible with membership in the Lutheran church but also must try to provide a basis for agreement with Roman Catholicism. Such theological agreement but would be meaningless unless the listening congregation accepts the gospel that it hears. In addition, the task of critically understanding the gospel requires us to consider the Roman Catholic position. It was indeed once true that Roman Catholics and Lutherans could not reach agreement, no matter how hard they tried. Since then, however, there have been changes on both sides. Under these changed circumstances, it will certainly be possible to reach a better understanding—even if this only means that we now have a better understanding of what separates the confessional churches. At the same time, we must consider whether the differences that separate us today are still the differences that separated the churches in the sixteenth century.

GOD'S GRACE AND HUMAN FREEDOM—THE ROMAN CATHOLIC DOCTRINAL FORM

The Relationship Between the Roman Catholic Doctrinal Form and Its Contradiction by the Reformation

The relationship between divine grace and human freedom is the characteristic issue of Western theology in the Augustinian tradition. The various models of late medieval theology and religious practice that prevailed at the beginning of the Reformation and that determined the Reformation position—usually in terms of its disagreement with its theological roots—cannot be described here. I can only assert that the concern for human merit was a dominating factor in the late medieval world of thought. God's grace had, of course, not been forgotten. The church mediated this grace through its sacramental acts. At the same time, however, human freedom was thought of in terms of people doing everything possible to gain certainty that they were saved. How is it possible, however, for anyone to be certain that they stand in God's grace and will be eternally saved? Is it enough that someone says, "You may hope in God's grace"? That was small comfort for people who knew that they had not really met God's moral and religious standards and were therefore dependent on God's forgiveness.

Under these circumstances, the appeal to human freedom was especially significant. "Do as much as you yourself are able to do. Then you can be certain that God will be gracious to you."[3] Doing as much as possible was in turn related to receiving grace from the church, especially through the sacrament of penance. Through contrition—sorrow for sin and intending not to sin in the future—people can prepare themselves to receive this sacrament. They can confess all the sins that they remember to the priest and thereby humble them-

31

selves before God and the church. Even more important, they can conscientiously carry out the satisfactions prescribed by the confessor, usually prayer, fasting, and acts of charity. These human works, contrition of heart *(contritio cordis)*, oral confession *(confessio oris)*, and satisfaction *(satisfactio operum)* can in some ways be described as being the matter *(quasi materia)* of the sacrament of penance. The form *(forma)* of the sacrament is provided when the priest speaks the words of absolution.[4]

Human work and the divine freedom that accepts this activity are joined together by this understanding of the sacrament of penance. In this context, human merits that deserve God's grace may be called "condign merits" *(meritum de condigno)* and are distinguished from human merits that God rewards with grace even though the works themselves do not deserve this reward and are therefore called "congruent [sometimes, "congruous"] merits" *(meritum de congruo)*.

The necessary condition for condign merit is that God has promised to reward a certain action, that the person wants to do this work and then actually does it. It was a consistent teaching of late medieval theology and Roman Catholic theology that the only real condign merit, the merit that actually meets this definition in its strict sense, is the merit gained for us by Jesus Christ. Recognizing that this is true, it is still possible for people to gain condign merit in a certain sense of the term, even though human works never fully deserve the reward of God's grace. God's promise to reward good works is so effective that even these works which in and of themselves do not deserve rewards are accepted by God if they are done by someone who has done these works while in the state of grace created by receiving supranatural grace.

In contrast to condign merit, congruent merit is not based on any such correspondence between the promise, the work, and the reward. Congruent merit arises in a twofold context. On the one hand, there is the human effort to do what we can ("facere, quod in se est"). On the other hand, there is God's freedom to accept a completely unsatisfactory human action and graciously reward it. This latter congruent merit can be received even by someone who is not in a state of grace. It is even possible for someone to receive congruent merit because of the intercessory prayers and corresponding actions of others. It is at this point that human freedom and divine freedom intersect. People are free to do something on their own initiative in order to gain God's grace, but it is the very definition of this grace that God is under no obligation to respond to this human action and the desire for salvation that it expresses. If God responds graciously, he does so freely.

The Reformation rejected this method of teaching and all the patterns of piety and church life that had developed on the basis of it. The Reformers objected that the medieval system emphasized human works at the expense of God's grace and trusting in the merits of Christ. They were correct in understanding the medieval system as basing the certainty of salvation on human works. However, it was not fair for the Reformers—and for Lutheran polemicists ever since—to misinterpret so crudely the medieval doctrine as though it based salvation on people's good works. It was very clear that Jesus Christ had completed the work of salvation and that it was communicated to people through the sacraments. The reception of the sacraments, however, involved human action and medieval theologians had emphasized that it was important for people to receive the sacraments. The Reformers were correct in observing that good works, or human capacity and action, had so become the focus of the popular religious practice that God's grace and Christ's merits had lost importance.

In response to the criticisms of the Reformers, the teaching and practice of the papal Christians had changed. The Lutherans were careful to point this change out to papal theologians and there was truth in their observations. For example, Article XX of the Augsburg Confession asserted that their opponents no longer praise "childish and useless works like rosaries, the cult of saints, monasticism, pilgrimages, appointed fasts, holy days, brotherhoods, etc.," as highly as they had sometimes been praised.[5]

The basic decision of the Reformation confession is directed against a papal theology and especially practice that had already been significantly changed in response to the Reformers' attacks. Tridentine Roman Catholicism was a result of the reform of the medieval church. Roman Catholicism, particularly its present complex manifestations, is no longer the church that the Reformers criticized. The abuses that provoked the Reformation have long since been done away with.

If we attempt to interpret the Lutheran confessions in terms of their historical context, this fact causes us some embarrassment. It is not difficult to understand how the Reformers at the beginning of the Reformation criticized the doctrine and practices of the medieval church as corrupt because they so often contradicted the gospel witnessed to by the Scripture. The situation is different, however, if we ask whether it is still necessary to maintain the opposition between the Lutheran and Roman Catholic confessional churches, that is, whether the Reformers' criticisms are still valid in view of the fact that the Roman Catholic Church is itself the result of a reformation. I personally think that it is still valid and my answer is based on more than my desire to assert that our Lutheran confessional church is the true church. For myself, I can see no way of escaping the conclusion that the Reformers gave a higher priority to preserving the truth than they did to preserving the unity of the church. They were convinced that the church exists and can continue to exist only on the basis of the truth of the gospel. What this means for our description of Roman Catholic doctrine is that we need to understand the teachings of the post-Tridentine church. It is easier to explain why we disagree with the late medieval church but we need to come to terms with the post-Tridentine Roman Catholic Church—a church whose teaching is more in agreement with the Reformation.

The Council of Trent's Decree on Justification

Space does not permit an extensive interpretation of the Decree on Justification adopted by the General Council of Trent on January 13, 1547.[6] I shall attempt to trace the meanings associated with the key concepts of God's grace and human freedom. Before beginning this discussion, I wish to emphasize that the Council of Trent made unusual efforts to demonstrate that its own formulation of Christian teaching was in harmony with Scripture. In so doing, it included a large number of quotations from the Bible in the text of this decree. Of course, the number of biblical references does not by itself demonstrate that a statement is in harmony with Scripture. Similarly, I wish to note that this decree on justification, from beginning to end, discusses God's grace. Before there was any human effort to gain salvation, God sent the Son in accordance with God's own plan of salvation.[7] After the Fall into sin, people were not able to free themselves from the power of sin by their own efforts.[8]

God's grace is the focus of Trent's description of God's work of salvation. Grace is also given the decisive role in our reception of salvation. Grace prepares people to receive and brings us into contact with grace. In this process, grace does not force itself on anyone. It does not take away our freedom as persons or destroy our conscious sense of ongoing personal identity. Rather, grace affirms our individual personalities and is necessary for the full development and realization of true personhood. Prevenient grace, the grace by which God makes grace available, always comes from outside the person. It comes through the church's ministry, which proclaims God's offer of salvation through Jesus Christ. Thus grace appeals to the limited freedom that we still have, even after the Fall into sin. When we hear God's offer of salvation, we are free to trust God and to respond to this offer. When we hear that God loves sinners, we begin to hate our own sin. God's grace in Jesus Christ becomes the object of our hope.[9] Our human freedom cooperates with divine grace—but it is only possible for us to turn to God because God has already been gracious to us. "Hence, when it is said in the sacred Scriptures, 'Turn ye to me, and I will turn to you' (Zach. 1:3), we are reminded of our liberty; and when we reply, 'Convert us, O Lord, to thee, and we shall be converted' (Lam. 5:21) we confess that we need the grace of God."[10] We are as humans most free when we choose to accept God's grace.

God's prevenient grace at first comes to us from outside ourselves. As saving grace, it becomes part of our inner reality. This happens first in the sacrament of baptism and, should we happen to lose this grace through mortal sin, is renewed through the sacrament of penance. All of this happens only because of what God in Christ has done for our salvation. This is always what makes justification possible. God makes us righteous by infusing his grace into us through the sacraments. This accomplishes more than the forgiveness of sins. The inner person is also sanctified and renewed.[11] Prevenient grace enables us to decide freely to come to the sacrament. God's grace is also present in the sacrament and gives us the supranatural gifts that enable us to renounce sin and live a new, God-pleasing life.

The infusion of grace is not the end of justification. Rather, this infusion of grace starts a new process in which we make the divine gifts of grace our own. The infusion of God's grace is God's gift to us and it must result in real changes. After we have been sanctified and renewed through grace, we are capable of things that were impossible for the sinner. The sanctified and renewed person can believe, hope, and love. Those are not mere capabilities that can be allowed to wither. Rather, it is in their very nature to express themselves through changes in our life. In terms of traditional scholastic terminology: The *habitus* (habitual character) of grace expresses itself in a corresponding *actus* (activity) in conformity with God's will.

Trent's decree on justification applies the traditional teaching on merit in this context: God rewards those who do God's will. It is firmly presupposed that people are able to do good works and to deserve rewards only because of the assistance of God's grace. Basically, God is so merciful that people are rewarded for having received the gifts.[12] The justified person is able to lead a new life only because God's grace has made this possible. The individual, however, must always take responsibility for leading this new life and it is therefore credited as the person's own meritorious act. Anyone who refuses grace by choosing not to lead a new life thereby loses grace. If we open ourselves to grace and permit it to have its good effects in our life, merit increases as grace makes us more and more able to do the good. The more the merit, the greater the reward. The reward we receive for having done good works is the increase of grace *(augmentum gratiae)* and, after death, the increase of glory *(augmentum gloriae)*.[13]

Freedom: We Are Responsible for Accepting or Rejecting God's Grace

Protestants are most likely to be offended by Trent's emphasis on the sacraments as the means through which we receive grace and by the definition of this grace as an infused habitual character *(habitus)*. In addition, the expressions referring to "merit" and "meriting" are strange. We do not use these terms because a taboo has been placed on the idea of merit as a result of the controversy with Roman Catholicism. We prefer to describe the reward that we receive for our works in terms of God's undeserved gift. This is, however, really not very much different from the Tridentine way of speaking. Once we leave this unfamiliar Tridentine terminology out of consideration, we have very few problems in stating our usual Protestant understanding of salvation in Tridentine terms: God graciously approaches the sinner in Jesus Christ. Through the gospel, God calls the sinner to come. God asks only that the sinner choose to accept the offer of salvation in Jesus Christ. God makes this positive decision possible and supports it with grace. Once someone has decided to accept God's offer of salvation, God gives power to live a new life.

Accordingly, present controversies between Protestants and Roman Catholics do not focus primarily on the doctrine of salvation. Rather, the discussion focuses on the doctrines of the church and ministry as being the really important differences. The controversies about the doctrines of salvation and the way in which we are saved had split the church at the time of the Reformation. Today, these doctrines no longer seem to be the major points of difference between Lutherans and Roman Catholics.

Now, I certainly have no intention of reviving an obsolescent controversy whose time has really passed. On the other hand, I also have no interest in glossing over a real difference—especially not if the boundaries drawn by this difference no longer coincide with the boundaries between the confessional churches. The fact is that Lutherans appear not to have any very clear knowledge about the issues at the time of the Reformation. To identify these differences would be to document the fact that we Lutherans ourselves are opposed to the gospel as the Reformation understood it. In that case, we would need to ask ourselves whether we still have any right to appeal to the confession of our Lutheran fathers. It is right and proper for us to analyze critically the Roman Catholic form of teaching if we are prepared to subject our own teaching to the same critical analysis. It is only through such a process that the Reformation's understanding of the gospel can be meaningfully presented to the separated confessional churches as a proposal for a better understanding of the Scripture.

Typical Roman Catholic teaching can also be described in these terms: We see people as being basically free in their responses to God's purpose and offer of salvation. People can and should accept this offer as free agents. In so doing, they will by the grace of God become truly human. In this process of salvation, people are seen as God's partners.

A statement from the work of Johann Adam Möhler, who lived from 1796 to 1838, clarifies this. Using the terminology of the nineteenth century, he asserted: "all differences between Catholicism and Protestantism, in the article of justification, may shortly be reduced to this; namely that the Catholic Church considers religion and morality as inwardly one and the same, and both equally eternal; while the Protestant Church represents the two as essentially distinct, the former having an eternal, the latter a temporal, value."[14]

Whether Möhler's conclusion is correct or not is not the issue. For our purposes, we need only recognize that he describes Roman Catholicism as placing the religious reception of God's grace and moral actions on the same level.

By receiving grace, we are enabled to act morally. Such activity preserves our condition as people who have received grace and attained our religious goal of eternal salvation in relationship to God. The human person is the independent partner of God both as the recipient of grace and as God's creation. Möhler asserted that Luther did not understand that. Luther was unable to see people as free and independent. "While he desired to oppose the self-will, he annihilated the free-will, of man; and, in combating his self-seeking, he assailed, withal, his self-existence and individuality."[15] Möhler concluded that the basic disagreement of Roman Catholicism with Protestantism is that it does not properly understand the relationship between God and human beings. Luther's position was that people are neither willing nor able to decide in favor of the good as human beings had once, through sinning, decided in favor of evil.

Thus the affirmation of human freedom is characteristic of Roman Catholic theology. Protestants very often agree. There is no inclination to examine the theological intersection of the actual experience of being held responsible with the freedom that is assumed on the basis of such responsibility. For this reason, Roman Catholic teaching sets limits on its affirmation of this human freedom. People are free to decide to accept the reality of their salvation when they are supported in the decision-making process by the grace of God. It is this supportive involvement of grace in the decision-making process that enables us to carry through on the decision rather than simply collapsing under the weight of the effort. God's grace is already active in evoking our awareness of our freedom; grace also makes it possible, supports it, and perfects it. Thus God and people are thought of as working together. Human beings were created for a relationship with God, but this relationship has been disrupted by sin. Because we remain God's creatures even though we are sinners, we both can and must seek the establishment of this relationship. God in grace is working to save us even before we consciously seek God and comes out to find us while we are still searching. God does this in such a way that our integrity and independence are not impaired. Rather, grace works in such a way that it really enables, strengthens, and perfects our personal independence and integrity. The ultimate expression of this occurs when we overcome our sinful inclinations and freely and joyfully fulfill God's will.

GOD WORKS ALL
IN ALL: THE LUTHERAN TEACHING

The Doctrine by Which the Church
Stands and Falls

Lutherans have traditionally described the teaching that the ungodly are justified for Christ's sake through faith as the doctrine by which the church stands and falls.[16] Lutherans have used this description to designate the doctrine of justification as expressing the decisive difference between themselves and Roman Catholics. From this perspective, we cannot give in on the smallest point of this doctrine without losing the whole gospel.

> Nothing in this article can be given up or compromised, even if heaven and earth and things temporal should be destroyed. For as St. Peter says, "There is no other name under heaven given among men by which we must be saved" (Acts 4:12). "And with his stripes we are healed" (Isa. 53:5).
>
> On this article rests all that we teach and practice against the pope, the devil, and the world. Therefore we must be quite certain and have no doubts about it. Otherwise all is lost, and the pope, the devil, and all our adversaries will gain the victory.[17]

It is especially important to understand two points about the Lutheran understanding of justification. First, Christ together with his saving work is received by the believer who is justified. Second, justifying faith joins us so closely to Christ that there is no possibility of thinking about the imputation or appropriation of the work of salvation as any kind of process in the individual person. "Inasmuch as this must be believed and cannot be obtained or apprehended by any work, law, or merit, it is clear and certain that such faith alone justifies us."[18]

Nothing stands between faith and the salvation that has been won by Christ and is offered to us in the gospel. For this reason, faith cannot be thought of as any kind of human work, knowledge, decision, or agreement to accept God's offer of salvation. Faith itself is rather to be understood solely as God's work in people. Each of us can and must say, "I believe." The fact that I believe, however, is not my ability, my competence, my decision, or some kind of independent act of my free human person. Rather, it is God's work, a work that creates the "I" of faith. I owe my faith totally and completely, solely and exclusively, to God, to the Holy Spirit. Luther's explanation of the third article of the Apostles' Creed makes this very clear.[19] Article V of the Augsburg Confession is equally clear, particularly in the Latin text. "For through the Word and the sacraments, as through instruments, the Holy Spirit is given, and the Holy Spirit produces faith, where and when it pleases God, in those who hear the Gospel."[20]

Christ together with his work of salvation is present in the gospel that comes to us as word and sacrament. When God the Holy Spirit works faith this faith unites us with the Christ who is thus present. No person can choose either to unite or not to unite themselves to Jesus Christ and his work of salvation through faith. God joins us together with Christ through faith. For this reason, the Reformation's doctrine of justification cannot describe the process in terms of the freedom and independence that Roman Catholic teaching presupposes. It is certainly true that Roman Catholic theology describes a freedom that is supported by God's grace and that precedes, accompanies, and perfects the freedom of justification. People, however, are still seen as independent in relationship to this grace and can decide in favor of both grace and good works and thereby gain the reward of an increase of grace. In contrast, however, Lutheran theology understands God as uniting people with Christ in faith. This does not even leave room for us to be free to reject grace. The God who works all in all is the God on whom we depend in faith.

Obviously, this Lutheran style of thinking can easily fall into the crassest doctrine of double predestination. Since God alone works faith and does so "when and where he pleases," God must be the only possible cause of the absence of faith. Since no one can believe in God unless the Holy Spirit has created faith, God must be considered to be the cause of unbelief in the same way that God is considered to be the cause of faith. This conclusion can easily be drawn on the basis of Lutheran teaching and it is not easy to avoid it. The strictly logical conclusion was explicitly drawn by the Calvinists who—on the basis of the Protestant doctrine of justification—taught an absolute decree of double predestination with all of its consequences. This predestinarian logic, however, ascribes a freedom to its own intellectual processes that it denies to faith. It presupposes that we are free to think about and capable of logically understanding God's own logic as God's absolute decree of election and reprobation. We need to ask whether that is really true. For the present, it is enough to have drawn attention to this problem and to have deferred its discussion as a problem that arises out of thinking about the accomplished fact of justification.[21] At this time, there are more important issues.

The Time and Place of Faith

Sixteenth-century Lutheran theologians gave much attention to the relationship between faith and freedom and independence. These discussions are reflected in the Formula of Concord.[22] As human beings, a sense of responsibility and decision is always part of our experience. That does not mean, however, that we need to think of our personal freedom in order to think correctly about the way in which we make salvation our own. In an attempt to resolve this issue more adequately, a somewhat unusual interpretation of what justifying faith really is will now be proposed. We can, for example, define faith in terms of the basic elements of the human person. If we begin with that assumption, we shall eventually arrive at conclusions very close to the Roman Catholic teaching. In one way or another, faith will be understood as part of the individual's personal life history. It becomes part of the definition of this person, who is now defined as a believer. We also need to be certain, however, that what we believe is really true. I have already pointed to the fact that the late medieval teaching of merit provided this kind of certainty. If we ever doubt whether we are really right with God or whether we have the right to hope in God's grace, we can remember what we ourselves have done. These remembered works make us certain of God's grace. "Do as much as you yourself are able to do. Then you can be certain that God will be gracious to you."[23] Even the decision to believe, together with the resulting religious and moral changes, can itself be thought of as such a good work. Protestants ordinarily do this whenever they try to define faith in terms of the basic elements of the human person.

Genuinely Lutheran teaching cannot permit itself to become involved in this way of thinking. Since no human being can believe, but can only confess the truth of Luther's teaching in the Small Catechism that we are not in and of ourselves able to believe, we can never define faith in terms of the basic elements of the human person. Faith is never a work that is within the realm of human possibility. If it were, anyone could require it and anyone who really wanted to could produce it. The presence of faith would depend only on the consistency of our personal will. The fact is that God decides whether this is the time and the place in which we are to believe.[24] The original intention of this assertion was to reject the papal teaching that the sacraments were effective *ex opere operato,* that is, simply by reason of their administration. The Lutherans affirmed that our administration of the sacraments does not set limits to God's freedom. This obviously implies that faith is not produced by human freedom but through God's freedom.

Roman Catholic theologians have expressed the concern that this Lutheran view denies our human freedom and independence. My opinion is that this doctrine preserves human freedom by placing it where it belongs, that is, in the activity of the triune God. It is only as God works in us to make us what we are in relationship to God that we become real persons.[25] Now it is no longer enough merely to make the general comment that God works faith "when and where he pleases." We are now able to say that the faith that God works becomes effectively present where it is most needed, in the troubled and anxious conscience. The doctrine of justification through faith will not appeal to everyone. Those who have not experienced the terrors of conscience will despise it. It brings real comfort, however, to all those who experience anxiety. "Although this teaching is despised by inexperienced men, God-fearing and anxious consciences find by experience that it offers the greatest consolation because the consciences of men cannot be pacified by any work but only by faith when they are sure that for Christ's sake they have a gracious God. . . . This whole teaching is to be referred to that conflict of the terrified conscience, nor can it be understood apart from that conflict."[26]

This identifies the place and time of faith as the "terrified conscience." In this situation we are tempted spiritually with the feeling that we are being attacked by God *(Anfechtung).* This kind of temptation cannot be overcome by assuring ourselves of what we have done, no matter how convinced we might be. In this situation our conscience finds comfort only when it is certain of the grace of God which preserves us in faith. We cannot understand the Reformation's way of teaching the gospel unless and until we have experienced this level of anxiety, this spiritual temptation, this awareness that we can do nothing at all. At least, that is what Melanchthon claimed: "Accordingly inexperienced and profane men, who dream that Christian righteousness is nothing else than civil or philosophical righteousness, have bad judgment concerning this teaching."[27]

Melanchthon's claim is, in some respects, obviously exaggerated. The fact is that the papal theologians then understood and Roman Catholics today understand Christian righteousness as the process of justification, which is begun, accompanied, and perfected by God—the process in which people fulfill God's will with the help of grace. At the same time, however, Melanchthon's polemical statement addresses the heart of the controversy. For Roman Catholics, certainty is based on human activity, the activity by which people confirm that they are really righteous. In contrast, the righteousness that comes through faith is always and only righteousness that we have received. The Reformers taught that we receive God's salvation in Christ only when we are past the point of being able to do anything. At this point, the point at which we are unable to do anything for ourselves, the Holy Spirit works faith. This kind of faith, therefore, comes only at a specific time and place. The time and place at which we experience spiritual temptation is the time and place at which God wills to create that faith which is God's own work in us.

When God works this saving faith in us, God thereby also makes it possible to follow God's leadership and life in the opportunities that God gives to us. "Whoever knows that in Christ he has a gracious God, truly knows God, calls upon him, and is not, like the heathen, without God."[28] If we live in the certainty of faith, we receive the world as God's gift. This certainty removes all the pressure to achieve a certain religious standard because we have been joined with Christ through faith. As a result, we can also face life with the new certainty that whatever happens, we are never outside of God's providential care. This enables us to face life with a new spontaneity. We can come to terms with whatever comes, because God comes to meet us in whatever happens.

The Gospel

Faith is God's work in us. It joins us together with God. This faith has its own time and place. Once this is understood, the danger arises that we consciously or unconsciously attempt to manipulate our own emotions in an effort to create the time and place in which we can enjoy the religious experience of unity with God. We are, however, not able to do that, precisely because faith is always and entirely God's work in us. This is why the Augsburg Confession says, "Condemned are the Anabaptists and others who teach that the Holy Spirit comes to us through our own preparations, thoughts, and works without the external word of the Gospel."[29] This rejection is necessary; only so could the Reformers maintain the distinction between God's work in the human person and the human person itself. Enthusiasm—whether consciously or, as is more usual, unconsciously—seeks to blur this distinction. In so doing, it thoroughly confuses God's leading with its own intentions, God's Word with human thoughts.

We need the gospel that comes to us as a Word from outside ourselves in order to recognize God's activity and differentiate it from our own inner feelings. The implication of this for our understanding of faith is that faith cannot in any way be determined by the believing person who is the subject of faith.[30] For as long as faith is something that the subject of faith knows or feels, faith is trapped in the ambiguity of all human experience. That kind of faith could not give us the certainty of participating in God's work for our salvation. Rather, faith must be determined by the same gospel in which faith trusts. This is the gospel of God's gracious acceptance of sinners. This faith can be described only in terms of what is believed: "that Christ suffered for us and that for his sake our sin is forgiven and righteousness and eternal life are given to us."[31] The content of this faith is the definite and clearly definable statement of the gospel. The Spirit works faith through our hearing of this gospel. "To obtain such faith God instituted the office of the ministry, that is, provided the Gospel and the sacraments. Through these, as through means, he gives the Holy Spirit, who works faith, when and where he pleases, in those who hear the Gospel. And the Gospel teaches that we have a gracious God, not by our own merits but by the merit of Christ, when we believe this."[32]

Insofar as these descriptions of the gospel are presented without reference to the time and the place of faith, they are abstractions. The meaning of these abstract statements of the gospel does not become clear until we experience spiritual temptation (Anfechtung). How this description of the very definite content of the gospel indicates the basic emphasis of Lutheran spirituality. Faith clings to the external Word of the gospel that is personally addressed to me. This also means that God does not simply encounter us in our internal processes—as though our exploration of our inner life would eventually bring us into contact with God. Rather, God comes to us from outside ourselves and establishes contact with us exactly at the point at which the Holy Spirit does his work in us. That which is outside me is the history of Jesus Christ, his life, suffering, and death. This is my righteousness. I can, however, never so make it part of myself that I am no longer able to distinguish it from myself.[33] No matter how much Jesus Christ becomes my righteousness through faith, he remains the other, in whom faith trusts and to whom it clings. The gospel is significant as the external means through which Jesus Christ encounters me.

This encounter with Christ provides the basis for a doctrine of the church. This encounter takes place through the office of the ministry. God has the gospel preached; God lets us hear it so that we may know how we stand with God. We need to know that when we have come to the point in life at which we need faith. This office of the ministry is not primarily the ordained ministry.[34] Rather, it is primarily understood as the function of preaching the gospel and administering the sacraments.

This understanding of the gospel as the external Word always provides the basis for at least a preliminary answer to the difficult question of the relationship between our experience of the spontaneity of human life and our consciousness of the continuity of our life.

The Reformation assertion that faith and the religious definition of our life are not under the control of our will and conscious self-awareness could be understood as denying the experience of spontaneity and as interrupting the continuity of our awareness of life. These difficulties do in fact result from the Reformation teaching. We may not attempt to avoid them by denying that religious reality is God's work and converting it into a human undertaking. At the same time, the ongoing engagement with the external Word does, however, create the context for the practice of a kind of religious discipline. This does not mean that such religious practices can establish the time and the place that are the necessary condition of faith. What we are able to say is that questions about the continuity and spontaneity of faith can be addressed on the basis of our understanding of the gospel and of the ongoing preaching of the gospel. Whenever we wish to gain certainty that we believe, we are dependent on the consolation of the gospel itself. And since this consolation comes to us in various ways, the troubled conscience is never without reassurance.[35]

In the context of the Reformation teaching, this description of the gospel once again shows the distinction from the Roman Catholic approach. The believer—the person who has been defined by God's working—is constantly directed to the gospel and thus to the encounter with God. The believer is primarily a receiver. This is totally the case in reference to salvation. As a receiver, the believer is never in control of the gift of being righteous before God. The believer can never be in control of the gift and thus the assurance of salvation never rests on anything that the believer might do. Assurance is based solely and alone on God's saving work in Christ—a work in which the believer has not participated in any way.

3

The Basic Decision of the Early Church: Biblical History Teaches that the World and Salvation Have Both Been Given to Us by the One and the Same God

The Reformation understood itself as standing in continuity with the early church and its doctrinal tradition. No extensive proof of this assertion is necessary at this point. The Book of Concord followed the pattern of earlier versions of the Lutheran *corpus doctrinae* and included the three symbolic Creeds of the early church. At the beginning of both the Augsburg Confession and the Smalcald Articles, the Lutherans presented the doctrine of the Trinity and the doctrine of the person and work of Christ and assumed that they were in agreement with the decisions of the councils of the early church. Luther's Small and Large Catechisms teach the faith on the basis of an interpretation of the Apostles' Creed. As a result, Lutherans tend to be more familiar with this creed and to use it more frequently as a liturgical creed than the Nicene Creed. Confirmation instruction still focuses on the Apostles' Creed.[1]

The superficial observer might, therefore, easily conclude that the statement of the faith in the Apostles' Creed may simply be taken for granted as the basis of Lutherans' statement of the faith. There are difficulties, however, particularly when historical study has questioned some of the "facts of salvation."[2] The early church has transmitted its basic decisions about the faith to us in the Creeds. Unlike the Reformers, however, we are no longer confident that we can reconstruct the larger outline of the teachings of the early church. As a result, we today are not as clear about the relevance of the basic decision of the early church in its historical context as we are about the relevance of the basic decisions of the Reformation. The ongoing presence of Roman Catholicism has constantly reminded us of the meaning of the Reformation.

In contrast, the controversial situation that forced the early church to make its specific doctrinal decisions seems to have passed away forever. This is true both of the decision that the world and salvation are gifts of one and the same God and of the conclusions drawn from this decision in the doctrines of the Trinity and of the person and work of Christ. The patterns of thought used by the Creeds are strange to us, but at the same time the basic decisions of the early church seem to be now accepted without question. This combination could mislead us into either merely accepting the formulas of the Apostles' Creed and the Trinitarian doxology or to adopting the stance of analyzing their meaning with the objectivity of historical observers. Still, it is worth the effort to make the basic decision of the early church part of our own way of thinking.

In this section, I shall follow the method outlined in the Introduction. I shall not present a dogmatics as the interpretation of the Creeds. That is, of course, one possibility—especially if the dogmatician presents this material in such a way that it can be understood by a larger circle of readers.[3] Rather, I shall attempt to clarify the significance of the decision that the Creeds both presupposed and expressed. This requires both historical and dogmatic understanding. Why did people at that time make this decision rather than some other? Why did this decision seem unavoidable? We shall become most aware of this problem at the very points at which we become aware of the consequences of these decisions for the doctrines of the Trinity and the person and work of Christ. I emphasize this in advance: We shall always find ourselves primarily concerned to see the right interpretation of Scripture as the norm and source of faith—although there may be times when the conciseness of this essay conceals that concern.

THE WORLD AND SALVATION
ARE HELD TOGETHER IN THE ONE GOD

The experience of the world in the classical age provided the context that gave meaning to the basis decision of the early church. This experience of the world is different from our experience of the world—although the differences may only be superficial. One reason is that we stand in the continuity of the Christian tradition and thereby have a relationship to the experience of the world in the classical age. In addition, both we and the early church live at the end of our respective ages. Many factors are therefore repeated. It is not our present task to find the analogies between that time and this, however. Rather, we are concerned to make the decision of the early church part of our own thinking. This decision still confronts us with its claim to be valid. That decision has served to preserve a content of the gospel that we may not abandon: Neither our concern for the world should lead us to exclude salvation from our faith in the one God, nor should our concern for salvation lead us to exclude the world.

Understanding as the Way of Salvation

The dual concept of "heaven and earth" comprehends the whole creation. The Nicene Creed expands this by using a second concept, "seen and unseen." This contrast between the seen and the unseen was used by Paul to describe the goal of salvation: "For this slight momentary affliction is preparing for us an eternal weight of glory beyond all comparison, because we look not to the things that are seen but to the things that are unseen; for the things that are seen are transient, but the things that are unseen are eternal" (2 Cor. 4:17–18). The values associated with the seen and the unseen are obvious: The task is to overcome the seen and the temporal in order to come to the unseen and the eternal. The ontological qualification "the things that are seen are transient, but the things that are unseen are eternal" explains why we should look for salvation in the unseen. The contrast between "visible and invisible," however, is used in Col. 1:16 to describe all that is created. The Nicene Creed used the Greek terminology of 2 Cor. 4:17–18 "seen and unseen" and interpreted it in the cosmological sense of "visible and invisible" of Col. 1:16. A long way led from Paul's use of the contrast between the seen and the unseen to the Nicene Creed's use of the same terms. Along this way, the terms attracted a wide variety of connotations that came from a different understanding of the world. Christian faith and thought needed to make themselves at home in this new world.

The "visible" is that which is available to our senses. The "invisible," on the other hand, is available to us only through thinking. This is one acceptable way of defining what is visible and what is invisible. As a result, we usually identify "reality" in terms of those things that are available to us through sensory experience. In contrast, thoughts are mere abstractions, "only" ideas. Is that an appropriate conclusion? Is this not really an absent-minded approach to life that seduces us into following the stimulation of our senses and prevents us from considering our own ability to think?

This question still confronts us today. It has ethical, philosophical, and religious dimensions. The ethical dimension emerges when we ask whether life is more successful when lived in an absent-minded sensuality or when carefully considered and well thought-through. The philosophical dimension emerges when we ask whether the true meaning of life reveals itself through sensory experience or through thinking. The religious dimension emerges as soon as we ask how we become aware of ultimate reality as a whole. If we ask the questions in this way, the answers seem clear. We become truly human though orienting our life to the invisible, to the world of thought. Animals also experience the world, but only through their senses; only human beings are able to transcend this sensory experience of the world by thinking about it. Certainly, not everyone is equally interested in the invisible world of thought. Still, the early church's challenge to find the meaning of life in the unseen found a broad echo among people who lived at the end of the world of classical Greek and Roman culture.

As time passed, the Platonic tradition became more and more influential. As a result, early Christianity had to present itself in a manner acceptable to this style of religious philosophy. This was the only way to gain entry into the cultured world of its time. Consequently, the kind of Platonism that was popular in the late classical world shaped the thought and life style of the early church. The early church was simultaneously attracted and repulsed by this late Platonism. The early church was not primarily affected by the scholarly traditions cultivated in the Platonic schools. The religious dimensions of this style of doing philosophy were the major attraction: Thinking pulls itself together out of an absent-minded approach to life and leaves the world of sensory impression with its interest in the many individual forms of existence behind; it thereby transcends the "many" and achieves an awareness of the One. This One is not one thing among others. It is the reality before all individual existences and beyond their inevitable limitations. It is the transcendent ground of being. No further description is possible. The One is not to be thought of as an individual something that could be described in some kind of language. Rather, this kind of transcendence is so indescribable that it can be spoken of only in negations, by saying what it is not.

The more thinking focuses on the One, God, the more it becomes aware of itself. Thinking God brings us close to the essence of God. This fulfills the goal of philosophy as defined in the Platonic tradition. Since all "real" reality has its ground in the transcendent One, human being also finds its goal there. As a result, salvation can be described in a meaningful way only on the basis of a cosmology that explains the world as coming from God. Similarly, we human beings can recognize that we are spirit and achieve our true spiritual being only by turning away from sensory experience. (Many Platonists accordingly lived in ascetic communities in which they abstained from eating meat and from sexual intercourse.)

This Platonic philosophy placed a limited positive value on the world. Since the world is formed through God's thinking, it is also possible for people to work their way through this world by a process of thinking. In so doing, we can find true godliness by leaving the transitory world behind us.

In contrast, the Gnostic movement raised the Platonic distinction to the level of a radical opposition between God and the world. The thinking self of the Gnostic defined itself as having broken with its physical being in this world. Physical nature cannot keep up with thinking that has been freed from the burden of the material. It is hopelessly captive to this world. The Gnostic religion asked and promised to answer this question: How can the thinking self be freed from its bondage to this material existence?

The first step in this process of liberation is taken when the thinking self becomes aware of its transcendent source. Some news reaches the thinking self that makes it aware of its origin and raises its consciousness of being captive to the flesh, that is, the material world. As a result of this understanding, the thinking self becomes aware that this condition of captivity is not the true life of the self. Rather the self recognizes that it is part of the reality of the totally transcendent God. The thinking self becomes aware of this because it is able to think about this God. Such thinking takes place only in the form of negative theology.

At that time, almost everyone—whether Gnostic, Platonist, or Christian— was fascinated by negative theology. The Gnostics, however, went even further:

> None of the names which are understood or said or seen or conceived, none is fitting for him, even when they are very splendid, prominent, honoured. Certainly it is possible to pronounce these [names] to his glory and honour, according to the capacity of each one among those who exalt him. He however, as he is and in what manner he finds himself, him no understanding can understand, nor can any word reproduce him, nor can any eye see him, nor any body encompass him, because of his own unapproachable greatness and his own unattainable depth and his own immeasurable height and his own inconceivable breadth.[4]

Such negative theology assures the thinking self that it is free of the world. Because it knows the Unknowable, it is delivered from ignorance and has begun the way of redemption. This presupposes, however, that the thinking self sees through the world in which it is imprisoned in its body and, as a result, recognizes its negative character. Enlightenment and knowledge is the way of salvation offered by Gnosticism.

Once the self begins to recognize its true nature, it also begins to realize that it is superior to the powers of the material world that hold it in bondage. This sense of superiority can lead either to an ascetic or to a libertarian ethic: The laws of this world and its ruler are not binding on the self that has been freed through Gnosis. This freedom is not fully gained until death. Dying means that we leave this material prison and—according to common Gnostic presuppositions—must still then rise to the transcendent world of light. Along the way, we need to avoid the guards who will try to keep us imprisoned in this evil world. If we have mastered the Gnostic teaching, however, we can succeed in rising to the light and finally escape this negative world.

God's Salvation in Jesus Christ

When early Christianity entered the late classical world, it brought along the rich inheritance it had received from Hellenistic Judaism. Hellenistic Judaism had already translated the Bible into Greek. It had also achieved the rethinking of the Old Testament tradition in the new categories required by translation into Greek. It had done so in ways that preserved basic characteristics of Judaism: faith in one God, the Creator, basic ethical principles, and eschatological expectation. Early Christianity built on this and added a new understanding of salvation. Whereas Hellenistic Judaism still described salvation as mediated through the law, Christianity described salvation as coming through the person and work of Jesus Christ. This confession and the corresponding proclamation of Christ became the enduring hallmarks of Christianity.

Given the context of late classical culture, how did the early church have to reshape the proclamation of Christ so that it could be heard as gospel? Whatever the situation of the hearer, it is certainly true that this gospel must always be rooted in the history of Jesus Christ. It is equally certain that its proclamation must be determined by the time in which it is heard. In order to be heard as a message of salvation by people in the late classical world, the gospel had to attempt to respond to their questions and to their needs; it tried to respond to their situation where they are. For this reason, then as always, the hearers helped to shape the form in which this gospel was presented. When this process of shaping the gospel to correspond to the world in which it is preached happens as it should, the vitality of the gospel is guaranteed, but the gospel is also still endangered.

In the late classical culture, the gospel was in danger of being caught in the assumption that salvation and the world are in a dualistic opposition to each other. We may describe this as the cosmological danger, that is, the danger that arises from the effort to restate the gospel in terms of a particular understanding of the world. In addition, there was the danger that the special offer of salvation in Jesus Christ would be absorbed into the assumption that everyone has the possibility of gaining salvation on their own. We may describe this as the soteriological danger. The confession of Christ defended against both dangers: Christ is the Redeemer whom God has sent as the way of salvation. The way by which people leave this world and go to God is available only because God has already entered into the world in Jesus Christ. This Redeemer who has been sent by God is the same Redeemer who has come to and is totally present with human beings.

This confession of Christ had to survive the threat of being falsified by Gnosticism. "By this you know the Spirit of God: every spirit which confesses that Jesus Christ has come in the flesh is of God, and every spirit which does not confess Jesus is not of God" (1 John 4:2–3). This criterion of the genuine Christian confession was directed against an understanding of the Redeemer that did not recognize that he was really and wholly human. If he were not, the real whole human person could not be totally saved. We might say that salvation involves an interaction between two selves that mutually define each other. For example, Docetism's teaching that the Redeemer did not share in our physical life meant that the whole human person was not saved but that its physical nature was excluded.

Such a Gnostic soteriology would also create presuppositions and consequences in the area of cosmology and in the understanding of God. If only the thinking self is saved, only the thinking self belongs to God. The world, the place in which we live and the necessary context of our physical life is no longer established by this God. Similarly, the confession that Jesus Christ has come in the flesh says more than that the Redeemer has entered into the totality of human physical life and accomplished our salvation (1 John 5:5–8). It also says that this human physical life and the world that is its necessary context are both established by God. No matter how much it may seem to us that the world and salvation are in opposition to each other, they can never fall apart. Thus a realistic Christology and soteriology presuppose a specific cosmology. If both the Redeemer and redemption are thought of as saving all of life, then the world itself must be the creature of the God who sent the Redeemer in the flesh—no matter how much the world has been spoiled by sin.

The confession of Jesus Christ as the Redeemer sent by God also has consequences for our doctrine of human beings (theological anthropology): People are not able to find redemption by their own powers. People are not capable of being equal with God—not even some special people who are particularly called to the spiritual life can achieve such equality. Redemption always comes to us from outside ourselves through Jesus Christ. The fact that people do not remain uninvolved but rather enter upon the way of salvation that has been opened to them can be understood only as their reaction to the redemption that has come to them from God. The reception of salvation in the sacraments of baptism and the Lord's Supper make a new godly life style possible.

As the confession of Christ unfolds, its truth is preserved and perversions are prevented. At first the truth of faith is experienced as a whole. As it unfolds, the truths that are familiar to us from the Creeds are revealed. It would obviously be a mistake to think that there was an agreed-upon text of the Creeds during the early period of the second and third centuries. The "rule of faith" or the "canon of truth" that guards against perversions of the faith is the living tradition of the faith in its entirety. The Scripture is part of this tradition of faith. "The 'rule of truth' is the larger context of the Christian faith. The two parts of the Scripture are its written documentation. In both forms, the one norm of faith appears. This norm of faith is ultimately identical with the reality of revelation."[5]

The Bible, with its two-part canon of the Old and New Testaments, together with the rule of faith define the basic decision of the early church. This decision is the truth of faith that the church must continue to maintain. The truth of faith cannot be understood on the basis of an arbitrary selection from the tradition (as in the biblical canon proposed by the Gnostic theologian Marcion) or on the basis of an arbitrary interpretation and combination of biblical passages. Rather, the truth of faith opens itself to us when the whole Bible is interpreted in accordance with the faith. Scripture and the rule of faith together preserve the gospel from being perverted. This gospel witnesses to us that God the Creator has come to save us in Jesus Christ.

Biblical History

I must still discuss one additional consequence of this decision of the early church.[6] Jesus Christ is confessed as the real Redeemer, who was totally incarnate, has suffered, has died on the cross, was raised from the dead, and ascended into heaven, the biblical witness to him must be understood in a historical context. Such an interpretation will often seem quite forced to anyone schooled in the historical-critical method of biblical interpretation. This is also true of the New Testament's references to the Old Testament. The confession of Christ requires us to read the Old Testament as a prophetic testimony to Christ.

The interpretation of the Bible was thus bound to the historical reality of Christ. An unlimited spiritual or allegorical interpretation of the Bible became impossible. The historical meaning of the Bible always needed to be taken into account. The rule of faith required such a historical interpretation to preserve the relationship between creation and redemption. The mystery of the divine purpose (see Eph. 1:10), God's plan or work of salvation, was to be thought of as the context within which God carried out God's work. God went outside God's self to create the world and the people in it and did so again in order to bring salvation to people who had fallen into sin.

In terms of this divine plan, any differences in God must be understood as differences only within God. God is the eternal, transcendent ground of all reality that is not God. God also is the Redeemer at work in Jesus Christ and as the Spirit who works in the believer. Because the divine plan is centered in the historical work of redemption carried out by Jesus Christ and described in the biblical history, the question arises as to how the God revealed in Jesus Christ the Redeemer is related to the God who is the transcendent ground of all reality. This in turns leads to additional questions about the consequences of the basic decision that the Creator has also brought salvation through Jesus Christ.

Once again we are concerned about the right understanding of Scripture. Precisely because the rule of faith establishes the christological center of the Bible, biblical interpretation must reach additional decisions. The fact that the early church found ways of making the gospel meaningful within the contextual horizon of the late classical world should not lead to a loss of the gospel within this horizon. The gospel could remain the good news of salvation only because the early church's basic decision preserved it from interpreting salvation as a process of rational understanding. On the contrary, this basic decision explicitly affirmed the biblical history that witnessed to God's plan. We today must make the same decision; otherwise salvation will disappear into an inwardness unrelated to the created world and we will abandon the world to its own autonomy.[7]

THE TRINITARIAN
DEVELOPMENT OF THE BASIC
DECISION OF THE EARLY CHURCH

The gift of the world and the gift of salvation are held together by the fact that they are both gifts of the same God. He is to be simultaneously thought of as the creator and as the redeemer. The plan of salvation includes both creation and redemption; this is the context in which Scripture must be interpreted. We must demand this of ourselves even when we have difficulty in really meeting this demand. For this is the point at which the universal dimension of the concept of God joins together with the specific character of redemption. Of course, the whole world is God's creation and every person is God's creature. The salvation that has appeared in Christ, however, does not reach everyone, but only a limited number of elect—those who are called into the church.

We still do not know how to think simultaneously about these two realities. The extensive modern discussion of the problem of a "natural" theology demonstrates this by its failure to come to any conclusion. The discussion about "natural" theology attempts to separate the order of creation from the order of redemption. In fact, however, these may be only distinguished, never separated, because they belong together in the same God. The order of creation includes every person and does so in such a way that each person can be conscious of being part of creation. In contrast, the order of salvation is available only when it is historically mediated through the church's proclamation of God's saving work in Jesus Christ.

At this point, we must limit our discussion of these issues to demonstrating that the modern form of this problem differs from the form of the problem to which the basic decision of the early church responded. The early church was not concerned about contrasting the revelation of creation that is universally available to reason with the revelation of salvation that is available only in a historical report handed down from one generation to the next. Rather, the early church never questioned that these two were joined together in the mystery of God's plan. The description of this plan could, however, be distinguished from theological statements about the Trinitarian nature of God. The plan of salvation assumes and reinforces this Trinitarian theological perspective.

If we succeed in comprehending the basic difference between the problem that confronted the early church and the problem that confronts us in the modern world, we may be able to resolve the apparently irresolvable problem of the relationship between reason and revelation. We have been struggling with this problem since the time of the Enlightenment at the very latest. Gaining insights into the Trinitarian theology of the early church expressed in its basic decision may help us find new approaches to this question.

God's Presence in the World

Thinkers of the late classical period found the transcendence of God a fascinating idea. The idea of the transcendent God permitted them to assert God's un- and other-worldliness by negating the categories of this world and applying these negated categories to God. The resulting theology was called negative (or, in a term derived from the Greek: apophatic) theology. If this method is consistently followed, we would have to conclude that God cannot be comprehended even in these negative statements—rather, God is totally and absolutely indescribable or ineffable.

Christian thinking properly uses this method of negative theology—up to a point. At the same time, God's presence and activity in the world must be affirmed. Christian theology thereby remains oriented to Jesus Christ as the focal point of God's presence in this world. The opening sentence of the *Second Letter of Clement*—a Christian sermon from the middle of the second century—is a programmatic statement: "Brothers, we ought to think of Jesus Christ as we do of God—as the 'judge of the living and the dead.' And we ought not to belittle our salvation."[8] The salvation procured by Jesus is really God's salvation. The universality of its claim is expressed in the assertion that we shall all—the living and the dead—be subjected to an eschatological judgment.

Having said this, the question arises as to how we may properly describe the presence of God in Jesus. In the Old Testament, God appears through the Angel of God. Should we then describe God's presence in Jesus Christ as the presence of this angelic messenger who reveals God? God is also described as having given the Spirit to certain people. Was it, then, the Spirit of God that was present in the world with and through Jesus? We might cite Isa. 11:1–3 as a prophecy that the Spirit would rest on the coming Messiah. Then we would be able to say that some part of God is present in Jesus. But that would not be God as such. Or do we want to say that none other than God was really present in Jesus Christ? Then Jesus would be a form in which God, the creator of the world, once appeared in this world by coming to redeem people from sin and death by his own suffering and dying. If we choose this formulation, can we still describe God as transcendent? The Scripture clearly describes Jesus' relationship to his Father as a relationship to someone different from Jesus: Jesus spoke to the Father, prayed to the Father, and obeyed the Father.

We can easily identify difficulties in the various attempts to describe the relationship between God and Jesus that failed to gain acceptance in the church. Some of the advocates of these ideas were called "Monarchians" because they emphasized the uniqueness and absolute sovereignty of God. One group of these was called "dynamic Monarchians." This name was derived from their description of Jesus in terms only of a divine power—but not God as present and working in Jesus. The "modalistic Monarchians" felt that the one God had been present in the world in three different modes: as Father, as Son, and as Holy Spirit.

Jesus was, of course, always called the "Son of God" and the use of this title was religiously significant. This title, however, needed to be defined more clearly before it could provide the basis for greater conceptual clarity about the relationship between Jesus and God. Should it be understood metaphorically? The faithful were also described as "sons" or "children" of God and prayed to God as the Father. Or was it an expression describing a special relationship between Jesus and God's being?

The description of Jesus as the Word (Logos) led a step further in the direction of describing Jesus as being in a special relationship to God. When Jesus was described as the Word of God, there were already biblical precedents for speaking about the Word of God and the Wisdom of God. The Greek word for "word" was *logos*. The fact that this term was used both in the Gospel According to John and in the description of deity in Hellenistic philosophy became the basis of a connection between the two. This connection was useful for, no matter how much emphasis Christians placed on God as transcending the material universe, Christians still had to describe some connection between God and the world. In Hellenistic thought of the time, the Logos was the transcendent ground of all being in the whole universe. This definition made Logos a term that could be used to describe God for it could be redefined to mean that God is in some way involved in all that is grounded in God. The transcendent One had to unfold into the reality of the world.

Logos, the Greek term for word, also described the divine dimension of the universe, the divine structure that shaped the world. And the conceptual bridges from this meaning of *logos* to the biblical concepts of "word" and "wisdom" were easily established. Jesus as the Word of God was then thought of as the unfolding of the transcendent One into the concept of multiplicity, which always remained only an idea within God—but determined the multiple forms of the reality that is available to our sensory experience. The Logos or Word of God then reveals the One in terms of the multiplicity that is the only kind of reality which human thought can comprehend.

The description of Jesus as the Logos also expressed the gospel's claim to address all people. Just as the Hellenistic Logos was expressed in the whole world, so Jesus was related to every person.

Naturally, this terminology immediately raised the controversial question as whether Jesus was properly called the Logos. The Logos was present and active in the world and in people from the very beginning. How was it possible that this new revelation of Jesus Christ was superior to the ancient truth? It could be taken for granted that this question would arise but it is not the issue here. Rather, the problem for the early church was how to more precisely define what was meant by calling Jesus the Logos. The assertion in John 1:14 that the divine Logos had become flesh raised a new kind of question. A Hellenistic cosmology could leave the question open as to whether the Logos was present only as one of God's thoughts or whether it was an independent something alongside God that had come from but was also different from God. Christians had to be more precise. Clearly, the incarnate Logos had to be thought of as having an independent existence. Similarly, the Hellenistic Logos should be seen as present in everyone as the capacity to think and reason—the Stoics had described this as the scattered Logos (the *logos spermatikós*). How could the Logos be described as being exclusively present in Jesus? On the one hand, the designation of Jesus as the Logos provided the possibility of describing God's presence in Jesus Christ in a proper and understandable way. On the other hand, however, new problems were created. For now it was absolutely necessary to more exactly explain how this Logos that existed independently *(hypostasis)*[9] was related to God's being.

The Son-Logos and the Father

The designation of Jesus Christ as the Logos did not displace the designation as Son. The symbolic Creeds—which became the definitive statements— described Jesus only as the Son, not as the Logos. Even when Jesus was called the Son of God, however, some of the elements of the concept of the Logos were included in its meaning. In attempting to define more closely the relationship of the Son-Logos to the Father, it was necessary to decide whether the Son was on the side of the world or of God.

The designation of Jesus as the Logos expressed his universal significance in cosmological terms: The ordered structure that God has given to the world appeared in human form in Jesus Christ. The Logos was thought of as having being for as long as there has been and will be a world. He is the mode in which God's transcendent being relates to the world. He is the mediator of creation; many biblical texts were available to support this. The question then was: How does this simultaneity of the Logos, the mediator of creation, with the beginning and end of the world relate to the eternal being of God. Should we think of the Logos as being present in God, just as a thought, before it is thought, is present in the human mind *(logos endiathetos)*. The Logos would then have been eternally present in God's mind until expressed by God's creating act and given independent existence *(logos prophorikos)*. If we say that, we also say that the Son-Logos was not always an independent entity and God can be thought of as being God without the expression of the Son-Logos. Such a God would—before the expression of the Logos—have no relationships. What kind of God would that be? The great theologian Origen therefore rejected this solution. He resolved the problem by saying: Since God is in

God's very nature unchangeable, God was always in relationship to the world. This means that world—in the very specifically defined aspect of the ideal world of the spirit—is eternally present. The church was, however, not willing to accept Origen's solution. The church's thinking was determined by its historical interpretation of the Bible. As a result of that understanding of the Bible, the church—contrary to Origen—always understood the creation as the beginning of this history and therefore as an event within time.

Therefore, the early church attempted to combine the emphasis on the function of the Logos as the cosmological mediator with the requirement that the creation be understood as an event within time by which the world began. The complex of ideas resulting from this effort has been historically identified as Arianism.[10] Arians taught that the Son-Logos belongs on the side of God's creatures. He had a beginning and was not eternal as the Father is. It is characteristic of his being that it is not contemporaneous with God, but rather contemporaneous with the world. Proverbs 8:22 was one of the most important—and therefore also most disputed—biblical proofs of this position. The church had commonly identified Wisdom with the Logos. In this passage, as it had been translated into Greek in the Septuagint, Wisdom says: "The Lord created me at the beginning of his ways, the first of his works." The very nature of the Son-Logos is therefore different from that of God. As a creature, he is subject to suffering and to change. This corresponds to the life of the incarnate Logos. He is thereby clearly distinguished from God, even though he has the most eminent position of the first of God's creatures.

There were many variations on this way of thinking that were popularly accepted, even after the Council of Nicea rejected it as heretical. This was only partially due to the influence that theologians who supported Arianism exercised at the imperial court. The combination of a strict monotheism with the emphasis on the cosmological valuation of Christianity's claim to be of universal significance seemed to meet the needs of the time very well. It seemed an appropriate position for a Christianity that was then in the process of becoming the new state religion of the worldwide Roman Empire.

And yet, although this way of obviously subordinating the Son to the Father satisfied these cosmological concerns, it was an equally unsatisfying answer to questions related to salvation. If the Redeemer, the incarnate Logos or Son of God, was really to be able to redeem people from the world and lead them to God, he himself could not be part of the world. On the contrary, he must come from the God to whom he would lead the redeemed. The goal of God's plan of salvation that reached its climactic fulfillment in the incarnation of the Son is not to provide a religious basis for the existence of this world but rather to rescue people from this world.

The decision of the Council of Nicea of 325 ultimately prevailed and became the generally accepted position of the church. This decision was determined by this concern for salvation. The symbolic Creed adopted by the

Council of Nicea is not, however, the Creed which we today commonly use and refer to as the Nicene Creed.[11] The creed used in the church's liturgy comes from a later period and reflects an advanced stage of the controversy.[12] The Nicene Creed of 325 emphasized the nature of the Logos as God. "And in one Lord Jesus Christ, the Son of God, only-begotten, born of the Father, that is, of the being *[ousias]* of the Father, God of God, light of light, true God of true God, born, not made, of one being with the Father, through whom were made all things in heaven and earth."[13] The Creed presently used in the liturgy is somewhat different. "We believe in one Lord, Jesus Christ, the only Son of God, eternally begotten of the Father, God from God, Light from Light, true God from true God, begotten not made, of one Being with the Father. Through him all things were made." The Creed emphasizes that being "begotten" or "born"[14] is quite different than being "made." And it places special emphasis on the Son being "of one being with the Father" *(homoousios to patri)*. That assertion in turn required further interpretation. This much was clear in any case: The Son-Logos belongs completely and totally on the side of the divine being. He is not a mediator between the world and God. And he absolutely must not be placed on the side of the world or of created being. The Son is not defined by his existing as long as the world but rather by his being as eternal as God is eternal.

The Holy Threesome

The decision of the Council of Nicea could be implemented only through significant interpretative work. For the God whose Being is one with the Being of the Son cannot be thought of as transcending the world in the same way that the Father does. As the incarnate Logos, this divine Being is also present in the world. Taking this into account required more than asserting the unity of the divine Being in terms of the Nicene *homousios*. The Son also had to be thought as being different from the Father in the context of the divine plan of salvation, in the course of which the transcendent God became immanent in this world. Otherwise the Nicene Creed would have been a relapse into the concepts of Modalistic Monarchianism—a viewpoint that had already been proved inadequate.[15]

Since the work of redemption was carried out by the incarnate Son-Logos, it was necessary to describe the Son as different from the Father—in spite of the assertion that he was of one Being with the Father. This provided the church an opportunity to express its cosmological interest. The first assertion was that the Logos was different from the Father even in the work of creation. More precise terms were needed, however, to express adequately such an ontological concept. This terminology was difficult to create, because the formulas of faith are something different from the technical language of theologians. Still, it was almost impossible to avoid the task of finding terms that would adequately express both the unity of the Logos with and the difference from the Father. This was done by using the terms that we translate as one "Being" and three "persons." The concept of "person" as used here is very difficult to define. Even the original Greek terms were difficult to explain; it was hardly possible to find adequate Latin translations, and it is even more difficult to express these ideas in English. The Greek term *hypostasis* has already been mentioned.[16] The closet Latin term is *substantia*. The basic meaning of *substantia* is that something exists as a specific, separate individual. Thus the Latin terms describes the one Being of God. The Greek that it translates describes the distinctiveness of the Father, Son, and Spirit. A simple diagram may help to clarify this significant difference in the frame of reference:

Greek: *ousia* + *hypostasis*

Latin: *substantia* + *persona*

As a result, Eastern theologians always thought of the one-ness even when they spoke about the three-ness. Western theologians in contrast always thought of the three-ness even when the spoke about the one-ness.

The work of developing terms that could be used to describe both the one-ness and the distinctiveness of the three-ness in God was carried on in the context of the discussion of the relationship of the Holy Spirit to God. On the one hand, it had long been customary to describe the Holy Spirit as divine. The Trinitarian baptismal formula of Matt. 28:19 as well as the threefold doxology made that unavoidable. On the other hand, the growing acceptance of the doctrine that the Son was of one Being with the Father made it increasingly difficult to speak of the Holy Spirit as God. The Son was the only-begotten *(monogenes)* Son of the Father. How could they say that there was a third divine *hypostasis* or person alongside the Father and the Son? Was this Spirit a kind of second son, the younger brother of the Logos? Since the term that we translate as "begotten" or "born" was reserved for the Son's relationship to the Father, how could the Spirit's relationship to God be described? Was not the Spirit really an impersonal power or a gift of God to the believers? If so, it was difficult to know what kind of "Spirit" this was; for the Greek word for "Spirit" is *pneuma* and always made people think of the "blowing of the wind."

Those and similar arguments against the deity of the Holy Spirit—proposed by the so-called Pneumatomachians—were certainly significant. Yet, none of these arguments could overcome the moment of the traditional inclusion of the Spirit in the threesome of Father, Son, and Spirit in the liturgy of baptism and in the doxology. Our so-called Nicene Creed is part of that tradition. Its historical origins are disputed, but there is no question about the fact that it has been widely adopted in the church. It is not the Creed adopted by the Council of Nicea but rather a later version attributed to the Second Ecumenical Council, the First Council of Constantinople in 381. It is therefore often called the "Nicene-Constantinopolitan Creed." This Creed does not explicitly say that the Spirit is of one Being *(homousios)* with the Father. At the same time, the Spirit is "worshiped and glorified" with the Father and the Son. The Spirit is also described as "the Lord, the giver of life." The Spirit's role in the history of salvation is described in the sentence "He has spoken through the prophets." The difficult question as to how the Spirit's origin in the Father can be different from the Son's being begotten of the Father was resolved both theologically and liturgically by the assertion that the Spirit "proceeds from the Father."[17] This resolution of the problem expressed a decision appropriate to the issue. The Holy Spirit must be thought of as being of "one Being" with the Father in the same way that we think of the Son.

I have already referred to the way in which the difference between the Greek and Latin terms used in the doctrine of the Trinity resulted in differing emphases in this doctrine. Eastern theologians also tried to think of God as being triune in his very Being in the way that the Western theologians did. They did this by describing the so-called personal properties *(proprietates personales)*, those qualities that define the person. The so-called Athanasian Creed lists these: "The Father was neither made nor created nor begotten; the Son was neither made nor created, but was alone begotten of the Father; the Spirit was neither made nor created, but is proceeding from the Father and the Son."[18]

One way of understanding the triune God is in terms of the relationship of the persons to one another—theologians often call this the "immanent" Trinity. It must be complemented by a parallel description of the persons of the Trinity in relationship to the world—the "revealed" or "economic" Trinity.[19] If the transcendent God were not active in the world, we never think nor need to think about any of the differentiations within God—that is, about the "personal properties" and the resulting relationships between the persons. The terms that we use in speaking about these differentiations are quite clear. Our understanding of the reality of these relationships, however, is much more confused. Because the Son, both as Creator and as the incarnate Redeemer, continues to be begotten of the Father, we need to speak of the Son as "eternally" begotten. Similarly, because the Spirit proceeds—the procession is less frequently described as an "aspiration" or "breathing upon"—from the Father and the Son even when sent by the Father and the Son into the believers, we must also speak of an "eternal" procession of the Spirit. This way of speaking guarantees that we are thinking of God as being present in the world.

At the same time, understanding God as the Trinity also requires that we think about the transcendent God in relationship to the world. Negative or apophastic theology[20] cannot be the final word that Christian theology speaks about God. Rather we need to think about God as a living God, who becomes

59

known to us through presence and activity in the world. As Basil the Great said, "There is one Source of things that are, creating through the Son, and perfecting in the Spirit."[21]

As discussed earlier, our contemporary attempts to think about God struggle with the burden of the unresolvable questions that have been created by theologians' efforts to define God's claim to be the savior of everyone.[22] One possible way out of this endless discussion is to interpret the Scripture in terms of the early church's perspectives on God as both transcending and as being active in the world.

THE IMPLICATIONS
OF THE DOCTRINE OF
THE TRINITY FOR CHRISTOLOGY

The early church's doctrine of the person and work of Christ (Christology) was part of the traditional theology that the Lutheran Reformers took for granted as valid. In this case, the differences between the approaches of Eastern and Western theologians are even more significant. The doctrine of the Trinity was basically developed by Greek theologians. Western theologians were, however, deeply involved in the controversies that resulted in the decisions about the person and work of Christ made by the Council of Chalcedon in 451. The dogmatic formulations of this council left many important questions unresolved. As a result the christological controversies continued and finally led to the still-existing division between those churches who could and those who could not accept the decision made by the Second Council of Constantinople in 553 (the fifth "ecumenical council").[23] Generally, the Eastern churches accepted and the Western churches rejected this council.

We often speak as though the "doctrine of the two natures" of Christ were the primary theological model of the early church. And some dogmaticians write as though the difficult paradoxes approved by the Council of Chalcedon were the last word in christological thought. In fact, these decisions do faithfully preserve the mystery of the unity of God and the human person in Jesus Christ. Every attempt to think through the accepted formulas, however, quickly and inevitably ends in logical contradictions. It is much easier to say, "I believe that Jesus Christ, true God, begotten of the Father from eternity, and also true man, born of the virgin Mary, is my Lord," than it is to know what this really means.[24]

Who is this Jesus Christ who is described both as God, eternally begotten of the Father, and as a human person, born of Mary? Can both be said of the same subject? It is, of course, possible to stop the discussion at this point and say that this is the mystery of Jesus Christ and that these christological statements express this mystery. We cannot, however, let this be the end of the matter. When we speak of Jesus Christ, we do not think only or even primarily about Jesus Christ as though these sentences told us who he is. We think of him as a historical person. We know who he is because the stories of the Gospels tell us many things about his life as a historical person. That has always been the case since the Gospels were written. The image of Jesus that has been given us through the Gospels has been of great significance for our piety and theology.

Of the four different images of Jesus presented by the four Gospels, the image of Jesus in the Gospel of John has been the most influential. This began to change only recently. Historical-critical analysis of the New Testament reduced the dominant influence of the Gospel of John on the church's image of Jesus and strengthened the influence of the tradition represented by the Synoptic Gospels (Matthew, Mark, and Luke). This does not necessarily mean that the image of Christ which determines piety and religiosity has become more "human." It is still quite usual for pious Christians to worship Jesus as the Son of God and to call on him in their prayers. There is little popular awareness of the difficulty of harmonizing these religious practices with the humanity of the Jesus described in the Synoptic Gospels. The description of Jesus Christ as God has apparently prevailed in Christian piety in spite of all the modern criticism of the content and, especially, of the metaphysical form of the early church's dogma. For this reason alone, it is important that we be clearly aware of the problems or, more accurately, of the inner contradictions of the early church's christological doctrines. This awareness will help us clarify our own thinking. This will be especially true if our awareness of these inner contradictions leads us to try a new way of thinking.

The Hellenistic Concept of the Logos as a Handicap for Theological Reflection

Although the development of the doctrine of the Trinity began with the christological issue, theologians could for a time bypass the original issue while they were working on the doctrine of the Trinity. Eventually, though, it was necessary to pay attention to the christological issue. The basic Trinitarian question may be formulated in this way: What is the meaning for our understanding of God that we also ought to think about Jesus Christ as God (2 Clem. 1:1)?[25] The basic christological question is: What does it mean for our understanding of the historical person of Jesus Christ that we also ought to think about him as God? These two questions are both different and inter-related. Historically, the development of christological teaching had to proceed on the basis of the already-accepted doctrine of the Trinity. The embarrassing contradictions that resulted are easy to predict.

The christological statements of the Athanasian Creed exemplify these problems. The christological section of this Creed begins with the assertion:

"It is necessary for eternal salvation that one also faithfully believe that our Lord Jesus Christ became flesh."[26] The Creed then describes this Lord Jesus Christ as God's Son and as both God and a human being:

> That our Lord Jesus, God's Son, is both God and man. He is God, begotten before all worlds from the being (substantia) of the Father, and he is man, born in the world from the being of his mother—existing fully as God, and fully as man with a rational soul and a human body; equal to the Father in divinity, subordinate to the Father in humanity. Although he is God and man, he is not divided, but is one Christ. He is united because God has taken humanity into himself; he does not transform deity into humanity. He is completely one in the unity of his person, without confusing his natures ("Unus omnino non confusione substantiae, set unitate personae").[27]

The statement of the Athanasian Creed is modeled closely after the decrees of the Council of Chalcedon.[28] It is also designed to conceal the real problem. This concealment is intensified by the German translation of the Athanasian Creed in the Book of Concord which translates the Latin substantia with the German natur.[29] This makes it seem that the deity (divinitas) and humanity (humanitas) are two abstract elements which are thought of as having been combined together into the specific person of the God–human being. The appearance is deceptive. The reality is that this description of the person of Jesus Christ does not take the presuppositions of Trinitarian theology seriously enough. In thinking about the incarnation, it is necessary to remember that the person (hypostasis) of the Son-Logos already was a specific being. The incarnation therefore could not mean that the deity, with all its divine attributes, was joined together with the human being, together with all its human attributes, and became a specific person. Rather, the specific person of the Son of God—in a manner still to be described—united himself with human being.

The Creed adopted by the Council of Nicea in 325 made it very clear that it was the "Son of God . . . Who for us men and our salvation came down, was incarnate and made man and suffered, and rose again the third day, and ascended into the heavens, and will come to judge the living and the dead."[30] The common liturgical Creed is even more detailed: "For us and for our salvation he came down from heaven; by the power of the Holy Spirit he became incarnate from the virgin Mary, and was made man. For our sake he was crucified under Pontius Pilate; he suffered death and was buried. On the third day he rose again in accordance with the Scriptures; he ascended into heaven and is seated at the right hand of the Father. He will come again in glory to judge the living and the dead, and his kingdom will have no end."[31]

These Creeds are speaking about historical events. The subject of these events is the one Lord Jesus Christ, God's only begotten Son, of one Being with the Father. This historical process of salvation is the necessary presupposition of the christological formulas. The description of this process sets the limits for the development of the christological formulas. The description of the process by the councils of Nicea in 325 and Constantinople in 381 is the true faith and has since been repeatedly affirmed. It cannot be revised because of any decisions made in the development of the christological formulas. It expresses the church's Trinitarian faith. It also expresses the basic doctrine of the person and work of Christ. Whatever came later could at best explain and clarify this Christology but could not revise the Creed of Nicea. No additional symbolic creed was needed. The participants in the Council of Chalcedon acted accordingly when they began their statement clarifying christological issues by confessing the creeds adopted at Nicea and Constantinople. This confessional statement is all that is needed for a knowledge of salvation. It is a complete doctrine of the Father, Son, and Holy Spirit and of our Lord's incarnation—adequate for all those who accept in faith. Any new definitions are only needed as answers to new heresies.

Although the Council of Chalcedon intended to preserve the continuity of the tradition, it is necessary to ask whether its decisions made there succeeded in doing so. Not only did this council really fail to solve the basic dogmatic questions; its decisions have never been as widely accepted by Christians as the Trinitarian Creeds have been.

The Real Humanity of Jesus Christ

Christ really came in the flesh. This was one of the basic assertions of the confession of faith in Christ. The church permitted no doubt at this point. Still, it was necessary to find ways of thinking about God's coming in the flesh. One could use the comparison to the unity of body and soul in the human being as an analogy to describe the incarnation. The Athanasian Creed did this: "For as the rational soul and body ("anima rationabilis et caro") are one person, so the one Christ is God and man."[32] That was intended as an analogy. It should not be taken literally. The analogy had been previously used both in Arian Christology as well as in the Christology of Apollinaris of Laodicea, who accepted the doctrine of the Trinity. The Logos was thought of as having played the role of the rational soul in Jesus Christ. That might seem to be an acceptable and insightful solution of the christological problem. Just as the body and soul of the human being are two separate and specific beings and yet form a unity, so Christ is the unity of a body and of the Logos. That solution obviously presupposes that the soul is thought of as an independent *hypostasis*—an assumption that we today can no longer make.

In the fourth century, this apparent solution was opposed for reasons related to the doctrine of salvation. It contradicted the basic axiom that only that which had been assumed in the incarnation had been saved. Since human being is totally sinful it can only be completely redeemed by totally sharing in the being of the God-Logos. This is how it was always understood: The Logos had come in the flesh and assumed human being in order to conquer sin and death and to save men and women who had fallen under the power of sin and death. Now the anthropological question had been raised. How is the humanity that the Logos assumed to be defined? The more definite the answer to this question, the more impossible it became to resolve the christological question. Does not this humanity have to be defined as a specific person if Jesus is described as really a whole human being? What was involved at this point was not the definition of what a human being is: That question could be answered in terms of body, soul, and mind. Rather, the question was whether the particular human being to whom Mary gave birth was really a human person. This ontological question was reformulated in religious terms and in this form aroused the emotional involvement of the believers: Is Mary really the Mother of God *(theotokos)* because in giving birth to this child, she really brought God into the world? Or is Mary the mother of the human person Jesus, a person whom God chose to unite with the Son of God? The result would be a union of God and a human person in which God would remain God and the human person would remain human. Of course, the human being would be so thoroughly dominated by the Logos that the Logos would control the Christ in everything that he did or did not do. God and the human being would then remain two entities, although they would be—as the saying goes—"of one heart and one soul."

One solution to this difficulty was proposed by the Monophysites. This tradition was very widespread in the church and satisfied an equally widespread religious need. The Monophysites asserted that the Christ had only one single unified nature. This was the incarnate nature *(physis)* of the divine Logos. This enabled them to affirm that the God-Logos was the subject who came in the flesh and became man. It rejected the possibility that the humanity assumed by the Logos had its own specific personal existence. This humanity is the flesh of the Logos, the incarnate God. Therefore Mary is properly called the Mother of God in the fullest sense of this term. The search for the reality of the humanity of the Logos was correspondingly limited. We ought not think that the Being of the Logos had changed itself in any way in order to become flesh or that he had transformed himself into a human being. Rather the Logos had united itself with full humanity made up of a body and a rational soul. This unification was described by Cyril of Alexandria: "We do say that the Word united himself in his Person *)henosis kath' hupostasin)* in an explicable and incomprehensible way with the flesh animated by a rational soul . . ."[33] This description is the source of the technical term "hypostatic union" often used by theologians in discussing Christology. Such an artificial expression was needed to express a meaning that could not be expressed in ordinary terms. That was probably unavoidable if the church was to find as exact a statement as possible that would meet all possible objections. In any case this much is clear: The specific person spoken of in discussing the Christ is and always will be the Logos. The church had avoided using the problematic concept of "nature" (*physis*) by speaking of the *hypostasis* of the Logos.

Cyril's approach received only limited approval at the Council of Chalcedon. The definitions made by this council were not concerned with the unity but rather attempted to describe the complete deity and the complete humanity of Jesus Christ. He was perfect both in his deity and in his humanity, one in Being with the Father according to his deity, one in Being with human beings according to his humanity. According to his deity, he was eternally begotten of the Father; according to his humanity he was, in these last times, born of the virgin Mary, the Mother of God. Although Mary was given the title of "Mother of God," (*theotokos*), it was in the context really a honorific title rather than a description of her function.

According to the Council of Chalcedon, this one Christ is to be thought of in two natures, which are "unconfused, unchangeable, undivided, and inseparable."[34] The difference of the natures was never to be described as though it had been abolished in order to achieve the unity. Rather, the properties of each nature were preserved. Having achieved this goal, could this formula still make it possible to speak of one person in these two natures? For even though this definition attempted to speak of the deity and the humanity as abstractions, it could not avoid describing the *hypostasis* of the Logos as a specific entity. It then was also necessary to think of the humanity as an equally specific entity, as the human being named Jesus who was born of Mary.

Given this context, the unity of the humanity and deity could not be thought of or at least not imagined in rational terms. The Council of Chalcedon made this very clear by approving not only Cyril's *Second Letter to Nestorius* but also Pope Leo I's *Dogmatic Letter (Tome) to Flavian*, the Patriarch of Constantinople. Leo described Jesus' saving work in this way: "Each of the two natures does what is proper to it in communion with the other, the Word doing what pertains to the Word, and the flesh doing what pertains to the flesh. One of them shines out with miracles, the other is subjected to insults. And as the Word does not leave the equality of glory with the Father, so also the flesh does not abandon the nature of our race."[35] Leo described the natures as though they were the independent subjects of their working and suffering. How was it still possible for him to think of them as being in unity with each other?

The interest in asserting that Jesus was a full and complete human being is understandable. How else could we think about the sufferings that Jesus endured in his body and soul? The idea that God suffered would have completely contradicted the then-current metaphysical assumptions about God. Such an assumption would have simply negated the meaning of the whole concept of God. As a result, it seems that the theologians at the Council of Chalcedon overlooked the fact that the Trinitarian concept of God had developed larger and broader ideas about God in the context of God's transcendence of and immanence in the world. Under those circumstances, Chalcedon could assert the real humanity of Jesus Christ only at the cost of the unity of the two natures. The price they paid to achieve this was very high, far too high— even though they succeeded in eliminating the trace of Docetism (denial of the real humanity of Christ) that was always an element of the emhasis that Cyril and the Monophysites characteristically placed on the unity.

The One Lord Jesus Christ

The doctrines of the person and work of Christ adopted at Chalcedon did not facilitate both clear thinking and a religiously satisfying view of Christ. Thinking was limited to following the once-traveled path of distinguishing the natures: We should think of the deity and of the humanity as being alongside each other in Jesus Christ. Both the deity and the humanity, however, are to be thought of as completely and totally independent of each other. The one Lord Jesus Christ, whom the church confesses, is hardly thought of as a personal subject. This is true even though the decree of Chalcedon says that Jesus Christ is still to be thought of as a single person or *hypostasis*.

The decree of Chalcedon proved to be a trap for later christological thinking. This is clearly revealed by the decision made at the Third Council of Constantinople in 681.[36] It was simply not possible to have a clear view of Christ as the object of religious meditation that was also in harmony with the gospels as long as theologians insisted on speaking of only one will and one active principle. For that reason, this council decided that each nature has its own active principle and its own will. The Logos is the subject of the divine active principle and of the divine will and the human nature is the subject of the human active principle and human will. The council cited John 6:38 in support of its assertion that the human nature has its own will: "For I have come down from heaven, not to do my own will, but the will of him who sent me." This passage from John obviously distinguishes the will of the Son from the will of the Father. The Gospel of John, however, was saying something quite different than the Council of Constantinople in 681 was saying when it distinguished the will of the divine nature from the will of the human nature in the person of Jesus Christ. In making this distinction, the council certainly did not think of these two wills as being opposed to each other; rather, it assumed that the human will completely obeyed the divine will. Still, this clearly located the obedient relationship within the person of Christ in the human will's obedience to the divine, that is, in the relationship between the divine and human "natures." That certainly was very meaningful viewed from the perspective of the then commonly accepted metaphysical presuppositions; however, it is of little use in understanding the dynamic process of God's work of salvation. In the words of Paul's christological hymn, was it the human nature that "became obedient unto death, even death on a cross" (Phil. 2:8)? Paul, at least, was speaking of Jesus Christ, who took on the form of a servant. In contrast, the council decided that the subject of this obedience was "the form of a servant" that had been assumed by the Son of God. (The phrase "the form of a servant" comes from Leo's *Letter to Flavian* and was at this point used by the council instead of "human nature.") It is clear that such a description, dominated as it was by the static categories of metaphysics with their rigid limiting distinctions, had taken the dynamic processes of salvation captive.

The Reformation theologians were careful to express their respect for the doctrinal formulations of the early church. That did not mean that they felt themselves bound to these formulations. The view of Christ based on religious meditation prevailed.[37] During the Osiandrian controversy, the righteousness of Christ that is imputed to faith was explicitly placed in the life, suffering, and death of the earthly Jesus.[38] The obedience of the earthly Jesus is imputed to faith as righteousness.

> Hence, since in our churches the theologians of the Augsburg Confession accept the principle that we must seek our entire righteousness apart from our own and all other human merits, works, virtues, and worthiness and that our righteousness rests solely and alone on the Lord Christ, it is important to consider carefully in what way Christ is called our righteousness in this matter of justification: Our righteousness rests neither upon his divine nature nor upon his human nature but upon the entire person of Christ, who as God and man in his sole, total, and perfect obedience is our righteousness.[39]

After the Council of Chalcedon, the church was concerned to provide a basis for reconciliation with the Monophysite churches. The council also tried to make it possible for Christians to create a view of Christ that would be suitable for religious meditation and yet remain within the limits of the decrees of the council. These were the dominant motives of the council's broad interpretations of the decrees of Chalcedon. In order to achieve these goals, the church had to move in the direction of Cyril's interpretation of the council's decrees. Thus the attempt was made to understand the *hypostasis* of the Logos as the *hypostasis* of the one incarnate Lord. It was agreed that this one person had suffered and that, to this extent, God had suffered. This was expressed in the so-called Theopaschite Formula: "One of the Holy Trinity has suffered." The council, however, characteristically added, "in the flesh" or "through the flesh." This demonstrated that the doctrines of the person and work of Christ were not an adequate basis for religious meditation on Christ. As a result, neither basic goal was achieved: The Monophysite churches remained separated—there were also national and political reasons for that schism. The intellectual problem also remained unresolved. There was still no adequate way of simultaneously describing the Son as of one Being with the Father and as the acting subject in the work of salvation, while at the same time maintaining his full deity and his full humanity. Formulas that tried to preserve the unity of the Christ as the subject confused the metaphysical distinction between God and human beings. Formulas that focused on the deity and the humanity were unable to describe the unity of the person. At their best, they could only leave religious meditation free to create its own object. Religious meditation, however, required unity in its object; the theologians were making distinctions.

Ultimately, the church could not tolerate a situation in which religious devotion and theological thought were going down such radically different paths. In case of doubt, theological thought was well advised to follow the lead of religious meditation on Christ. This meant, however, that the basic issues of Christology could not be defined in terms of categories of "real" deity and of "real" humanity. These categories were not useful because they had been developed in other contexts and then applied to the discussion of the person and work of Christ. The inevitable result of trying to do so was that the unity of Jesus Christ became a problem. The truth is, however, that the unity of this one Lord Jesus Christ who is made known to us in the Scripture is the presupposition of all theological reflection on his person and work. The only question that needs to be resolved is what "humanity" and "deity" mean in terms of the reality of this Lord.

4

The Theological and Anthropological Implications of the Reformation's Basic Decision

The Reformation took it for granted that the early church's basic decision and the consequent conclusions in the doctrines of the Trinity and of the person and work of Christ were valid. The creeds in which this decision was affirmed were included in the Lutheran *corpus doctrinae*. The Lutheran Reformers also took this basic decision of the early church into consideration as they interpreted the Scripture and expressed its meaning for their own situation. This went beyond the then-usual custom in the church of teaching people the Apostles' Creed as well as the Commandments and the Lord's Prayer. In addition, as the Reformation theologians implemented the Reformation's own basic decision, they also rethought the dogmas of the early church—the doctrines of the Trinity and Christology.

For example, Luther began the Smalcald Articles with a brief summary of the early church's statements on the Trinity and Christology and then concluded, "These articles are not matters of dispute or contention, for both parties confess them."[1] Luther had originally written "both parties believe and confess them" but then deleted the words translated as "believe and." This deletion reflected Luther's conviction that there could be no real agreement on faith in the triune God as long as there was disagreement about salvation.[2]

The issue here is not whether Luther's assumption was correct or not. Rather, we need to be clearly aware that the Reformation affirmed the decisions of the early church. As we explore the implications of the Reformation's own basic decisions for the understanding of God and of human beings, we shall clarify their continuity with the decisions of the early church. We must pay special attention to the way in which we think of God acting affects the way we think about human beings and the reverse.

69

THE TRIUNE GOD
ACTS TO SAVE HUMAN BEINGS

The Theocentric Understanding of Our Relationship to God as the Point of Departure for Interpretation

The Reformation's ideas seem to threaten human independence, responsibility, and freedom. This is due to the fact that the Reformers did not limit people to what we are and can do; rather, the Reformers described us as dependent on what God makes out of us. This kind of thinking contradicts the social disciplines of seeking our own best interests and taking responsibility for what we do. And indeed, it does seem natural to use the patterns of relationships that we learn from living together in society as the basis for understanding our relationship to God. For example, in society each of us is valued as a person to the extent that we meet certain social expections. Society recognizes and rewards our efforts to meet these expectations. It seems natural to transfer this social value system to our understanding of our relationship to God. This is particularly attractive because of the close interrelationship of religion and morality. It is easy to conclude that the principles governing social interactions between people and our relationship to God are equally close together. The Roman Catholic position is clear and understandable: Religion and morality affect and make demands of the same person.[3] Religion is the gracious process by which God enables us to live a moral life. The reverse is also true: Moral actions are a process of sanctification that confirms God's grace and deepens our relationship to God.

This process of human self-interpretation takes both our moral and religious responsibilities seriously. It also provides a basis for our thinking about God and God's relationship to people. It presupposes that we are able to fulfill the demands that are made of us. To this extent, it thinks of people as free. Such freedom is admittedly not unlimited. For we are able to gain salvation only because God's "prevenient" grace precedes, accompanies, and perfects all that we do. Still, people are free to turn to grace, to decide to accept God's offer of salvation, and to persevere in this decision by acting according to God's will.

God is thought of in a corresponding manner. The God to whom human beings relate is a free person. It is this free God who takes the initiative in coming out to meet people with his grace. This free God also confronts us as free people and holds us responsible for our own actions. This free God is a gracious as well as a challenging, helping, judging, punishing God. The human person corresponds to God; God corresponds to the human person. God has established this correspondence between himself and human beings through creation. It is, therefore, possible for people both to know God and to respond positively to God's offer of salvation. This correspondence between the Being of God and the nature of human being is often referred to in modern theology as the analogy of being, *analogia entis*. In thinking about this, it is important to always remember that this correspondence is not an equality, "For between Creator and creature no similarity can be expressed without including a greater dissimilarity."[4]

It is then clearly possible to think about God's freedom and personhood as comparable to human freedom and personality. As part of this pattern of thinking, our relationship to God in the process of gaining salvation is understood as comparable to the relationship between human persons. At the same time, this way of thinking emphasizes that the gracious God also encounters people in his grace in a different way and on a different level than people do when they encounter one another and make reciprocal demands on one another. Most important of all, God's purpose in his gift of salvation is incomparably more glorious than anything that people can give to or do for one another.

This approach to the understanding of the process of achieving salvation is so significant precisely because it is supported by our ordinary experience of life and matches the ways in which we interpret our own lives. Because of this relationship to human experience, we may think of it as anthropocentric or human-centered. This way of thinking appears in commonly accepted Protestant doctrines of salvation—with changes in detail but not in substance; it is identifiably present in various statements in the Lutheran confessional writings. Modern scholars usually attribute these aberrations from the basic Reformation position to Melanchthon. There is some reason to do that. Yet, the Formula of Concord made these statements precisely when it was explicitly attempting to correct these Melanchthonian aberrations.[5]

On the other hand, Reformation thought intended to establish barriers that would prevent the breakthrough of this kind of human-centered thinking. Calvinism, for example, used the doctrine of double predestination as such a barrier: Before the beginning of time, God decided whether each person was one of the elect, who would reach the goal of eternal salvation, or one of those whom God's saving choice would pass over and who would, therefore, justly suffer the eternal punishment of sin. Even this apparently invincible barrier could not prevent the development of the practical syllogism in later Calvinism. This syllogism began by assuming the premise that the elect will never be without good works. On this basis, it concluded that anyone who does good works must therefore be one of the elect. As a result, the certainty of election, and therefore of salvation, was based on good works rather than God's grace.

The comparable Lutheran barrier was the assertion that the believer is at one and the same time always righteous and a sinner *(simul iustus et peccator)*. This is true only if and as long as God is carrying out his saving work in this person's life. This statement, however, is of questionable value as a description of the religious life. It is very true that the believers always remain sinners and always need to pray the fifth and sixth petitions of the Lord's Prayer. There are, however, also changes for the better in the life of the believer. These occur not only in the area of the relationship to God, an area beyond human observation; these changes also occur in the believer's life in this world and can therefore be observed. If there is no evidence that such changes have occurred, the genuineness of that person's faith will properly be called into question. Works and new obedience belong to faith. This fact raises the very questions that the Lutheran principle that believers are at one and the same time sinners and righteous was intended to suppress.[6]

This means that we cannot maintain the Reformation's basic decision in our interpretation of the Lutheran confessional writings simply by first identifying and then defending against the problems of a human-centered approach to salvation. Even the intellectual barriers that we have just described were not effective for very long. Rather, we need to clearly comprehend the God-centered (theocentric) approach and maintain it through the process of making the theology of the confessional writings our own theology. To do this, we need to use the Reformation's basic decision as the critical principle of our interpretation of the texts of the confessions. Doing this involves us in a circular process of interpreting the confessions just as interpreting the Bible does. Our interpretation of the texts provides us with a specific understanding of the gospel, and we then use this understanding as our standard in critically evaluating our understanding of these documents. This approach can validate itself only by making a convincing interpretation of the whole collection of texts. This interpretation must, for example, also provide an explanation of the fact that a particular statement of the confessions cannot be interpreted as agreeing with the interpretation of the whole.

I have described one possible approach to the understanding of salvation as "human-centered." In contrast, I shall refer to the basic characteristic of an adequate interpretation of the Lutheran confessions as "God-centered" or "theocentric." Such a God-centered understanding of our relationship to God sees humanity as supported and held by God. God approaches people, not merely through a gift of grace that it separate from God, but rather as the triune God in whom alone human beings can survive.

People can experience God's closeness as a threat. It can seem as though the human being no longer exists as a free and independent person but is rather completely absorbed by God. If that were the case, this kind of closeness would make it impossible to describe correctly either God or human beings as acting independently for themselves or as being in relationship to each other. Actually, human beings achieve full humanity through their relation to God—who is always the triune God. This presupposition of the doctrine of the triune God is so important because it describes God as always being in relationship to God self as Father, Son, and Spirit. This is the necessary presupposition of God-centered thinking about the process of salvation.

It makes it possible to think of the human person as both being in relationship to God and remaining a human person, without being absorbed into the abyss of God who works all in all. On the contrary, since it is God's very nature to be in relationship, the human being can be and remain a fully human person in this relationship to God.

The Granting of Salvation as the Work of the Holy Spirit

The Reformation's basic decision gave full weight to the early church's assertion that the Holy Spirit is of one Being with the Father and the son.[7] The early church thereby ascribed a special activity to the Holy Spirit that corresponds to his distinct character as a person of the Trinity. In contrast, a human-centered approach to salvation cannot ascribe such a special activity to the Spirit. This is because a human-centered approach must describe the free human person as a constant factor in the process of gaining salvation. Since the human person cooperates with the grace of God, the human person is always the active subject of this process. As a result, God's activity in people must be described as though it were different from and separable from God: God gives grace to a human subject who receives the gift and therewith also receives the possibility of salvation. When salvation is described in this way, the Holy Spirit recedes into the background. The actual result—even though the traditional doctrines never state this explicitly—is that the church takes the place of the Holy Spirit as the mediator of God's gift to people who need to be saved. The effectiveness of this process was guaranteed by the church's teaching that the sacraments are always effective when properly administered *(ex opere operato)*. This means that the church is always effective in mediating the divine activity in the sacraments to anyone who has decided to receive the sacrament and does not resist the work of grace.

Article V of the Augsburg Confession discussed this question. It replaced the gift of grace with the Giver, God the Holy Spirit. "To obtain such faith God instituted the office of the ministry, that is, provided the Gospel and the sacraments. Through these, as through means, he gives the Holy Spirit, who works faith, when and where he pleases, in those who hear the Gospel."[8] By understanding the gift of salvation in terms of the divine person of the Holy Spirit as the gift rather than in terms the impersonal activity of grace, the Augsburg Confession clearly changed the understanding of the process by which people are saved. The focus of activity in the giving and the acceptance of salvation shifted from the human person to God. A human being neither can nor should believe, love, and hope as a result of receiving grace. Rather God, the Holy Spirit, produces faith at the opportune time.

The Holy Spirit thereby became the subject of the process of salvation and gained a whole new significance in the divine plan of salvation. Luther's Large Catechism said, "As the Father is called Creator and the Son is called

Redeemer, so on account of His work the Holy Spirit must be called Sanctifier, the One who makes holy."[9] Luther implemented this principle by restructuring the third article of the Apostles' Creed in his explanation (also in the more familiar explanation of this article in the Small Catechism). The Apostles' Creed has simply listed a series of items: Holy Spirit, church, forgiveness of sins, resurrection, and eternal life. Luther restructured this in a form parallel to that of the second article of the creed by subordinating the latter items to the Holy Spirit. The third article thus became a recognizable statement about the Holy Spirit and his work. "Just as the Son obtains dominion by purchasing us through his birth, death, and resurrection, etc., so the Holy Spirit effects our sanctification through the following: the communion of saints or Christian church, the forgiveness of sins, the resurrection of the body, and the life everlasting."[10] Thus Luther's interpetation of the third article clearly revealed a new evaluation of the doctrine of the Holy Spirit. The church, the forgiveness of sins, the resurrection of the dead, and eternal life were no longer objects of faith alongside the Holy Spirit. Rather, as God the Father is characterized by creation, and the Son by the saving events from his incarnation through his ascension into heaven, so the Spirit is characterized by these facts that describe the process of receiving salvation.

The special work of the Holy Spirit may be described: *God* makes a saving relationship to God possible. The interaction between God and human beings is therefore not to be described in any way that is human-centered. For example, it would be in error to say that God and a human person interact as though the human person still possessed a God-given capacity for such interaction that has not been lost through the Fall into sin. Such a capacity for interaction with God was referred to and understood by people at the time of the Reformation as "free will." Modern theology, insofar as it is human-centered, speaks about the human personality or the human capacity for transcendence. Both ways of speaking mean the same. Each asserts that human beings retain some capacity to turn to God that has not been destroyed by sin, some point of contact at which they are open and receptive to God's work. This view, of course, recognizes that no one is able to act on the basis of this capability. To do that, people need God's grace, which comes to human beings and enables us to use our innate capacity. Even when stated in this guarded way, the saving relation of human beings and God is always thought of as being possible because of something that is innately present in human beings.

The basic decision of the Reformation guarded against this error. It defined the saving relationship of God and human beings as coming not from the human person but only from God. It was for this reason that salvation was described at the work of the Holy Spirit. Both the process by which we gain salvation and the process by which we make it our own were described as the work of the Holy Spirit. The Holy Spirit, the Creator Spirit who creates life, demonstrates this life-giving power by awakening sinners and making us alive to God in faith. The Reformers thought of this process as being solely God's work, both made possible and executed only by God. Still, it is neither possible nor permissible for us to stop at simply asserting that such a living relationship to God is present wherever the Holy Spirit is present. Least of all may we participate with the enthusiasts in attempts to use various techniques of meditation to force God to enter into such a relationship with us. Those efforts are again totally human-centered. They are not possible because a saving relationship with God also has its external side. The Holy Spirit works only through the external word, the gospel of Jesus Christ.

The Gospel of Jesus Christ

We can only think of one thing at a time. Even though we must describe the work of the Father, the Son, and the Holy Spirit separately, however, their work is indivisible. The Father, the Son, and the Holy Spirit are one undivided Being of the one God; similarly, their works belong inseparably together. Separating one from the other would make everything false. For example, we cannot describe the granting of salvation as the work of the Holy Spirit without simultaneously binding the working of the Spirit to the external Word. This external Word in turn has to be understood in terms of the person and work of Christ. And as certainly as the Holy Spirit works faith in people through the gospel, the spoken Word of promise, so this Word must be thought of as God-centered.

The Augsburg Confession, Article I, asserted that the Lutheran teaching about the Trinity is orthodox and rejected a variety of other positions. The list of rejections did not simply copy traditional catalogues of past heresies but was also intended to condemn errors that were then present realities.

> Therefore all the heresies which are contrary to this article are rejected. Among these are the heresy of the Manichaeans, who assert that there are two gods, one good and one evil; also that of the Valentinians, Arians, Eunomians, Mohammedans, and others like them; also that of the Samosatenes, old and new, who hold that there is only one person and sophistically assert that the other two, the Word and the Holy Spirit, are not necessarily distinct persons but that the Word signifies a physical word or voice and that the Holy Spirit is a movement induced in creatures.[11]

The Holy Spirit is God Working personally in people. The Word of God is God personally addressing God self to the sinner. The Augsburg Confession, in its statement on justification, said, "We receive forgiveness of sin and become righteous before God by grace, for Christ's sake, through faith."[12] "Through faith" was an implicit assertion that salvation is the work of the Spirit. Similarly, "for Christ's sake" bound salvation to the work of Christ. The faith that the Spirit works in us binds us to the gospel of Jesus Christ.

The kind of interaction that the Holy Spirit establishes between God and people is not a relationship that people need to fill with content. That would be enthusiasm. On this point, the Reformers said, the pope and the enthusiasts agreed. Both described God's spirit as relating to people apart from Jesus Christ. Such a relationship would inevitably—whatever the intention of this teaching—be opposed to Jesus Christ. Under those conditions, humanity would be related to God, God would be present and active through a kind of Word of God that claims obedience and faith; the problem is that such a humanity would not be the humanity of Jesus Christ in whom God is really present and the Word would not be the Word of God that Christ spoke. Only the Word that he spoke has the right to claim our obedience and our faith. Everything else "is the old devil and the old serpent who made enthusiasts of Adam and Eve. He led them from the external Word of God to spiritualizing and to their own imaginations, and he did this through other external words. Even so, the enthusiasts of our day condemn the external Word, yet they do not remain silent but fill the world with their chattering and scribbling, as if the Spirit could not come through Scriptures or the spoken word of the apostles but must come through their own writings and words."[13]

The external Word that mediates and annonces the activity of the Holy Spirit in people is the Word in which the scriptural witness to Jesus Christ is interpreted and applied. Christ himself is present in this Word. Therefore the gospel appears not only in the form of a sermon or an interpretation of Scripture, but also in the form of the sacraments.[14] Jesus Christ is present in the sacrament in bodily form. Article III of the Augsburg Confession described the person and work of Christ and basically repeated the statements of the creeds of the early church. However, it added an explanation of the meaning of Christ's sitting at God's right hand: "That he may eternally rule and have dominion over all creatures, that through the Holy Spirit he may sanctify, purify, strengthen and comfort all who believe in him, that he may bestow on them life and every grace and blessing, and that he may protect and defend them against the devil and against sin."[15]

This firm relationship between the doctrines of salvation and of the person and work of Christ, a relationship in which they interpret each other, is characteristic of Reformation theology. Melanchthon's statement in the first edition of his handbook of theology (1521) is well known. Melanchthon then thought—although he "corrected" himself in later editions—that it really was not right to focus all theological energy on the sublime doctrines of God, his unity and the Trinity, the mystery of creation, and the way in which the incarnation occurred. "But as for the one who is ignorant of the other fundamentals, namely, 'The Power of Sin,' 'The Law,' and 'Grace,' I do not see how I can call him a Christian. For from these things Christ is known, since to know Christ means to know his benefits, and not as *they* teach, to reflect upon his natures and the modes of his incarnation."[16] This made it very clear that soteriology and Christology belong together. We cannot begin our teaching about the way in which we gain salvation by stating our basic doctrine of

Christ's merit and then focusing our treatment of the doctrine of grace in terms of the people who receive this grace and on their justification. We cannot think clearly about the justified person without thinking about Christ. Once again the God-centered thinking of the Reformation resulted in a decisive shift of emphasis. The righteousness, the works, the fulfillment of the law in which we can and ought to trust is the righteousness of Jesus Christ. The human being who corresponds to God is not the abstract human being discussed above. That abstract human being is still described as being in the image of God and therefore free and able to enter into a saving relationship to God. Rather, the human being who corresponds to God is Jesus Christ, true God and true man. When faith trusts in God's grace, it does so by recognizing the work of this Christ.

These two approaches are opposed to each other. This opposition is repeatedly described in the Reformers' controversies with the papal theologians. We may say either that Jesus Christ himself is the source of our certainty that God is gracious to us or we may say that our certainty comes from ourselves, with our own works and activity, because God cannot refuse to give us his grace. Trusting in our own works means that we are robbing Christ of the honor due him in the same way that justifying faith gives him this honor. Article XX of the Augsburg Confession described the righteousness of faith: "We begin by teaching that our works cannot reconcile us with God or obtain grace for us, for this happens only through faith, that is, when we believe that our sins are forgiven for Christ's sake, who alone is the mediator who reconciles the Father. Whoever imagines that he can accomplish this by works, or that he can merit grace, despises Christ and seeks his own way to God, contrary to the Gospel."[17]

The authors of the Roman Confutation rejected this accusation. They listed a whole series of Bible texts that say good works merit the forgiveness of sins. In addition they protested: We do not "reject Christ's merit, but we know that our works are nothing and of no merit unless by virtue of Christ's passion."[18] And yet, as correct as that assertion may have been in the context of the medieval doctrine of grace, the resulting certainty is still based on what we ourselves do rather than on receiving what Christ has done.

The only righteous humanity that enables the righteous God to enter into a saving relationship with sinful people is the humanity of Christ, the God-man. The issue was clarified later in the Osiandrian controversy.[19] The Formula of Concord then determined: The living, suffering, dying, and rising of the God-man Jesus Christ is the righteousness of the believer. This meant that it was no longer sufficient to speak of the divine Word that comes to us through the gospel and of the fact that this Word lives in us and makes us righteous. We must be clear that this gospel is always grounded and completed in the person and work of Christ. We have seen above that the activity of the Holy Spirit is always bound to the external Word. Now we need to emphasize that this Word is always bound to the history of what Christ has done. The Spirit and Christ belong together. Salvation is based on this togetherness. That which we can only think of as a human concern about our relationship to God has been assumed by God. God has made it God's concern and brought it to a successful conclusion. That is the christological component in the God-centered focus of the Reformation's basic decision. This christological component points us back to God the Creator, who thereby establishes that God's creature belongs to God.

God the Creator

This is a particularly difficult topic. Modern theology has typically defined our faith that the creation is God's work by stating this faith in subjective terms. Because I experience myself as God's creature, I also see my world as having been created by God.[20] In support of this position, reference is frequently made to Luther's explanation of the first article of the Apostles' Creed in the Small Catechism: "I believe that God has created me and all that exists."[21] This usage of Luther's statement runs the danger of modernizing his and the entire Reformation's existential affirmation of the doctrine of creation. This kind of modernization is not acceptable. The heritage of the Reformation doctrine provides us with a way of overcoming the modern impasse in the discussion of this doctrine. When we modernize this doctrine, however, we are no longer able to recognize the various opportunities it offers of overcoming this impasse. By beginning this section with a discussion of this problem, we become aware that every modern subjective description of the doctrine of creation too easily resolves the questions that arise when we attempt to define the relationship between our faith that God has redeemed the world and our faith that God has created the world.

Every discussion of God the Creator must begin on the basis of the claim that God makes on the creature through the law.

I cannot here summarize the debate about the relationship between law and gospel. This debate has extended over the last decades and is a product of the renaissance in Luther studies and the development of dialectical theology. There have been no end to the contributions to and no results from the whole discussions.[22] This debate gives us some indication of the significance of the topic but does not really introduce us to the basic concepts of the Reformation's confession. More is to be gained from being instructed by the Reformation itself about the meaning of the law and the gospel and the distinction between them at the time of the Reformation. In accordance with the goals of this study, I shall try to base my presentation on Melanchthon's statements in the Augsburg Confession and the Apology of the Augsburg Confession.

In his arguments defending the Augsburg Confession's doctrine of justification, Melanchthon introduced the distinction between law and gospel as a principle of biblical interpretation. He used this principle to interpret and disarm the numerous biblical references made by the Roman Confutation in support of its rejection of the Lutheran position. Melanchthon interpreted these same passages as supporting the teaching of the Reformation. In order to make this argument, Melanchthon had to give a more exact definition of the law. The law *(lex)* referred to in this theological controversy is this revealed will of God summarized in the Ten Commandments. Melanchthon refused to adjust the divine demands so that they match human ability; that is, he refused to interpret the law in such a way that people are able to fulfill it.

Obviously this was not intended to deny that people can do some things and are required to do what is right. What Melanchthon disputed is the assumption that such human actions in any way help to put people into a right relationship to God. Anyone who thinks that God's law can be either understood or fulfilled as a statement of what people are able to do has not understood the law and actually misuses it. Melanchthon accused the opponents of looking at the law from the perspective of human reason, as though it were a guide to doing what is right and that they could gain forgiveness of sins and be justified by keeping the law. "But the Decalogue does not only require external works that reason can somehow perform. It also requires other works far beyond the reach of reason, like true fear of God, true love of God, true prayer to God, true conviction that God hears prayer, and the expectation of God's help in death and all afflictions. Finally, it requires obedience to God in death and all afflictions, lest we try to flee these things or turn away when God imposes them."[23] Melanchthon interpreted the Decalogue, the Ten Commandments, on the basis of the First Commandment. This reminds us of Luther's explanation of the First Commandment in the Small Catechism. "We should fear, love, and trust in God above all things."[24] The real meaning of the Ten Commandments is not that they command us to do this or to avoid that. Melanchthon agreed that people could to some extent fulfill such commandments. The Ten Commandments require much more. The first demand is that our will is in harmony with God's will.

Melanchthon discussed this conformity of our will to God's in terms of prayer and submissive obedience. Fearing and loving God means asking for help with the certainty that God will hear our prayers and, as a result, can be expected to help. This very basic religious attitude lets God be what in fact God is: the Almighty, the Creator of heaven and earth. It distinguishes God from everything else, whether we like it or have to put up with it, those which threaten us and those which are helpful. Our prayers should not—as we might easily think—seek help in the form of being rescued from any of these things. Rather, prayer rises above these things and subordinates them to its petition. Whatever I may encounter in this world—whether it is helpful or harmful—is not the God from whom I receive my life and my death. Prayer is addressed to this God of life and death. Melanchthon accordingly did not encourage us to pray—rather he interpreted the First Commandment. This means that all prayer should be made in the certainty of being heard. For this God is in control of everything, whether it suits us or we must endure it, whether it is helpful or threatening. For this reason, we should seek our help only from this God and not from anything else.

Melanchthon interpreted the Ten Commandments not only in terms of petitionary prayer but also in terms of submissive obedience. We will have even more difficulty in understanding what he said about submissive obedience. Obedience does not have a good reputation among us today. Melanchthon, however, spoke of taking life as it comes. He specifically named hard times, spiritual afflictions, and death. Since these come to us from God, we are to accept them in submission to God's will.

Two interpretative notes are needed. First, we are to submit ourselves to God's will and not to an unchangeable course of events. Modern thought especially is tempted to equate these two—particularly in discussing religious attitudes. Schleiermacher, for example, said: "The religious self-consciousness, by means of which we place all that affects or influences us in absolute dependence on God, coincides entirely with the view that all such things are conditioned and determined by the interdependence of Nature."[25] Melanchthon, however, spoke about God's personal will. Furthermore—and this brings us back to the quotation from Melanchthon—the Apology asserted: People are not able to obey by submitting their will to God's in the way the law demands. Precisely for that reason, we cannot agree with Melanchthon's opponents, scholastic theologians who soften the will of God expressed in the Ten Commandments. Melanchthon said they were following the lead of the philosophers and, therefore, taught only about the kind of righteousness that we are capable of *(iustitia rationalis)* and which is fulfilled with merely moral works *(civilia opera)*. In addition, they maintained that "without the Holy Spirit reason can love God above all things."[26]

The interpretation of the law rejected by Melanchton does not recognize the Ten Commandments as God's law.[27] This is especially the problem for any attempt to understand the law as God's will. We can do that as long as we are not troubled and are apparently in control of ourselves—as though we had the time to love God above all things without God working such love in us through the Holy Spirit. We know from our own experience that it is possible to feel this way. Then we can seriously intend to do what is right and to love God. "As long as a man's mind is at rest and he does not feel God's wrath or judgment, he can imagine that he wants to love God and that he wants to do good for God's sake."[28] It is exactly this fiction that we are in control of ourselves that the law is struggling to overcome. We only recognize that this as the real nature of the law when it scores a bull's-eye by striking us "in the agony of conscience and in conflict."[29] Then we become aware that all the philosophical speculations about what we are able to do, about our freedom and capacity to make decisions, is empty talk. They do not help us find salvation. "Paul says (Rom. 4:15), 'The law brings wrath.' He does not say that by the law men merit the forgiveness of sins. For the law always accuses and terrifies consciences. It does not justify, because a conscience terrified by the law flees before God's judgment."[30] I add: The law that is active in this way is not a general experience of the world or of destiny that overcomes my human will to live. Rather, it is the preached law, the Ten Commandments as Melanchthon interpreted and applied them in the Apology of the Augsburg Confession. Obviously the law will be not always be experienced in this way even though it is being interpreted to us—something similar is true of our experience of the gospel. Whenever the law becomes God's Word to us then we know that we are not capable of doing the most simple thing of all, that is, letting God be God. Rather we then begin to seek information and help from other things and from ourselves. We neither thank God for the good that we experience not do we submit ourselves to what is happening in our lives.

Obviously, we have more to say than that God makes demands on us and that our experience teaches us that we are not able to keep them. Simultaneously with this experience of being unable to fulfill the law, we also experience God's work of fulfilling these demands in faith. The law forces us to stop depending on ourselves, destroys the fiction that we are free, and puts us in the place where we belong: in faith. For this reason we speak of the pedagogical function of the law. Paul called the law "our custodian until Christ came" (Gal. 3:24). Faith accomplishes exactly what we are not able to do as long as we maintain the fiction that we are free, willing, and able to do it: We let God be God. "Whoever knows that in Christ he has a gracious God, truly knows God, calls upon him, and is not, like the heathen, without God."[31] Faith comes as God's own work through the Holy Spirit, "where and when it pleases God."[32]

There is absolutely no value to any of our attempts to decide that this is the time for us to believe, the time for the Holy Spirit to be active in us. Before we even begin, such efforts are trapped in the fiction of our own ability, in the fiction that we are able to decide to believe and, in this faith, let God be God. No one can do this. When our mind is at rest (homo otiosus), we act as though we could. We really need to remain patient and composed in those times when things are going well in life so that we neither fall back into the fiction of being able to trust in God ourselves nor drive others into it. Rather, we must always ascribe the fact that we have faith when we need it to God and to God's work. Otherwise we will immediately relapse into the fiction that we have kept the law and thereby once again come under the condemnation of the law. "For who loves or fears God enough?"[33] Melanchthon answered his own question: We all know very well that this question condemns us. We rebel often enough against the affliction which God lays on us, doubt that God cares about us and hears our prayers, and are angry because the godless prosper and the righteous suffer. We all know that we are lazy in our calling, neglect our neighbor, and are driven by our passions. In spite of our best will and all our good intentions to obey God and keep the Commandments, we are always trapped in our own inability as soon as we rely on what we are able to do. We are able to let God be God only when God enables us to do so by giving us faith. Faith makes it simple and easy to keep the First Commandment by enabling us creatures to acknowledge that God is the Creator.

In concluding this section, I refer again to a factor that is always significant in our interpretation of the Lutheran confessions. Our theological reflection on these confessions is our effort to understand the basic decision of the Reformation. We will understand this basic decision only in terms of its presuppositions. The basic decision of the Reformation was to reject any kind of human-centered approach. Only as long as we consistently read the confessions as God-centered will we recognize the inner logic and compelling truth of the assertion that we become fully human beings solely through God's work in our lives.

Both God's withdrawal and granting of the experience of salvation are to be understood from this perspective. These experiences always go together—a fact that becomes especially clear when we think both about our times of experiencing withdrawal of salvation and about our times of feeling that we are saved in God-centered terms. This total experience of God withdrawing and granting salvation to us should be described in terms of the Trinity. Obviously, it can also be described simply by speaking about God. Trinitarian thinking, however, helps us keep our thinking from sliding into a human-centered approach. Such Trinitarian thinking can help us think about the Reformation's basic decision in terms of the theological meaning of the early church's basic decision. Thinking of them together obviously makes it necessary for us to rethink the basic decision of the early church. The new emphasis given to the work of the Holy Spirit in Reformation theology illustrates this. This emphasis on the Holy Spirit requires us to think about God in terms of the relationship between God and people. It is not useful to think about God and people separately from each other and then to think of them as being related. The end result of such a process can be seen from the way in which the early church's human-centered understanding of the person and work of Christ continually led to irresolvable dilemmas.

The basic decision of the Reformation was to reject such a human-centered approach. To say that God and people are in relationship means to speak of Jesus Christ as the person who corresponds to God. This Jesus is the living example of the justified person. His life is the basic form of our life in God— the life that God gives to us. Once we think as the Reformation did, then we will—at the right time—also think of God in the only way that lets God be God, Father, Son, and Holy Spirit.

WE ARE DEPENDENT ON
GOD'S WORK TO BE REALLY HUMAN

In his theses prepared for an academic disputation on the nature of human beings, Luther said: "Paul in Romans 3 [:28], 'We hold that a man is justified by faith apart from works,' briefly sums up the definition of man, saying, 'Man is justified by faith.' "[34] If being really human is defined theologically in terms of being justified by faith, every aspect of our humanity is defined in terms of our being dependent on God. Human beings are not defined in terms of being free in relationship to God but rather in terms of being caught up in God's activity through faith. This work of God can be described in Trinitarian terms—as in the previous section. In any case, being human is not to be defined in terms of what we already have or still might make out of ourselves. Rather we are defined in terms of what *God* can make out of us. Thus Luther in the same series of theses described being human from an eschatological perspective. "Therefore, man in this life is the simple material of God for the form of his future life."[35] The concept of "material" is derived from an Aristotelian system of ontology and refers to possibility. Luther's usage of the term was, in terms of that system, a misuse. Luther was saying that the human being is a possibility that God both wills to and actually will make a reality.

Luther's statements were clearly formulated. Obviously, they could not become part of the confessional writings, precisely because they were pointed. The confessional writings needed to be written in such a way that as many people as possible would accept them. In order to do that, they had to use theological language that was commonly used and that fit with the current understanding of people. The following discussion will show how difficult that was. The statement of Reformation theology made it necessary not merely to contradict people's experience of themselves but their experience of themselves as social beings who were able to respond to the demands of social relations. I have, however—at the very beginning of this discussion—referred to Luther's theses to indicate the direction of the Reformation's interpretation of being human that we are trying to understand. These theses also indicate the way in which the Reformers' basic decision influenced their view of people. We are not speaking about humanity in general from a philosophical perspective. Rather, we are speaking theologically about the individual in whom God is working salvation.

Human Beings as Sinners

In discussing sin, we must be careful not to think of sin in moral terms, as the evil which we do even though we ought to do the good. Rather, sin is to be understood in terms of our relationship to God. We once again see a difference between a human-centered and a God-centered approach. A human-centered approach establishes the basis for a relationship between God and people on the basis of the nature of the human being. For this reason, sin must be described in such a way that this basis for the relationship is not destroyed. At the same time, the serious disturbance in this relationship resulting from the sinner's loss of grace must be taken into account. Roman Catholic doctrine defined sin in a way that combined both God's grace and human freedom. It described a twofold image of God in human beings, the image of God *(imago dei)* and the likeness of God *(similitudo dei)*. Before the Fall into sin, human beings were related to God both through their natural being and the accompanying image of God and through the likeness of God, God's gracious gift that enabled people to orient their lives to God. It is this latter likeness to God, God's gracious gift, that was lost through the Fall into sin. Human beings still are God's creatures and retain the image of God that is part of creation. As a result, original sin can be described as the loss of the righteousness and holiness in which human beings were created. This and all its results were clearly described, for example, in the decree on original sin of the Council of Trent.[36] This definition, however, specified that the freedom of the will, which is the decisive element of the human creature's image of God and the point of contact for God's grace, dare not be questioned. For this reason, the Lutheran assertion that the will of human beings is not free was rejected by Trent as heretical.

The papal bull which threatened Luther with excommunication, *Exsurge Domine,*[37] included Luther's thirteenth thesis from the Heidelberg Disputation of 1518 among the statements of Luther that it condemned as heretical: "Free will, after the fall, exists in name only, and as long as it does what it is able to do, it commits a mortal sin."[38] The decree on justification adopted by the Council of Trent explicitly repeated this condemnation: "If anyone shall say that after Adam's sin man's free will was lost and destroyed, or that it is a thing only in name without a reality, a fiction introduced into the Church by Satan—*anathema sit.*"[39] These statements clearly establish the human-centered viewpoint of Roman Catholic teaching: No matter how deeply human beings are trapped in sin, they are still always able to seek God's grace. They are free to take the initiative and always remain responsible for their actions in relationship to God. The Lutheran confessions did not completely adopt these statements of Luther that Roman Catholics condemned as heretical. Rather, they sought a compromise between theological necessity and their own personal experience.

The second article of the Augsburg Confession described original sin by reversing the interpretation of the First Commandment. "Our churches also teach that since the fall of Adam all men who are propogated according to nature are born in sin. That is to say, they are without fear of God, are without trust in God, and are concupiscent."[40] This original sin is then described as "truly sin, which even now damns and brings eternal death on those who are not born again through Baptism and the Holy Spirit."[41] This statement could be understood as agreeing with traditional medieval teaching and was therefore approved by the Roman Confutation. The definition of original sin, however, was rejected, "because it is manifest to every Christian that to be without fear of God and without trust in God is the actual guilt of an adult rather than the offense of a recently born infant who does not as yet possess the full use of reason."[42] This argues that we must become responsible rational persons before we can either fear and trust in God or not. The inherent ability to generate fear or trust in God is presupposed, however.

In the Apology, Melanchthon explained that the second article of the Augsburg Confession was explicitly designed to reject this assertion. "This passage testifies that in those who are born according to the flesh we deny the existence not only of actual fear and trust in God but also of the possibility and gift to produce it."[43] Melanchthon asserted that the issue is not whether we do or do not do something that, as the authors of the Roman Confutation claimed, we have the natural ability to do. Rather, Melanchthon denied that sinners have the capacity to fear and trust God. People are really trying to do the opposite of what God intends. Concupiscence is concerned about the created world rather than about God. "In this sense the Latin definition denies that human nature has the gift and capacity to produce the fear and trust of God. . . . When we use the term 'concupiscence,' we do not mean only its acts or fruits, but the continual inclination of nature."[44] This clearly defined the point at issue. Melanchthon's opponents presupposed that people have the capacity to seek God and described sin as people not taking the appropriate action to do what they are able to do. The Lutheran confession explicitly denies that people have this ability. This is the logical conclusion of the Reformation's basic decision.

Melanchthon felt that a clearer definition of the freedom of the will was needed. If we are not free to respond positively to God's offer of grace, do we have any freedom at all? The Augsburg Confession responded to this question in a special article that offered a compromise between the necessary statements demanded by their theological position and the confessor's experiences of the realities of human life. As is usual in theology, this article made a basic distinction. In this case it affirmed that the human will has certain freedom in matters related to peoples' relationships to one another. At the same time, it asserted that in relationship to God, human will has no freedom at all. It can produce an external righteousness in social life and can act morally (iustitia moralis). On the other hand, it cannot produce the kind of spiritual righteousness that is acceptable to God. That righteousness is possible only through the work of the Holy Spirit.[45] This distinction made it possible to meet the theological need of denying people every capacity to cooperate in the process of being saved. This was necessary because it was the only way of maintaining that God is the sole cause of people's salvation. At the same time, it was still possible to meet the social need of holding people responsible for their actions. Doing that, however, made it necessary to describe people as being free to choose the good and to reject the evil. Given the situation in which the Augsburg Confession was written, this was probably the only possible compromise.

The Augsburg Confession needed to defend itself against its opponents' polemical assertion that the Lutherans denied all freedom of the will and therefore taught an error long condemned in the church. This accusation has been made in the first version of the Roman Confutation—a version not accepted by Emperor Charles V. This version of the Roman Confutation document distinguished between the Augsburg Confession as the confession of the princes and real thinking of the Lutheran theologians which—this draft asserted—was not clearly stated in the Augsburg Confession.[46] The authors of the first draft of the Roman Confutation provided many quotations from the writings of the Reformers to demonstrate this fact. For example, in their discussion of Article XVIII of the Augsburg Confession, they quoted this statement from Melanchthon's *Loci Communes Theologici of* 1521: "Since all things that happen, happen necessarily according to divine predestination, our will *(voluntas)* has no liberty. For all creatures act according to God's predestination."[47]

It is of decisive significance for our understanding of this solution that the effect of the distinction made by the Augsburg Confession between freedom in relation to the world and freedom in relation to God was to prevent a thorough discussion of the controversial issue: How is the spontaneity of human action related to God's activity? If we think of human actions as being determined either by human spontaneity or by God's activity—as a human-centered approach does—it necessary to overcome this either/or by describing their interaction in such a way that human spontaneity and God's activity work cooperatively rather than in competition with each other. Such a competitive either/or is established whenever human decision is described as being productive, that is, as discovering possible courses of action and life styles that can be implemented by the action of the will. The result is that we determine the nature of our reality. Luther rightly rejected this position in the controversy with Erasmus about the freedom of the will. "It follows now that free choice is plainly a divine term, and can be properly applied to none but the Divine Majesty alone; for he alone can do and does . . . whatever he pleases in heaven and on earth."[48] Any way of thinking about God and human beings as coordinate ontological entities requires us to think about some kind of competitive relationship between divine and human freedom. We may then describe how this competition is overcome by cooperation. The other possibility is to think of human spontaneity as being made possible by God's activity. Then there is no possibility of thinking of these two as either competing or cooperating.

The above-quoted statement from Melanchthon was taken by the authors of the Roman Confutation out of its larger context. In this context, Melanchthon speaks of the human heart as the seat of affect, of love, hate, fear, sorrow, etc. As we know from experience, these affects are not under our control. At most, a stronger affect is able to suppress a weaker. Any attempt to decide what we want to feel on the basis of our knowledge of how we ought to feel at best produces an external attitude that is hypocritical. As Melanchthon says, "The Pharisaical Scholastics will preach the power of free will)(arbitrium). The Christian will acknowledge that nothing is less in his power than his heart."[49] Melanchthon described our concept of spontaneity as the "affects," or as the biblical "heart." No human being can control these by the power of reflective consciousness. Rather, they are determined by what comes to the person from outside, that is, from God. Thus faith is dependent on the external Word of the gospel. In this dependence, it experiences the liberated spontaneity of loving God. If we think about the relationship between human spontaneity and God's activity in this God-centered way, we do not need to mediate the relationship in some process of cooperation.[50] At the same time, the Augsburg Confession's distinction between divine and civil righteousness is called into question because it places civil righteousness under the control of reflective consciousness and thereby opens the door to a human-centered approach.[51]

The distinction under discussion between the freedom of the will in civil matters and its bondage in relationship to God was not only a conscious concession that was unavoidable in the situation of 1530. Rather, it described an unresolved problem of Reformation thinking. On the one hand, Luther had presented a doctrine of the human person from a God-centered perspective in *The Bondage of the Will*—a book that he highly valued.[52] Many Lutherans did not agree with Luther's position in this book. They dealt with the problem in another way. They developed the distinction discussed above—distinguishing between an area in which the will is free and another area in which the will is in bondage. Melanchthon's presentation of this distinction demonstrated its advantages.

The distinction typified by Melanchthon was an extraordinarily useful theological position. It provided the theological basis for a Christian theory of education. Everyone "ought to know that God requires this civil righteousness and that, to some extent, we can achieve it." At the same time, it "points out the need for the Holy Spirit."[53] Melanchthon claimed that this freedom of the will makes civil righteousness possible. It must therefore mean that the human will is free to agree and cooperate with God's will. Melanchthon maintained that this cooperation occurs in the area of civil righteousness and not in the area of spiritual righteousness. However, the application of this distinction was difficult and generated its own problems. Basically, it opened the door to a human-centered approach to life and to the interpretation of the meaning of this life. This problem must be very explicitly recognized. One area of life has now become independent. It is bound to God's activity only through the voluntary agreement of the human will with the divine will. Whether that agrees with a God-centered understanding is still an important question today. It must be addressed to and answered by every attempt to apply the Reformation's basic theological decision to the understanding of human life.

Faith as God's Own Determination of the Person

During the sixteenth-century controversies, the Reformers needed to make their position understandable to those opponents who represented the medieval approach to theology. Thus the texts of the Lutheran confessions—especially the Augsburg Confession and the Apology, which are most important for the following interpretation—were determined by this need as well as by the inner necessity of theological thought. These documents were written as contributions to an ongoing conversation. Melanchthon had learned much from his experiences during the Diet of Augsburg in 1530. It was a situation in which he was responsible for defending the teaching of the Reformation rather than attacking the teaching of its opponents. The difficulty in clarifying the Reformation's understanding of what faith is makes it clear that it was very difficult even to present the Reformation's position in such a way that it could be understood. This is indicated by the fact that the controversy repeatedly raised the question as to whether faith could coexist with mortal sin.

The Roman Catholic understanding of faith said that faith and mortal sin could coexist. This is because faith was understood primarily as a knowledge of God's gracious will and the trust that the offer of salvation as mediated by the church is true. Faith thus stands at the beginning of justification and is the beginning point of this process in the human person.[54] This process of justification must go further. That grace which faith affirms must become an internal reality in the human person and determine the whole course of life. The natural person is capable of unformed faith (*fides informis*), but this faith must be transformed into faith formed by love (*fides caritate formata*) through sacramental grace. That love which is beyond the capacity of nature must perfect faith so that it becomes "faith working through love" (Gal. 5:6). The human person is righteous only if both its cognitive functions, that is, faith, and its will, that is, love, are transformed and thus fulfill God's intention. If this righteousness is lost through a mortal sin, faith remains as unformed faith which can once again become the basis of repentance and a return to the state of grace. This distinction between unformed faith and faith formed by love demonstrated how human-centered thinking defines faith as something that is the possession of the human person.

For the Lutherans, it was unthinkable that someone could simultaneously believe and sin. "Receiving the forgiveness of sins for a heart terrified and fleeing from sin, therefore, such a faith does not remain in those who obey their lusts, nor does it exist together with mortal sin."[55] For faith is the opposite of sin. If sin is understood as turning away from God, trusting in things, and seeking the desires of life, then unbelief is the way in which this turning away from God occurs, the bond with Jesus Christ and the gospel broken, and the saving relationship to God abandoned. Therefore, we probably need to say that Canon 28 of the Council of Trent's Decree on Justification—as well as many other of these canons—misunderstood the Reformation teaching and condemned a nonexistent error: "If anyone shall say that with the loss of grace through sin faith is also lost, or that the faith that remains is not a true faith, even if it is not a living one, or that he who has faith without charity is not a Christian—*anathema sit*."[56] In any case, it is clear that the participants in this controversy really did not understand one another. As a result, the controversy was really unprofitable.

The following analysis of the Reformation's teaching about faith presupposes the earlier discussion of the time and place of faith and of the fact that it is not under the control of the individual. Faith is withheld from a person and granted at the proper time, when it is needed.[57] Two additional factors are characteristic of this faith—although they appear to be contradictory. It is precisely this contradiction that reveals the distinctive character of the Reformation's understanding of faith: (1) Faith is always totally present; (2) Faith is totally determined by the object of faith.

The Reformation understanding that faith is always either totally present or totally absent is clearly different from the Roman Catholic teaching that describes faith as an act of the intellect and love as an act of the will. Rather than seeing faith merely as an act of the rational intellect that must be completed than an act of the will, the Lutherans saw faith as a characteristic of the whole person. Justifying faith is not only the knowledge of facts *(notitia historiae)*; rather it is the intentionality of the whole person who trusts in the gospel. "Faith means to want and to accept the promised offer of forgiveness of sins and justification."[58] The whole person is thus involved in faith. The believer is totally and completely defined by this relationship to Jesus Christ. It is simply inappropriate to ask whether faith takes over any special capacity of the soul, for example, whether it is a function of the intellect or of the will. We cannot even say that faith is a function of the thinking and willing personal self, but that the body does not participate in it. Melanchthon described the exemplary situation in which faith is given in terms of the "terrors of the conscience."[59] Just as these terrors express themselves in the whole person, including the body, the whole person is also affected by the peace that faith gives to the terrified conscience. Precisely in faith, therefore, the whole person is involved; we can say that we pull ourselves together in faith. In this process, we experience ourselves as totally free persons who are able to act spontaneously.

This freedom of faith is not like the freedom ascribed to the will without faith as though it were able to choose and thereby to generate possibilities. This is the fiction that we have some ability in and of ourselves—a fiction that

89

shatters when it comes into contact with reality. Rather, faith is our experience that we are totally free when we are aware that we are totally determined by our relationship to God.

The other factor in faith, that we are totally defined by the object of our faith, only appears to contradict this total determination of the person through faith. The reality of faith does not lie in the process that we have just described as taking place in the believing subject. Quite the opposite, this reality lies outside the believing subject, that is, in the object in which faith trusts. Melanchthon said that justifying faith has three objects: the promise, the unconditional nature of the promise of grace, and the merits of Christ. Whenever we speak of saving faith, we are always dealing with the promised mercy. "For faith does not justify or save because it is a good work in itself, but only because it accepts the promised mercy."[60] This means that we cannot define faith as the total definition of the human subject if we thereby mean that faith consists in a condition of the believing subject. Because faith binds us to Christ, the spontaneity of faith is bound to the promise of the proclamation of the gospel in which faith trusts and from which faith receives its reality.

Here too the Reformers had difficulty in stating their teaching in such a way that representatives of the medieval tradition could understand it. In trying to do this, Melanchthon made a number of very problematical statements. For example, he said that human beings please God through faith. As believers, we are what God wills us to be. "God wants us to believe him and to accept blessings from him; this he declares to be true worship."[61] That statement is not a problem—as long as we remember that such faith and acceptance does not have its source in a human capacity to believe but rather that this "true worship" is a gift from God. The danger is that faith itself becomes our work that pleases God. However, we receive our righteousness through faith because the rigteousness of grace is given to us through faith. That is how God wants it to be. If this will of God becomes the object of faith, however, faith is in turn described as obedience. "We must speak technically because of certain carping critics: faith is truly righteousness because it is obedience to the Gospel. Obedience to the edict of a superior is obviously a kind of distributive righteousness."[62] Melanchthon then continued the discussion by emphasizing the object of faith. The problems remain: Once faith is defined as obedience, the emphasis is placed on the act of faith produced by the believing human subject. Under some circumstances, this makes it easier to reach an understanding with the Roman Catholic partner in the conversation. Roman Catholics always define faith as such an act of the human subject—whether this act of faith is possible because of the natural freedom of the human being or because God graciously enables us to believe. The price for such an understanding is too high, however. This approach shifts the emphasis in faith from God as the active subject in the process of salvation to the activity of the believer as the subject of faith.

We must, therefore, carefully observe the limitation that faith justifies only because of the object of its trust. Certainly it is true "that faith is the very righteousness by which we are accounted righteous before God." This is more carefully defined, however: "This is not because it is a work worthy in itself, but because it receives God's promise."[63] Justifying faith is, therefore, the way in which God defines and shapes the believing person as the subject of faith. This faith needs the object of faith because it is God's coming out to meet us that provides the basis of faith. Since this object of faith is the gospel, the Word of the gospel is all that is important. "But one cannot deal with God or grasp him except through the Word. Therefore justification takes place through the Word, as Paul says (Rom. 1:16), 'The Gospel is the power of God for salvation to every one who has faith,' and (Rom. 10:17), 'Faith comes from what is heard.' "[64] The total spontaneity of the believer can be understood only as dependence on the gospel, which is God actively coming out to meet us. If we as believers were to think about our faith rather than focusing on the gospel, the reality of faith would disintegrate.

The Active Life

The understanding of faith is shaped by the perspective from which it is viewed. This is even more true of the understanding of good works. Although the arguments were carried out in an energetic and aggressive manner, the opponents of the Reformation did not merely disagree with but never really understood the Lutheran position. The Reformation needed to reject "works-righteousness," that is, any attempt to achieve certainty of salvation by religious activity. This argument could obviously be misunderstood as meaning that the Reformation's way of salvation was easier. If salvation is the free gift of God's grace, then we have no need to trouble ourselves with trying to lead a God-pleasing life. Rather, we are free to do or not do whatever pleases us. This reproach was close to the surface and was easily confirmed by experience—for people's religious and moral activities are always open to criticism. The statement that Lutheran preaching resulted in immorality was an effective argument and the Lutherans had to defend themselves against this accusation.

Thus it is understandable that the Augsburg Confession presented the Reformation's basic decision in Articles IV and V and then immediately followed them with Article VI, "The New Obedience." This article in particular demonstrated how difficult it was to present the Reformation teaching in such a way that the opponents could understand it. As a result, it was, on the one hand, necessary to separate human activity from the giving and receiving of salvation and must therefore again focus on faith. On the other hand, it was also necessary to emphasize that believers neither can nor may neglect doing God's will. The necessity of acting according to God's will must be maintained. From this perspective, Article VI of the Augsburg Confession was not very well formulated. The identity of the subject who obeys God's will is not clear. At first, faith is named as the doer of good works. Soon, however, this is changed to a general *man müsse,* "one must," in German or *quod oporteat,* "it ought" in the Latin.[65] This article would have been clearer if it had consistently spoken of faith as the subject of the new obedience as the Schwabach Articles and the Marburg Articles (documents that were used as sources of the Augsburg Confession) both did.[66] Once that had been clarified, it would have been possible to comprehend the human activity that fulfills God's will in the activity of the Holy Spirit, who creates such living and active faith. The unclear statements of Article VI were improved in Article XX. "It is only by faith that forgiveness of sins and grace are apprehended, and because through faith the Holy Spirit is received, hearts are so renewed and endowed with new affections as to be able to bring forth good works."[67] Melanchthon went on to say that this new focus of the human being, or of the new affects, as Melanchthon said, enables a new kind of activity. "For without faith and without Christ human nature and human strength are much too weak to do good works, call upon God, have patience in suffering, love one's neighbor, diligently engage in callings which are commanded, render obedience, avoid evil lusts, etc."[68]

How is it possible to think of such activity without also thinking of the person who does these works as in control of her- or himself? Undoubtedly one can then admonish this person not to trust in these works or to assume that they merit grace.[69] Such an admonition is certainly not adequate protection against sliding into human-centered thinking. Two basic ideas must be emphasized that remind active persons of their basic dependence on God. First, the Lutheran Reformation's own implementation of its basic decision emphasized that good works, works which conform to God's will, are works that have been commanded by God.[70] This meant that religious activities do not have any unusual value or gain any special merit. This may well have been the most revolutionary result of the Reformation's basic decision: The distinction between actions in a "religious" and in a "secular" realm was eliminated. Everything that late medieval piety thought of as a religious work, "like rosaries, the cult of saints, monasticism, pilgrimages, appointed fasts, holy days, brotherhoods, etc." are "childish and useless works."[71] It is obvious that the religious intention is dominant in such works. They are intended to do something to please God, whether as a sacramental act of penance *(satisfactio operum)* or as a way of being certain of one's own salvation. In every case, such works are distinguished by their religious purpose.

In contrast to this position, the Lutherans taught that good works which come from faith have no such special character. The good works that God wills us to do are those meaningful works that must be done in any case if life is to go on.[72] These works are the kinds of things that people need to do every day—farmers, blue-collar workers, homemakers, servants, and princes, as cabinet makers or as jailers, as preachers or as hearers of the gospel. The need for doing these works can be taken for granted. There is nothing special or unusual about the works that are done in faith.[73] No one needs to try to think up things that we can do to please God. Life itself shows us what is to be done on each day. We are in harmony with God's will when we do these things and do not run away from these everyday tasks to do some special religious work. By focusing our attention on the ordinary walks of life rather than on some special religious work, the Reformation oriented the course of our lives to that which comes to us from God. The special work that we choose for ourselves because it seems so religious is not God's will, but rather the work that we take for granted.

We shall follow this way of thinking one more step. We have asked how our own activity can be put into the context of God's activity. Melanchthon dealt with this question in his interpretation of the Ten Commandments as well as of the Creed. He says the human heart and its affects are and can be present with God only if God makes this possible through the Holy Spirit. Faith leads us to be able to accept our whole life in this world with all its special characteristics as God's will. In contrast, unbelief rebels against God. "The flesh distrusts God and trusts in temporal things; in trouble it looks to men for help; it even defies God's will and runs away from afflictions that it ought to bear because of God's command [mandatum]; and it doubts God's mercy. The Holy Spirit in our hearts battles against such feelings in order to suppress and destroy them and to give us new spiritual impulses."[74] Melanchthon is struggling to find a way of speaking both about what goes on inside and outside people, in the way in which we want to live and the way in which we actually do live. The "flesh"—our humanity as determined by sin—presents us with the contradiction. This contradiction expresses itself in the efforts of our will to control what we do. The points at issue in this conflict do not always have to be expressed in the context of religious works. This context clearly shows how the human will worries about and desires salvation and tries to do those things that will lead to salvation. The conflict can also appear in the form of unbridled passion, in trusting in "temporal things" in such a way that our will to live leads us to amass the possibilities of life in the form of possessions and money so that we will have them when we need them. The Holy Spirit works against these tendencies. The Spirit starts "new spiritual impulses" in our heart. Through this work of the Spirit, there can be some correspondence between what we want to do and what we actually do. The heart can now accept what comes to us from God. Our will to live focuses on the tasks that need to be done now and thereby we actually do what God wants. By thus accepting life as it comes to us from God, we are able to do the right things in life. Then our life's work is a doing of what is good through loving God and our neighbor. In the same way that we become whole in faith—because we are wholly focused on the object of faith, the salvation that comes through Jesus Christ—we also become whole in love, because we accept life as it comes to us and are in harmony with God because we enjoy depending on God.

5

The Augsburg Confession
as a Document
of Church Renewal

An Introductory Note on the Interpretation
of the Augsburg Confession

In the two following chapters, individual Lutheran confessional documents contained in the Book of Concord will be analyzed. This analysis will not take the form of a running commentary on the whole text—although that would be very rewarding. Instead, the focus will be on specific characteristics of the individual documents.

The Augsburg Confession is the first confessional writing to be evaluated. The comments made earlier on the original purpose of the Augsburg Confession as a defense *(Apologia)* of the reforms in the life of the church in Electoral Saxony are presuppoed.[1] The supporters of late medieval theology at the time of the Reformation not only rejected these reforms but also accused the Reformers of false teaching. Because of these attacks, it was necessary to add an extensive introductory statement on doctrine to the statement that the Lutherans originally planned to submit to the Diet of Augsburg in 1530. This statement on doctrine is contained in Articles I–XXI and was based on the Schwabach Articles.[2]

This presentation of the Lutheran doctrine was shaped by the fact that it was a defense against attacks. As such an apology in response to the charge of heresy, it was intended to demonstrate the orthodoxy of the Lutherans. In preparing it, Melanchthon presupposed that there was general agreement on these teachings and that the accusations of heresy were malicious and without foundation. "The whole dissension is concerned with a certain few abuses."[3] It is difficult to say how true Melanchthon's claim was. The union negotiations that were carried on during the Diet of Augsburg indicated that agreement had been achieved on many points. The discussions of the proposal that the Roman Catholic Church might observe the four-hundredth anniversary of the presentation of the Augsburg Confession in 1980 by recognizing it as a Catholic confession confirm this impression. The supporters of this proposal wisely suggested tht only Articles I–XXI be recognized. Otherwise, we may assume that it would quickly have become obvious that Roman Catholics could not possibly recognize the whole text of the Augsburg Confession.

The second part of the Augsburg Confession (Articles XXII–XXVIII) did much more than merely report on the abolition of a few abuses. Rather, it described a far-reaching program of church reform. To a large extent, this had not yet been put into practice in 1530. At the same time, the reform had gone so far that there was no longer any way of imagining a reunion with the late medieval church. This reform shaped the Lutheran church. The Roman Catholic and Lutheran churches differ from each other primarily in the forms of church life. Differences in doctrine play a comparatively subordinate role. The following interpretation of the Augsburg Confession will show that these reforms of the life of the church were directly related to the Reformation's basic decision. This assertion will be proved on the basis of a discussion of the reasons that were given for every part of the reforms. A study of individual doctrines would focus more attention on the details of the Reformation's teachings. The main result of the Reformation, however, was not a new theology but rather a thorough reformation of the church and of religious life. This is clearly documented by the Augsburg Confession.

This interpretation of the Augsburg Confession will therefore not take the form of a basic doctrinal statement. That is what theologies of the Lutheran confessions have usually done. It is, however, more appropriate to the Augsburg Confession's self-understanding to emphasize the basic principles of this reshaping of the life of the church. This will necessarily require reference to the first, doctrinal part of the Augsburg Confession.

Because the Augsburg Confession was basically written as a defensive, or apologetic document, many matters, such as the controversial question of the papacy, were not discussed at all; others were referred to only very cautiously. Melanchthon wrote the Apology of the Augsburg Confession as an explicit answer to the Roman Confutation produced by the opponents who, in varying degrees, supported the late medieval understanding of the church's life. As a result, the Apology said many things much more clearly than the Augsburg Confession itself did.[4] This characteristic of the Apology was facilitated by but was not basically due to the fact that it is so much longer than the Augsburg Confession. For this reason, the Apology of the Augsburg Confession will often be used as a primary resource in interpreting the Augsburg Confession itself. Any discussion of the regulation of church life among Lutherans must also refer to the Smalcald Articles of 1537[5] and the Treatise on the Power and

Primacy of the Pope.[6] Although both of these latter documents were considered at the meeting of the Smalcald League in 1537, only Melanchthon's Treatise—not Luther's Smalcald Articles—was at that time officially recognized as an addition to the Augsburg Confession and the Apology. Luther's articles were only subscribed to by some theologians.[7]

It is admittedly not usual to give so much emphasis to the second part of the Augsburg Confession in interpreting the whole. The decision to do so is not merely based on the historical development of the Augsburg Confession or on the effects of the church reforms described in the second part. Rather, Luther himself set the precedent for this approach in his outline of the material in the Smalcald Articles. No justification is needed for following Luther's approach.

The second part of the Smalcald Articles listed the items that Luther felt could not be discussed by the kind of council in which the Lutherans were then preparing to participate. Luther first named the chief article of justification by faith as this is based on the person and work of Christ. Luther next referred to the liturgy of the mass, or more accurately, to the misuse of the Sacrament of the Altar as defined by the papal theologians. Luther described the sacrificial character of this sacrament as the decisive point of difference. "If the mass falls, the papacy will fall with it."[8] Luther attached his criticism of the form that the church had taken as a result of the doctrine of the sacrifice of the mass. He followed this with a critical analysis of monasticism and the papacy. Luther felt that there was no possibility of negotiating these issues. The best that could be done was to reaffirm that the Reformers condemned the Roman Church on these points because of the Reformation's basic decision.

Only in part III did Luther list the doctrinal topics that well-intentioned and intelligent people could discuss at the council. Luther's outline was impressively comprehensive and gave a balanced treatment of the various issues, especially when it directly related the reform of the church to the Reformation's basic decision.[9] This conclusion is assumed as a basic presupposition of the following interpretation of the Augsburg Confession.

THE GOSPEL IN WORD AND SACRAMENT

Sixteenth-century Lutherans described themselves as *evangelisch*. They thereby identified themselves in terms of their teaching of the gospel.[10] They thereby also defined the gospel as the basis of the church and the basic element in its form.

At the same time, the gospel was not the only factor that determined the life of the Lutheran church. As a result, this church is, at least partially, a malformation. Several obvious factors can be specifically named. The church is never made up only of people who need the gospel, who are driven by the question of their salvation and who therefore turn to the church. Some people are in the church only because they earn their living by offering to satisfy the needs of those people who seek salvation from the church. As a result the church is not formed only by the reality that the gospel is preached there and God's salvation in Jesus Christ made available to people. The church is always also formed by the self-interest of those people who represent this offer and expect to earn a guaranteed income from it. The more demand there is for what the church has to offer, the better and more certain the income of those who represent the church; and the more people are able to make their living by offering the church's services. This is probably not always quite so clear in the German *Volkskirche*—which assumes that everyone is a member of the church who has not explicitly declared otherwise. This factor, however, appears quite clearly in statements of the church's financial officers expressing concern that so many of the people leaving the church are those who would otherwise pay an above average amount of church tax.[11] Similarly, discussions about ways in which participation in the life of the church can be increased and congregational life strengthened are always partially motivated by the desire to provide a secure basis for meeting the church's financial needs; this financial basis depends on developing as strong an interest in the church as possible among as many people as possible. And since the church tax is theoretically owed by all those who have been baptized, it also seems important to baptize as many people as possible. Thus the church has a great interest in maintaining the custom of baptizing as many children and/or infants as possible.

This long introduction focuses attention on the interrelationships that determined the form of the church at the time of the Reformation. We are generally aware that the Reformation was occasioned by the sale of indulgences. That practice was obviously a misuse of the gospel for the sake of increasing the church's wealth. The self-interest of those who claimed to control God's offer of salvation thereby led to a terrible distortion of the church and was one of the reasons why the Reformation so quickly established itself in Germany. These are some of Luther's theses on indulgences:

62. The true treasure of the church is the most holy gospel of the glory and grace of God.

63. But this treasure is naturally most odious [to merit], for it makes the first to be last [Matt. 20:16].

64. On the other hand, the treasure of indulgences is naturally most acceptable [to merit], for it makes the last to be first.

65. Therefore the treasures of the gospel are nets with which one formerly fished for men of wealth.

66. The treasures of indulgences are nets with which one now fishes for the wealth of men.[12]

Luther's play on words brilliantly characterized the perversion of the church's life: Jesus called the treasures of the gospel nets the apostles were to use in fishing for people, including rich people. Indulgences, however, are the nets that are used to fish for the riches of people.

Because the selling of indulgences is so familiar to us as the occasion of the Reformation, we easily overlook the fact that the liturgy of the mass, more exactly the sacrifice of the mass, was of far-greater significance for the financial support of the church. Once the mass has been interpreted in terms of being a sacrifice, it could be offered for both the living and the dead. As the Council of Trent decreed: "If anyone shall say that the sacrifice of the Mass is only one of praise and thanksgiving; or that it is a mere commemoration of the sacrifice consummated on the cross but not a propitiatory one; or that it profits only him who receives Communion, and ought not to be offered for the living and the dead, for sins, punishments, satisfactions, and other necessities—*anathema sit*."[13]

This meant that the sacrifice of the mass was offered to God on behalf of specific individuals—some living, some dead. The sacrifice was offered with the intention of reconciling God to these people. This understanding of the sacrifice of the mass naturally led everyone who was concerned about the salvation to try to receive as many of these sacrificial masses and as much of their reconciling effect as possible. As a result, more and more masses needed to be read. Individual persons purchased these one at a time or established endowment funds and designated their income for the purchase of regularly celebrated masses for the benefit of a specific dead person. Noble families even hired a priest who was responsible for regularly reading masses for the benefit of their members. Less-wealthy persons formed societies for the benefits of their members. Since canonical law permitted each priest to say mass only once a day, this led to a great increase in the numbers of clergy. These "mass priests" *(Messpfaffen)* formed a proletariat of poorly trained and poorly paid clergy. We must keep this background in mind when we read the Reformers' attacks on the doctrine of the sacrifice of the mass. The basis economic interests of many people were damaged by any such criticism. Any effective critical analysis and reform of the practices related to the celebration of the mass negatively affected the whole system of the church as then organized, including the systems created for the support of the clergy.

The Reform of the Mass

Article XXII of the Augsburg Confession described a very basic change in the previous custom of administering the Lord's Supper. Asserting that it was necessary to celebrate this sacrament as it had been instituted, this article said that both the bread and the wine had to be administered to the laity. One could not be administered separately from the other. Withholding the chalice from the laity violated the express command of Christ. This was also the reason why the Lutherans no longer held processions on Corpus Christi. In these processions, only the bread contained in the monstrance was exhibited to the people as the sacramental presence of Christ. The decisive problem of the mass was, however, first addressed in Article XXIV. The Augsburg Confession emphasized that the Lutherans had not done away with the celebration of the mass—as they had been accused of doing. On the contrary, they had preserved the liturgy of the mass and all the usual ceremonies. They had added a few chorales that were sung in German for the instruction of the common people. In addition, they were diligent in teaching the people about the mass and admonishing them both to attend mass and to commune.

Having said that, Article XXIV did not try to avoid the real point of controversy. The buying and selling of masses was an evil business and most of the masses that were celebrated were read only for the sake of the money. "Then when our preachers preached about these things and the priests were reminded of the terrible responsibility which should properly concern every Christian (namely, that whoever uses the sacrament unworthily is guilty of the body and blood of Christ), such mercenary Masses and private Masses, which had hitherto been held under compulsion for the sake of revenues and stipends, were discontinued in our churches."[14] The reason the Lutherans gave for no longer selling or celebrating masses that had already been purchased is given in the reference to 1 Cor. 11:27. Since the priest saying the mass must also commune, Lutheran clergy experienced such an unworthy reception of the body and blood of Christ as a burden on their conscience.

This introduction was followed by a critical theological analysis of the doctrine of the sacrifice of the mass. The enormous number of masses resulted from the fact that people thought Christ had suffered sufficiently to take away original sin and had instituted the sacrifice of the mass as a way of dealing with actual sins.[15] That was certainly not the official teaching of the late medieval church. The Roman Confutation complained about this distortion. True Catholics protested that the church had never taught anything even similar. "For the mass does not abolish sins, which are destroyed by repentance as their peculiar medicine, but abolishes the punishment due sin. . . ."[16] This statement, however, confirmed Melanchthon's description of the public teaching of the church: The mass was "a work which by its performance [ex opere operato] takes away the sins of the living and the dead."[17] There is no doubt that late medieval theology distinguished between the forgiveness of sins received through the absolution in the sacrament of penance and the satisfaction required of the penitent—a requirement that could be met through applying the sacrifice of the mass. The authors of the Roman Confutation were absolutely right about that. This distinction, however, was also certainly unknown among the common people and it was their common opinion—well described by Melanchthon—that provided the basis for the buying and selling of masses. This became especially clear when people expressed the opinion that although a mass could be said for the benefit of many people at once, it was really better to say a special mass for each individual.[18]

At this point, individual assertions could be argued for and against: Did the Reformers' polemical description adequately express the late medieval teaching? Were their opponents ready to admit such errors and prepared to correct them? What was the relationship of the Christ's unique sacrifice on Golgotha to the sacrifice of the mass? These are no longer the significant questions—especially since the Roman Catholic Church has made significant changes both in the doctrine as well as in the liturgical practice of the mass. (I think, for example, of the Constitution on the Sacred Liturgy, adopted by the Second Vatican Council on April 12, 1963, and the far-reaching effects of that action.)[19]

The really decisive question is rather: To whom is the celebration of the sacrament addressed? The fact that it is called the Eucharist, the "giving of thanks," indicates that it is celebrated in praise of God. That, however, is not the question. Every service of worship properly contains elements of praise of God. Rather the question is: To whom do the gifts of the Lord's Supper, the bread and the wine, belong? Are they a sacrifice to God, offered by the priest who takes the place of Christ? That was the position of the Council of Trent. The basic canon has already been quoted. This third canon on the mass was sharply and negatively formulated: The sacrifice of the mass is not merely thanksgiving or mere commemoration of the sacrifice consummated on the cross. Rather, it has a reconciling effect. It is of use not only to the communicants. Rather, it is "to be offered for the living and the dead, for sins, punishments, satisfactions, and other necessities."[20] The basic movement in the celebration of the mass so described is from the people through the priest who represents Christ to God. The decisive role is that of the priest who offers the sacrifice of the mass in the presence of God.

The Lutheran understanding and celebration of the mass—that is, the Sacrament of the Altar or, as it is called in Luther's Small Catechism and most frequently referred to by Lutheran worshipers, the Lord's Supper—moved in the opposite direction. It is God's gift to people. The promise of the gospel comes from God and moves through the pastor who represents Christ to the worshipers. These worshipers must also be present. The sacrament cannot really be celebrated without them. What is the value of a private mass without a participating congregation? What is the use of whispering the promise of the gospel into a corner of the church? That would be the exact opposite of the intention of the institution of the sacrament and its proper use. As a result, the Lutherans said, they celebrated the mass for the whole parish on Sundays, holidays, and at other times when people desiring to commune were present.[21] Since the Lord's Supper is God's action in relationship to people, there is no other way of doing it. The presence of the assembled congregation, which is the addressee of God's action, is essential for the celebration of the sacrament.

The authors of the Roman Confutation are only attacking straw people when they say: "But if they regard one mass advantageous, how much more advantageous would be a number of masses, of which they nevertheless have unjustly disapproved."[22] If that statement was meant seriously, we can only conclude that the authors of the Roman Confutation simply did not understand what the argument was all about. The issue was not the number of masses; the issue was the basic direction in which the celebration of the sacrament moves. It was for that reason that the Lutherans needed to abolish the custom of saying private masses.

Word and Sacrament

The actual result of the developments described above is that the emphasis in Protestant services of worship shifted to preaching. In comparison to preaching, the Sacrament of the Altar was deemphasized. People spoke of the "church of the Word" and asked whether the Sacrament of the Altar contained anything that was not contained in the Word. If it did not, was this sacrament still needed? These questions about the sacrament were always asked about the Sacrament of the Altar, the Lord's Supper.

Quite apart from the institution of this sacrament and the reality of its use in the church, there was a good answer to such questions. The sacrament makes the gospel, which is based on the person and work of Christ, present in an especially clear way. The sermon may contain only the law and represent the subjective thinking of the preacher, but the "Christ for us" is always at the center of the sacrament. This is true of both the constitutive elements of the celebration: the repetition of the words of institution and the distribution of the sacramental gifts. It is, of course, always possible to convert even this sacrament of the gospel into a law, for example, into a law of human communication. That can happen only if the nature of its institution is radically changed. It is much easier to protest such a distortion of the sacrament than against a sermon that claims to proclaim the gospel but only preaches the law.

The sacrament is, therefore, the promise of the gospel defined in terms of the person and work of Christ. The Lutheran Reformers repeatedly emphasized this fact. Understood in this way, this sacrament also keeps the preaching of the Word about its business. For what is proclaimed in the sermon can be nothing else than this gospel that has been defined in relation to Christ. On the other hand, the sacrament needs the Word in order to be and remain what it is: distribution of the gospel. This happened in the Reformation when preaching came to the assistance of the sacrament and set it free from its distortion. Preaching must be heard. There is no sense in sermons preached in some corner of the church in whispers that only the preacher hears. Given the fact that the Word and Sacrament are both ways of distributing the gospel, it is clear that private masses said in some isolated corner of the church are a meaningless misuse of the sacrament. This is also true of all of the ways in which people have manipulated the consecrated elements, for example, carrying the consecrated bread around in a monstrance or saving them in a tabernacle on the altar so that they can be reverenced. The Word is the process of speaking and hearing; the sacrament is the same kind of process and seeks to be nothing else.

This is the way in which the Reformation inseparably joined preaching and the sacrament to the gospel. The Word and the Sacrament both come to us from outside ourselves and touch and move our hearts. If the Word were merely preached without being received and understood it would be empty sounds. The sacrament also needs to be received and understood in a similar way. For this reason, no sacrament can be effective merely because it has been celebrated *(ex opere operato)*. The sacrament does not do something to us in a process in which we remain passive. Just as hearing the Word presupposes our activity, so the reception of the sacrament involves our active participation. For both Word and Sacrament intend to create faith. Faith, however, is our total personal involvement in orienting our whole life to God. "Through the Word and the rite [the sacrament] God simultaneously moves the heart to believe and take hold of faith, as Paul says (Rom. 10:17), 'Faith comes from what is heard.' As the Word enters through the ears to strike the heart, so the rite [the sacrament] itself enters through the eyes to move the heart. The Word and the rite have the same effect, as Augustine said so well when he called the sacrament 'the visible Word.' "[23] The Sacrament is joined to the Word with the purpose of strengthening that faith which comes from hearing the gospel. Thus faith is an integral part of the sacrament's effectiveness just as it is of the effective preaching of the gospel.

It is for this reason that Article XIII of the Augsburg Confession, which describes the use of the sacraments, focuses attention on faith. "The sacraments were instituted not merely to be marks of profession among men but especially to be signs and testimonies of the will of God toward us, intended to awaken and confirm faith ["ad excitandam et confirmandam fidem"] in those who use them."[24] Melanchthon apparently made an addition to the first printed edition of the Augsburg Confession—in order to make it very clear that this statement was directed against the late medieval doctrine and practice of the sacrament: "Our churches therefore condemn those who teach that the sacraments justify by the outward act and who do not teach that faith, which believes that sins are forgiven, is required in the use of the sacraments."[25] The interrelationship of promise and faith, of gospel and faith, thus required that Word and Sacrament be given equal significance.

In contrast, the papal theologians were not able to ascribe the same significance to the Word as to the sacrament. The preached Word was regarded as important as the means and sign of prevenient grace. This meant that it informs us and calls us to faith. The information is that God has graciously turned to us through Jesus Christ. An appeal is then made to our free will, calling us to decide in favor of God's gracious offer by receiving the sacrament offered by the church. This approach clearly distinguished between Word and Sacrament. This issue was clearly revealed in the controversy as to whether faith can coexist with mortal sin. Roman Catholic teaching speaks of unformed faith (*fides informis*) as already being faith. It is that faith that comes from hearing and that is generated by the information and appeal to believe discussed above. Such a faith is, however, not sufficient for salvation. It needs to have the sacrament and the infusion of grace which will convert unformed faith into faith formed by love. This difference in the way in which Word and Sacrament work, as well as the understanding of the receiving of the salvation gained by Christ as a process, results from the understanding that people are involved in this process as participants who are free to respond positively to the Word's appeal.

The Reformation—at least its Lutheran branch—joined Word and Sacrament together as equally important. This was typical for the way in which its understanding both of the theory and practice of receiving salvation focused on God's activity. The gospel as distributed in Word and Sacrament joined together both the objective side of the gospel, based on the person and work of Christ, and the subjective side, based on the work of the Holy Spirit. Christ is personally present in the gospel together with the Word and Sacrament, each of which helps us understand the other. We received this presence of Christ through the faith that the Holy Spirit works in us. In this process, giving and receiving, speaking and hearing, distributing and eating and drinking are two complementary sides of a single process.

Roman Catholic theology and practice primarily focused on the objective side of this process. For example, this is shown by the way in which the bread—the sacramental Christ—is kept and preserved in the tabernacle or carried about and displayed in the monstrance. The sacrament, however, has been given to be received not to be reverenced. Treated in that way, it is not even the sacrament. Rather, the gospel is present in the sacrament so that it can be received together with the bread and wine.

In contrast, Zwinglian theology and practice, which viewed the sacrament as a sign of confession and faith and of the membership of those who (already) believe in Christ, may be described as emphasizing the subjective side of the sacrament. (This would be true of Calvinist theology only in a limited way.)[26]

The gospel, however, joins both the subjective and the objective side of the gospel into a single process. That is why Lutherans have insisted on the real presence. The objective and the subjective sides of savlation, the work of Jesus Christ and the work of the Holy Spirit, may not be separated from each other.

If it is true that Word and Sacrament belong together and interpret each other as two forms of the one gospel, it would be good if we would keep them together in our liturgy. It is easier to preach if the celebration of the sacrament keeps both preacher and sermon focused on the gospel. At the same time, the preacher is relieved from the burden of excessive expectations. It is easier to celebrate the sacrament among those who have already gathered together to hear the sermon and remain together to commune. Such communicants do not think of the celebration of the sacrament as an appendage to but rather as an integral element of their worship.

The Gospel and Sacramental Practice

This basic understanding of the sacrament provides the basis for a critical examination of Lutheran liturgical practice. I shall undertake this task by first examining the other actions that Roman Catholic theology designates as sacraments. I begin with "penitence."[27] The Reformers were at first uncertain as to whether to call it a sacrament. The Augsburg Confession discussed confession and penance between its discussion of the Lord's Supper and its article on the use of the sacraments. It thereby included them among the sacraments without explicitly designating them as such. The more general teaching about the sacraments in the Apology of the Augsburg Confession made up for that. It named the factors that the Lutherans generally considered to be necessary in a sacrament. On that basis, it was easy to conclude which were to be recognized as sacraments: Baptism, the Lord's Supper, "and absolution (which is the sacrament of penitence)."[28] This list did not set the pattern for Lutheranism, however. The ceremonial element in confession and absolution was too weak. Penitence had no external element similar to the water of baptism or the bread and wine of the Lord's Supper. It is more properly described as a special form of the proclamation of the Word. And "penitence" was as a result preserved in the Lutheran church in the form of a common confession of sin and a public absolution.

Individual confession fell into disuse—although the Reformers tried to preserve it. The Augsburg Confession reports that it was their custom not "to administer the body of Christ except to those who have previously been examined and absolved."[29] Instruction was, however, focused on the comfort given by absolution and the importance of respecting the promise given in the absolution. Penitents were not expected to follow the late medieval requirement of trying to enumerate all sins. "Our wretched human nature is so deeply submerged in sins that it is unable to perceive or know them all, and if we were to be absolved only from those which we can enumerate we would be helped but little. On this account there is no need to compel people to a detailed account of their sins."[30] The insight is convincing. It does not, however, explain why private confession is no longer practiced in the Lutheran church. Attempts have been made to reintroduce it but have not been successful. We might refer to the fact that the examination was attached to preparation for communion and quickly became a mere external matter.[31] In any case, the late medieval rule requiring every Christian to commune at least once a year during the Easter season and therefore to have gone to private confession beforehand was abolished. Probably, the absence of such a rule requiring private confession was the main reason that private confession did not survive in the Lutheran church.

That did not mean, however, that the Reformers placed a low value on penitence. The opposite is really the case. I quote Luther's first two of the Ninety-five Theses on Indulgences (1517), theses that significantly influenced the Reformation's teaching and practice of penitence.

1. When Our Lord and Master Jesus Christ said, "Repent" [Matt. 4:17], he willed the entire life of believers to be one of repentance.

2. This word cannot be understood as referring to the sacrament of penance, that is, confession and satisfaction, as administered by the clergy.[32]

Luther emphasized that penitence is not a discrete sacramental process, which is repeated from time to time. He rather saw it as a description of the whole Christian life.

This style of teaching was directly related to the Reformation's understanding of the time and place of faith. True penitence occurs whenever God leads people to repentance through law and gospel. Contrary to the Roman Catholic teaching, repentance was not something that people do, can do, and that the church requires them to do. The Fourth Lateran Council had established the "Easter duty." Whenever the canonically determined time for repentance comes, the Roman Catholic Christian must repent. Thus Roman Catholic theology understood repentance completely in human terms. People are free to repent and the church's regulation requires them to exercise this freedom.

The Lutheran teaching about penitence focused on God's activity.[33] In order to free confused consciences from the erroneous teachings of the late medieval teaching about penance, the Reformers emphasized that penitence has two parts: contrition and faith. Contrition is the real terrors that the conscience feels because God is angry with sin and the sorrow because we have sinned. "This contrition takes place when the Word of God denounces sin."[34] The time for contrition comes when the Word that creates it is effective. God works contrition in sinners with the purpose of leading us to salvation. Faith that trusts the gospel must be added to this contrition with its terrors of conscience. "This faith strengthens, sustains, and quickens the contrite according to the passage (Rom. 5:1), "Since we are justified by faith, we have peace with God.""[35] The saving path of penitence that leads to salvation and to God can only be found when contrition and faith are both present. If only contrition is present, the result is destruction and death. "This faith shows the difference between the contrition of Judas and Saul on the one hand and that of Peter and David on the other."[36]

This is also the context of the office of the keys and its rite of individual absolution. Melanchthon rightly emphasized the high value that Lutherans placed on the absolution. For the value placed on absolution indicates the value placed on the gospel. This meant that the Lutheran doctrine of penitence intended to transform the late medieval sacrament of penance into the sacrament of penitence that would serve the gospel. "So faith is conceived and confirmed through absolution, through the hearing of the Gospel, so that it may not succumb in its struggles against the terrors of sin and death."[37]

Now it is possible to describe what happened to the sacrament of penitence in the Lutheran church. Penitence was understood as the most characteristic factor of the Christian life. The call to repentance, as the promise of forgiveness, was preserved in the ministry to the Word. Thus, although the sacrament of penitence disappeared, penitence itself gained in importance.

The Reformers did not recognize confirmation, marriage, and ordination as sacraments—although they survived as pastoral acts. Only extreme unction disappeared completely. Its function was preserved in the custom of communing the sick and thereby providing them with this final nourishment for their journey. Given the Lutheran definition of a sacrament, these pastoral acts were no longer recognized as sacraments. A sacrament was a rite instituted by God or by Christ that was joined to the promise of the gospel. The denial of sacramental character to these acts was not only based on this formal criterion. There was obviously no direct relationship to the gospel, no conjunction of the objective side of the sacrament, related to the person and work of Christ, with the subjective side, related to the work of Holy Spirit. For this reason, confirmation, marriage, and ordination could not be recognized as sacraments.

In this context, I need to discuss a problematical statement made by Melanchthon in the Apology of the Augsburg Confession. Melanchthon had criticized the late medieval order of ordination because it was understood as establishing a priesthood that brought sacrifices to God rather than as the priesthood of the ministry to Word and Sacrament. Then he continued: "If ordination is interpreted in relation to the ministry of the Word, we have no objection to calling ordination a sacrament. The ministry of the Word has God's command [mandatum] and glorious promises."[38] Even if we ignore the fact that the promises cited by Melanchthon are ascribed to the Word and not to the ordained minister, Melanchthon clearly abandoned the concentrated focus on the gospel that usually characterized the Reformation's discussions of the sacraments. Where was the faith that such a sacrament of ordination supposedly would awaken and strengthen? Lutherans could describe that faith only as the kind of faith that unites us with Christ. Such faith is not directed to nor does it joins us to the minister. Thus this statement of Melanchthon, which does not fit with the Reformation's understanding of the sacraments in the context of the gospel, clearly shows us why ordination can not be defined as a sacrament. The same is true of marriage. I shall not discuss confirmation—a custom that is closely related to infant baptism.

The question naturally remains as to why confirmation, marriage, ordination, and even the custom of communion of the dying have survived as in the Lutheran church. Apparently these pastoral acts met basic human needs that the church could not deny. Obviously, the fact that the Lutheran church still finds it necessary to shape its ministry to meet these needs is a special problem. The office of the ministry is exclusively a ministry to the gospel. And the clergy have the task of once again defining their task in these terms.[39] That can be done only on the basis of a very clear and precise understanding of the gospel.

The Relationship Between Promise and Faith and the Problem of Infant Baptism

Our response to the question that we have now raised is also of great significance for our understanding and practice of baptism. This is an unusually critical matter for the Reformation's focus on the gospel as it is distributed in Word and Sacrament and received in faith. The problem is that the church's practice of infant baptism makes it impossible for us to see God working in the unified process of giving and receiving. This difficult issue cannot be dealt with by repeating the popular assertion that infant baptism demonstrates God's working in a special way because it is obvious that the child contributes nothing to its baptism. For example, Werner Elert said, "In baptizing infants the church clearly states that baptism is solely God's doing. It happens to but not through the child being baptized."[40] This argument is not convincing because it does not provide the necessary context to describe the fact that must still at some point appropriate this baptism. In discussing faith under these presuppositions about baptism, we cannot avoid the appearance that this faith is really the work of the person who has been baptized. The question as to how the church's practice can be conformed to this theological insight remains an open question. I have already drawn attention to the fact that German churches have a special interest in preserving the custom of infant baptism as the best way of assuring the membership of as many citizens as possible in the *Volkskirche*.[41]

It is quite understandable that the Lutheran Reformation was not able to question the practice of infant baptism. For the Anabaptist movement in its various forms was characterized by the demand for adult, that is, for believers' baptism. There were good theological and political grounds for not accepting this demand. Thus the Zwinglians, who were at many points much closer than the Lutherans to the Anabaptist position, continued the traditional practice of infant baptism. This was not the right time for Lutherans to raise the theological questions about infant baptism. Any theological evaluation, however, of the ecclesiastical reforms that were based on the Reformation's understanding of the gospel must now ask how we understand baptism and what this means for our baptismal practice. It would not be good for us to avoid these questions by hiding behind the text of the confessional documents and to fail to ask whether this practice really agrees with the more basic assertions about the correlation of promise and faith in the sacraments.

The Augsburg Confession asserted that baptism is necessary to salvation, that it is offered through grace, and that children should be baptized because they are thereby brought to God and received in God's grace. The Latin text of Article IX was very clear: "Our churches condemn [damnant] the Anabaptists who reject the Baptism of children and declare that children are saved without Baptism."[42] Conversely stated, this meant that unbaptized children who die cannot be saved. It was for this reason that the Lutheran as well as the Roman Catholic traditions recognized emergency baptism. I have above demonstrated the basic Lutheran principle that the administration of the gospel in Word and Sacrament must take place in such away that the objective side of the gospel, related to the person and work of Christ, and the subjective side, related to the Holy Spirit, are kept together. This is confirmed by the addition to the Latin text of Article XIII in the first edition of the Augsburg Confession which explicitly denied that the sacraments are effective simply because they have been administered—whether or not they are received in faith (ex opere operato).[43] The practice of infant baptism, however, isolates the objective side of the sacrament that is related to the person and work of Christ. Thereby it places the salvation gained by Christ into the hands of the church so that it now has to be distributed by the church. If the church fails in its task and a child dies without being baptized, then this child misses out on salvation. The church's function then becomes a work that is necessary to salvation and God's freedom to work and through the gospel is set aside.

Such an understanding of infant baptism is inconsistent with the gospel. This argument, however, does not support the Baptist assertion that the effective administration of baptism presupposes that the person receiving baptism already believes beforehand. Such an isolation of the subjective side of God's activity related to the Holy Spirit also needs to be avoided. That understanding would make the acceptance of salvation a human work, for faith is no longer something that God works but rather has its source in the believer. This in turn leads to a human-centered understanding of the sacrament. Both this Baptist understanding and the practice of infant baptism destroy the unity of speaking and hearing, of giving and receiving. Having said this, it is now our task to think about ways in which the church could administer baptism that would most clearly express the correlation of the gospel and faith. This task is much more important than the work of formulating arguments against believers' baptism.

Even at the time of the Reformation, the discussion of infant baptism created all kinds of problems for the Reformers. Unfortunately, the Reformers were not consciously aware of the problems in their own position and did not recognize the weakness of their own arguments. In the Apology of the Augsburg Confession, Melanchthon concluded: (1) The promise of salvation is also given to children; (2) "The promise of salvation . . . does not apply to those who are outside of Christ's church, where there is neither Word nor sacrament, because Christ regenerates through Word and sacrament. [(3)] Therefore it is necessary to baptize children, so that the promise of salvation might be applied to them according to Christ's command (Matt. 28:19), 'Baptize all nations.' "[44]

The weakness of this argumentation is revealed as soon as we inquire about the understanding of the church presupposed in these assertions. The church is thought of as the space of salvation. Baptism is the way in which the child moves into this space. If we ask the next question about what makes the church such a place of salvation, Melanchthon would have to return to his usual way of thinking and refer to Christ's working through Word and Sacrament. Then he would actually have to say: The church is present wherever the gospel is offered and accepted. The same ought also be true of Baptism. Baptism is an effective work of God wherever it is offered and accepted in faith. It is God's working in the gospel that makes the church to be the church. Melanchthon's line of reasoning in Article IX, however, made it seem that God's working presupposes the existence of the church.

More arguments are not necessary at this point. The most significant additional point in the Lutheran confessional writings seems to be Luther's statement in the Large Catechism that we do not receive the sacrament on the basis of our faith but on the basis of God's promise and command.[45] This does not demonstrate the integrity of any particular baptism. All baptisms, however, become part of the obedient response of the congregation that baptizes in the expectation that God will do God's work. This does not solve the problem. For the isolation of the objective side of Baptism that is related to the person and work of Christ leads to a similar demand that the subjective side of Baptism related to the work of the Holy Spirit in the appropriation of Baptism be expressed in an equally isolated way. As Paul Althaus has said, "Infants are baptized in the expectation that faith and the confession of this faith will follow. Through these, the person who has been baptized comprehends the meaning of baptism and personally takes possession of it. . . . Infant baptism becomes full and complete baptism only when the baptized child publicly confesses its faith in [the rite of] confirmation."[46] Althaus's handbook of dogmatics is widely used in Germany today. It clearly demonstrates the way in which the practice of infant baptism threatens the Reformation's basic understanding of Baptism. The effect of infant baptism on infants is seen on an *opus operatum* that is completed only through confirmation, which then becomes the sacrament of confessing one's faith. Adding together two such isolated events, however, does not produce a Lutheran understanding of the sacrament in God-centered terms. All that is produced is a human-centered understanding. Thus the question of what would be a proper practice of Baptism and a corresponding doctrine of Baptism remains an open question—the statements in our Lutheran confessional writings do not provide an adequate answer to this question.

THE FREEDOM TO
BELIEVE AS THE BASIC
CHARACTERISTIC OF THE CHURCH

The Church's Rules of Religious Life

The Reformation's new definition of good works had far-reaching results—not only for the understanding of the ethical life but also for the kind of spirituality that was taught and practiced in the church. Special "religious" works were no longer described as fulfilling God's will. Rather, the Reformers taught that God wills us to do those works that are necessary to maintain life and to provide for the needs of all people. Once the nature of this new piety is understood, the ethical consequences will also become clear. Article XXVI of the Augsburg Confession was very clear about this. Its title, "The Distinction of Foods," indicates that it will deal with the church's rules on fasting. This article, however, also analyzes the whole scope of "religious" activities, that is, all the works that people do because they think they are especially pleasing to God. The late medieval church had taught that such works could earn grace and serve as satisfaction for sins. "For this reason new fasts, new ceremonies, new orders, and the like were invented daily, and were ardently and urgently promoted, as if these were a necessary service of God by means of which grace would be earned if they were observed and a great sin committed if they were omitted. Many harmful errors in the church have resulted from this."[47]

The Augsburg Confession named three evils that resulted from this idea and its associated practices. First, this emphasis on human religious activity obscured the grace of Christ and teaching about faith. Second, God's Commandment receded into the background. Third, people thought that the really good and necessary works were worldly and unspiritual, whereas the works required by the church's traditions were thought of as being the only holy and perfect works. The Augsburg Confession listed these good and necessary works: "the works which everybody is obliged to do according to his calling—for example, that a husband should labor to support his wife and children and bring them up in the fear of God, that a wife should bear children and care for them, that a prince and magistrates should govern land and people, etc."[48]

The reply of the authors of the Roman Confutation was characteristic. They asserted that such laws of the church make it easier to obey God's Commandments. "Fasts suppress the lust of the flesh" and help us maintain an orderly life.[49] The Lutherans were described as acting blindly. They are described as having taken fasting and the rules on food away from Christians and replaced them with three other commands: to bear children, to raise the next generation, and to govern the community. These, however, are rules followed by all the heathens, Turks, Tartars, and Persians. Lutherans have thereby erred by ascribing the highest praise to those works that everyone does, whether Christian or not.[50] The line of argument is typical of the Roman Confutation. Anything that needs to be done in any case, whether by Turks, Tartars, or Persians, cannot be a good Christian work! It might also have been noted that these nations also have their religious practices, fast, and observe rituals. The Roman Confutation did not carry the analysis that far. It stopped with the presupposition that good works must be unusual works and thereby confirmed the critical assertions of the Augsburg Confession.

The third issue raised by the Augsburg Confession dealt with the burden that the traditions of the church placed on consciences. Since it was impossible to keep all of them, conscientious people were in a very difficult situation. The late medieval church dealt with this problem through very learned casuistry. This in turn resulted in disagreements among the theologians. "But they were so occupied with such efforts that they neglected all wholesome Christian teachings about more important things, such as faith, consolation in severe trials, and the like."[51]

The first conclusion was that such ecclesiastical regulations could not be made a necessary worship of God as though keeping these rules would reconcile God and earn grace. "It is diametrically opposed to the Gospel to institute or practice such works for the purpose of earning forgiveness of sin or with the notion that nobody is a Christian unless he performs such services."[52] This discussion, like the earlier discussion of the reform of the mass, demonstrated the central significance of justification in the Lutheran's reform of the church's life. Since the late medieval patterns of church life encouraged a false understanding of justification, they could not be accepted as valid. For the church cannot detract from the truth of the gospel by establishing rules about what we must and can do in order to please God.

The Reformation could not stop at the point of rejecting practices of the late medieval church. Rather, it had to give expression to the unique characteristics of the Reformation's own spirituality, particularly when defining the godly life. The Lutherans emphasized that they do not forbid discipline and the mortification of the flesh. "They have always taught concerning the holy cross that Christians are obliged to suffer, and this is true and real rather than invented mortification."[53] Late medieval ascetic practices, as described, for example, in the regulations on fasting, were intended to permit the spirit to gain control over the flesh, that is, our physical nature with its orientation to sensory experience, by using the spirit's will and knowledge. Life can be lived in obedience to God only if the body obeys the spirit. This requires the kind of self-discipline that could be learned by the obedient conformity to the ecclesiastical regulations. This was an explicitly religious orientation to life; its requirement of the practice of this kind of God-pleasing life assumed that people were capable of meeting this requirement.

In contrast, the Lutheran Reformation described the Christian life in terms of God's leading the Christian along the way of life. The attempt of the human will to choose its own artificial spiritual disciplines reflected the will's attempt to direct and confirm its own life. Such an effort assumed that the will has powers which it in fact does not have. In contrast, true and really valuable suffering comes from God. This is not the kind of suffering that we choose for ourselves in an effort to shape our own lives but rather the suffering that comes to us from living in the world outside ourselves. True mortification of the flesh occurs as we seek to live our lives according to God's will. In the context of the Reformation's understanding of God, the resulting battle with sin that God lays on each of us can not be thought of us some other-worldly and merely internal spiritual process. Our selfish human will to live encounters the resistance of the world, of other people, of relationships, and of conditions that all go quite differently than we would choose for ourselves. For example, we experience the limitations of our own physical nature. These experiences that come to us against our will are the means that God uses for the real mortification of the flesh—the cross that God assigns us. This is the decisive emphasis in the Reformation's understanding of the Christian life—although special religious discipline may also be needed.[54] This, however, is only a means to end. It is not intended to enable us to carry out other religious works but rather trains us in obedience to our calling. Such practices help us focus our attention on what really needs to be done in this world.

Such reforms of the church's rules for the Christian life were of far-reaching significance. The rejection of all merely religious behavior was the decisive factor in shaping Lutheran spirituality. I shall return to this point later.[55] The liturgical rules were preserved in the Lutheran churches. Nothing more needs to be said about that. It was of decisive significance that in abrogating the church's rules as binding on the Christian life, our freedom to believe became apparent. Late medieval regulations had concealed this freedom because they focused the attention of the will to live a religious life back onto itself. They emphasized people's ability to lead a special, supposedly God-pleasing life by obeying the rules established in and through the church. This, however, distracted people's attention away from God's will and from the life that God gives to each of us. No attention was paid to those elements of life that it seemed could be taken for granted. Precisely because of that, the gospel, which seeks and creates faith, could not assert itself. A spurious freedom was ascribed to people, the freedom to obey the rules of the church. This was the exact opposite of the freedom to submit to God's working in their lives.

The Legal Authority of the Church and the State

The freedom to believe is not merely freedom from the church's laws and rules for life. It is primarily freedom to believe the gospel. This presupposes, however, that the church itself is free to focus on the gospel. It was for this reason that the Reformation needed to redefine the relationship between spiritual and secular authority. This is a central concern of Article XXVIII of the Augsburg Confession: The Power of the Bishops (or, in Latin, "Ecclesiastical Power"). "Therefore, the two authorities, the spiritual and the temporal, are not to be mingled or confused, for the spiritual power has its commission to preach the Gospel and administer the sacraments. Hence it should not invade the function of the other, should not set up and depose kings, should not annul temporal laws or undermine obedience to government, should not make or prescribe to the temporal power laws concerning worldly matters."[56] This demand was the beginning of a process that led to the dissociation of spiritual and temporal authority that characterizes our present legal system and understanding of government. The primary focus of this demand is on the freedom of the state and its right not to be interfered with by the church. Legal power belongs only to the state and not to the church.

At the time of the Reformation, this was a revolutionary demand. It found a strong echo even among those who were not Lutherans. The bishops at that time exercised a threefold authority. First, the bishops were princes of the empire who ruled over their own geographical territories and subjects. The Augsburg Confession accepted the reality of this lordship but was careful to emphasize that it was based on imperial, not divine law.[57] Some of these principalities continued as religious states under the rule of bishops until the time of Napoleon. Others—particularly in northern and eastern Germany—were absorbed into the territories ruled by the Protestant secular princes.

There were also a number of areas in which legal jurisdiction was ascribed to the church's legal system. The Augsburg Confession specifically named marriage and tithes—the income tax paid to the church.[58] Thus not only matters related to penance were under the control of the church's courts (the so-called *forum internum*) but also matters that we today assume are under the authority of the secular courts. The Roman Catholic Church still asserts its claim to jurisdiction in questions related to the marriage of its members and maintains its own system of ecclesiastical courts.

The last matter that was particularly significant was the so-called *privilegium fori*. This gave *the* clergy the right to be tried in an ecclesiastical court in both criminal and civil cases. If we think of the large number of clergy at the time, this represented a great extension of the jurisdiction of the ecclesiastical courts. It also created considerable legal confusion, since lay-persons involved in legal processes with clergy could be required to appear in the ecclesiastical courts and were subject to their punishments and judgments.

Having experienced this confusion of secular and ecclesiastical legal systems, the authors of the Augsburg Confession demanded a clear distinction between the two governments. Ecclesiastical law cannot be in conflict with secular law—neither as a different set of laws or as a different system of courts. We take this for granted today; at the time of the Reformation, it was a program for radical change. It was the beginning of a development that led to an increasing limitation of the church's legal authority and to an increasing emphasis on the legal authority of the state. In its early stages, this liberation of the state resulted in the autonomy of the state. It is understandable that many of the territories that were, at that time, struggling to assert their sovereignty supported the Reformation. It was obviously in their own interest to restrict the legal jurisdiction of the church in favor of extending their own legal authority. Simultaneously, however—and this was the original religious motivation for this move—the issue was the liberation of the church. The exercise of secular power by the church had forced the church to become involved in contemporary power struggles. By giving up its secular power, the church was set free to carry out its own task, the proclamation of the gospel.

The Office of the Ministry

The dissociation of the authority of the church from the authority of the state naturally did not lead to a solution of the basic problems of the church's own organization and structure. It led only to the principle of the separation of the organization of the church from the organization of the state. Competition between these two should no longer be possible or permissible. The Augsburg Confession made only very vague statements about the internal organization of the church. There were obvious reasons for this. On the one hand, the Augsburg Confession was written with the intention of reaching agreement with the churches that followed the late medieval traditions. That made it necessary to be considerate of the bishops who were all loyal to the papacy and played a significant role in the politics of the empire. Even at that time, it hardly seemed possible to find a solution to the problem of authority that would be acceptable to both sides. The statements of Article XXVIII of the Augsburg Confession, however, reveal extensive consideration for the position of the bishops.[59] In terms of the organizational structure of the church, the Augsburg Confession was not able to report that they had achieved any basic reforms—as they were able to do in the other articles of the second section

(Articles XXII–XXVII) of the Augsburg Confession. On the one hand, the organizational structure of the church had been dissolved in the Protestant territories. On the other hand, the Protestant *Landeskirchen* (established territorial churches, disestablished since 1919) were still far from being organized. The statements made by the Augsburg Confession and by the later Treatise on the Power and Primacy of the Pope[60] were—except for the criticisms of existing abuses—basically proposed programs for change. Not everything there proposed was actually carried out later.

Articles V and XIV of the Augsburg Confession had already spoken of the office of the ministry. Scholars disagree about the relationship of these two articles to each other. Article V was closely related to Article IV on justification. This fact gave a high status to the ministry of the church in the systematic statement of doctrine. The office of the ministry is necessary in the church so that justifying faith can become a reality. This is God's will. God therefore instituted the office of the ministry. To use the technical terminology, the office of the ministry exists by divine right. It is therefore a part of the church's structure that must be taken for granted in any plan for the church's organizational structure. All church law, every plan for the organization of the church's human activities, must respect this office as its presupposition.

Article XIV of the Augsburg Confession discussed the office of the ministry again under the title of Order in the Church or, in the Latin, "ecclesiastical order." This article is extremely brief: "It is taught among us that nobody should publicly teach or preach or administer the sacraments in the church without a regular call."[61] This established a definite order of the ministry. The office of the ministry is to be exercised by regularly called officials. Nothing was said about how they were to be called. The bishops had the right to ordain priests and nobody wanted to alienate the bishops by questioning their authority at this point.

It is therefore the task of a theological interpretation of the Augsburg Confession to provide a clarification of the relationship between Articles V and XIV. Does the divine institution of the office of the ministry require a certain ecclesiastical structure? Must there be a group of people who have been explicitly called to the ministry and who continue to function as ministers of the Word and Sacrament? If so, the call into this office would be subject not only to the church's rules but to divine law. This evaluation of the church's office of the ministry described in Article XIV would come so close to equating it with the ministry described in Article V that they would be almost one and the same. This would have implications for the relationship between the office of the ministry and the congregation as well as for the practice of ministry. The minister would then be an independent partner of the congregation and the congregation would be dependent on the minister in the same way that faith is dependent on the gospel. Accordingly, the office of the ministry is

higher in rank, although not earlier in time, than the congregation. This structure of the church assumes the duality of ministry and the congregation. If we
accept it, we would consider the congregation responsible to recognize the
authority of the office of the ministry as represented by the minister.

This is obviously not the only possible interpretation of the relationship
between these two. Another possibility is to derive the church's ministry from
the congregation. This would mean that there is no specially designated group
of ritually ordained ministers who administer the office of the ministry as representatives of God or Christ. Luther put it this way in 1520: In the Lutheran
understanding, baptism is the only ordination to the spiritual estate, "for baptism, gospel, and faith alone make us spiritual and a Christian people."[62] In
Christianity, there is no distinction between some spiritual estate and laypeo-
ple. Rather, all Christians are priests and have been called to this priesthood
through baptism. Since it is not possible for all to exercise the ministry publicly, however, they assign the exercise of this ministry to specific members
of the congregation. In this interpretaion, the church's office of the ministry
is created by the congregation. The congregation and its universal priesthood
is logically and temporally prior to the ordained ministry. Then the congregation designates certain members of the congregation to exercise its office of
ministry.

Obviously neither of these two models matches the viewpoint of the Reformation as stated in the Augsburg Confession. Our analysis must begin with
a discussion of the freedom to believe as the basic characteristic of the church.
Any understanding of the office of the ministry as existing by divine right too
easily destroys this freedom by subjecting it to the office of the ministry.
Ascribing such authority to the ministry requires the congregation to respond
in obedience rather than freedom. In the second model, freedom is threatened
in just the opposite way. The minister is dependent on the congregation and
his or her exercise of the ministry is under the control of the congregation.
The minister is obligated to say and do whatever the congregation demands.
The proper task of the ministry, however, is to administer the gospel in Word
and Sacrament.

Both of the above models for the establishment of the office of the ministry
suffer from a static view of the relationship between the ministry and the congregation. Either a ministry established by divine right confronts the congregation or the congregation establishes its own ministry on the basis of human
right. The office of the ministry, however, can never be defined merely in
terms of the people who exercise this office. The office of the ministry must
rather be understood as a process that is always determined by the gospel. Just
as the single process of speaking and hearing the gospel and of administering
and receiving the sacraments combines the objective side of God's activity
related to the person and work of Christ with the subjective side of God's

activity related to the Holy Spirit, so the office of the ministry is a similar process that joins the preacher and the hearers, the minister and the communicants, together with one another.

This interpretation corresponds to the basic principles stated in Article XXVIII of the Augsburg Confession. This conclusion must be prefaced by the assertion that there can be no hierarchical structure of the office of the ministry in the Protestant Church.[63] Article XXVIII spoke of "bishops" only because the situation at the time was so confused. Nothing was said about the bishops, however, that does not apply to all ministers. "According to divine right, therefore, it is the office of the bishop to preach the Gospel, forgive sins, judge doctrine and condemn doctrine that is contrary to the Gospel, and exclude from the Christian community the ungodly whose wicked conduct is manifest. All this is to be done not by human power but by God's Word alone."[64]

The power of the office of the ministry is derived solely from the gospel. The gospel establishes itself and the ministry supports the gospel in the process without using any human powers. When it is functioning in support of this process, the office of the ministry can demand obedience from the congregation: "On this account parish ministers and churches are bound to be obedient to the bishops according to the saying of Christ in Luke 10:16, 'He who hears you hears me.' "[65] The person functioning in the office of the ministry stands in the place of Christ and can therefore command unlimited obedience. Obedience, however, is due not to the person of the minister but to the Word of the gospel. In practice, that distinction is not easily made. Yet everyone must be clear that we are bound to obey the gospel and not the minister. That is why Article XXVIII continues, "When bishops teach or ordain anything contrary to the Gospel, churches have a command of God that forbids obedience."[66] The office thus loses the right to be obeyed, because it is the right of the gospel and not of the minister. The ministry has divine right only when it is proclaiming the gospel. Melanchthon's interpretation of Luke 10:16 in the Apology of the Augsburg Confession made that very clear. He pointed out that Christ did not give the apostles and their successors the right to rule in his stead and to establish laws as conditions of salvation.

Certainly the statement, "He who hears you hears me" (Luke 10:16), is not referring to traditions but is rather directed against traditions. It is not what they call a "commandment with unlimited authority," but rather a "caution about something prescribed," about a special commandment. It is a testimony given to the apostles so that we may believe them on the basis of another's Word rather than on the basis of their own. For Christ wants to assure us, as was necessary, that the Word is efficacious when it is delivered by men and that we should not look for another word from heaven. "He who hears you hears me" cannot be applied to traditions.[67]

One way of emphasizing that the authority of the office of the ministry is joined to the gospel is to describe the office of the ministry as a process. The minister is not the only participant in this process. The congregation that hears participates equally. The congregation must not only obey the gospel but reject demands made by the minister that are contrary to the gospel. The church's ministry is possible only if both the minister and the congregation are thus bound to the gospel.

Understood as this kind of process, the office of the ministry preserves the freedom to believe, a freedom that is not bound to the authority of the ministry but to the gospel. Melanchthon emphasized that in the above quotation. It is not what the bishops teach that has the right to be heard but only what Christ himself teaches. That is why he challenges the bishops to teach in such a way that the people hear Christ and his word rather than human traditions.

The office of the ministry is the process of the gospel. That is the basis of the rights of the ministry. For that reason, the congregation shares in the ministry of the gospel. That is the real meaning of rights in the church. All the superstructures of rights and organization that have been built around this process of the ministry must be subject to this basic right. If the bishops prove to be enemies of the gospel and refuse to ordain the Lutheran preachers, then the right of ordination that the bishops claim reverts to the congregations. "Consequently, when the regular bishops become enemies of the Gospel and are unwilling to administer ordination, the churches retain the right to ordain for themselves. For wherever the church exists, the right to administer the Gospel also exists. Wherefore it is necessary for the church to retain the right of calling, electing, or ordaining ministers."[68]

The congregation has the basic right to administer the gospel. Every issue involving the church's organization is important only if it is centered in questions related to the freedom to believe that is created and given to us by the gospel. That is why the church's ministry is needed. This office cannot be defined in ecclesiastical terms. There is no use in arguing whether the ministry or the congregation is more important. In every case, both presuppose God's activity for our salvation. That activity cannot be divided, as though the objective side related to the person and word of Christ established the priority of the ministry over the congregation or as though the subjective side related to the Holy Spirit made the congregation the source of the church's ministry. Rather, the unity of the ministry becomes visible in the process of administering the gospel.

The Congregation and the Larger Ecclesiastical Organization

It is understandable that the confessional writings hardly touch on questions related to a larger ecclesiastical organization that includes several individual congregations. This had taken the form of the episcopal dioceses. The diocesan structure in northern Germany had, however, already begun to disintegrate—even before the authority of the bishops was challenged because they were neither willing nor able to administer the church in a way that was compatible with the gospel. This created a legal vacuum that had to be filled. For life went on and needed to be regulated. It was necessary to install pastors, to arrange for their support, and to maintain church buildings. Marriages were to be performed and marital disputes resolved. The charitable activities of the church continually needed attention, etc. In addition, there was church property. The bishops—who were all loyal to the pope—claimed it for their dioceses. The Lutheran princes rejected this claim by citing canonical law, "The benefice is given because of the office."[69] The riches of the church were to be used to fulfill the tasks of the church. Those who were seeking to carry out these tasks had a legitimate claim on the church's property.

In the Lutheran territories, the secular governments assumed the tasks of the ecclesiastical organizations. At first, this was thought of as a transitional solution. It soon became permanent, however. Indeed, the bureaucracies of the Protestant churches in Germany have long survived the secular governments that created them. A twofold theological basis was given for this organization. First, the government officials were considered "the chief members of the church" and were therefore expected to be especially concerned for the church's welfare.[70] The church is, in this context, understood as the religious community of the baptized. The secular dimension of this community that was under the government of the secular princes could not be simply ignored. It was this primacy of the secular authorities that obligated them to intervene after the previous ecclesiastical authorities, that is, the bishops, failed to carry out their tasks. As far as we can see, that was the only real possibility at that time. No one else was organized to act. No one even thought of the possibility of the congregations being incorporated and becoming legal persons who could then act on their own behalf.

The theory was that the secular prince who assumed specific tasks in the life and work of the church acted as a "chief member" of the church. His authority to act was not based on his rights and duties in the secular government but in the fact of his baptism. He had authority as a baptized Christian, even though his position in secular government gave him the ability to get things done.

This was combined with a second understanding of the princes' intervention in the life of the church. The secular government was responsible for administering both tables of the law, that is, for all of the Ten Commandments including the first commandments dealing with religious life. In so far as possible, secular law was to encourage the fulfillment of the divine law. This obligation to enforce the first three commandments dealing with religious life included the regulation of the community's public worship. "For the first care of kings should be to advance the glory of God."[71]

Thus two somewhat contradictory ideas formed the basis for the government's intervention in the life of the church. On the one hand, the church was thought of as a religious community and responsible for the regulation of its own life. Its "chief members" were understandably expected to assume this responsibility. On the other hand, the secular government considered itself responsible for enforcing the divine law and therefore responsible for regulating the life of the worshiping community.

This is how it actually happened. The secular governments at first organized "visitation" committees who investigated and actively supervised the life and work of the congregations. These committees soon became permanent bureaucracies. Even today, their members represent both the church and the secular government—a reminder of the twofold basis on which they were originally organized.

All this has left the Protestant churches in Germany with a still-unresolved problem. In fact, these governmental bureaucracies still make decisions about the life of the church. In so doing, they assume rights and responsibilities that really belong to the congregations. That is true at least of all those tasks that the prince assumed as "chief member" of the church: the selection and the installation of pastors and church officials, the adoption of liturgies for the use in worship, and church discipline—the last is, admittedly, not very energetically administered. Obviously we cannot begin to guess how the situation would have developed if the congregations at the time of the Reformation had retained these responsibilities. The examples of all those Protestant congregations who have had to organize themselves under governments who have opposed their very existence demonstrate that the result would not necessarily have been chaos. The fact is, however, that the German Protestant churches have been under the control of the secular governments and that, as a result, even today the congregations have hardly any rights and responsibilities. We deceive ourselves if we expect mature congregations to develop under that condition. Perhaps, maturity will come only in situations in which the church is called to decision, for example, the *Kirchenkampf*.[72] Only then may the church be organized in a way that expresses the freedom to believe and rejects all the traditions that contradict this freedom.

THE HOLINESS OF SECULAR LIFE

The significance of the Reformation's basic decision became especially clear in its reshaping of ethics.[73] The Reformation set aside the practice of the religious life, the term that is commonly used for the spiritual life of monks and nuns. That was a revolutionary change and aroused a great deal of sensation. Monks and nuns left their cloisters, married, and participated in the affairs of the secular world. Luther himself was not the first monk or priest to marry. His marriage, however, to the former nun Katharina von Bora, who had left her nunnery, was a consciously demonstrative act that aroused public attention. The Reformers taught that monastic vows were not binding and the monasteries and nunneries were sometimes pressured into closing. The Augsburg Confession could not avoid dealing with this issue—as the following discussion of the Reformation's restructuring of ethics will show.

The Opposition to the Religious Life

This question is dealt with in Article XXVII of the Augsburg Confession under the title of "monastic vows." It is related to Article XXII, which dealt with "the marriage of priests." In the latter article, the argument made against the required celibacy of the clergy is that God had instituted marriage in order to guard against fornication. For only a few people have the gift of living a chaste life outside of marriage. The human command to remain celibate cannot undo God's command to marry.

Finally, Article XXIII referred to the rules of canon law which "show great leniency and fairness toward those who have made vows in their youth—most of the priests and monks entered into their estates ignorantly when they were young."[74] Article XXVII picked up the discussion at this point. It begins with a general reference to the then-current abuses in monastic life. That could be understood as an invitation to conversation. It left open the possibility to begin the conversation by discussing whether and to what extent monastic life actually met the requirements of canon law and of the church's tradition. This conversation could be carried on without getting into the actual point of controversy. Once the conversation reached that basic issue, agreement would be impossible. The Augsburg Confession is not reluctant to discuss these basic issues.

Late medieval theology claimed that the religious life was especially meritorius. "It was claimed that monastic vows were equal to Baptism, and that by monastic life one could earn forgiveness of sin and justification before God."[75] It was even claimed that more merit could be earned in the religious life than in any other kind of life established by God. That was because the "religious" not only kept God's Commandments but also the evangelical counsels and therefore produced supererogatory works. This distinction between the Commandments and the evangelical counsels was the basis of the religious life. Many biblical passages were cited in support of this distinction. For example, Jesus' word to the rich young man, "If you would be perfect, go, sell what you possess and give to the poor, and you will have treasure in heaven; and come, follow me" (Matt. 19:21); or, as Paul said, "So that he who marries his betrothed does well; and he who refrains from marriage will do better" (1 Cor. 7:38). These passages were interpreted to mean that there is one set of commandments that are binding on everyone. Alongside these is another group of standards. On the one hand, these are less binding; they are only advisory counsels that are found in the gospel. On the other hand, however, keeping these counsels is the better kind of obedience, of discipleship, of the way to salvation. This style of life is "more" and "better." This is the way in which the religious life was still described by the Second Vatican Council in *Lumen Gentium*, The Dogmatic Constitution of the Life of the Church, which described "religious life:"

> The People of God has no lasting city here below, but looks forward to one which is to come. This being so, the religious state by giving its members greater freedom from earthly cares more adequately manifests to all believers the presence of heavenly goods already possessed here below. Furthermore, it not only witnesses to the fact of a new and eternal life acquired by the redemption of Christ. It foretells the resurrected state and the glory of the heavenly kingdom. Christ also proposed to His disciples that form of life which He, as the Son of God, accepted in entering this world to do the will of the Father. In the Church this same state of life is imitated with particular accuracy and perpetually exemplified.[76]

Religious are therefore clearer witnesses to the eschatological dimension of faith than other Chistians are. They are freer of worldly cares and are seen as more clearly following Christ because they more closely imitate his life style—as he commanded his disciples. Obviously, this description of the pre-eminent character of the religious life is much more strongly formulated in terms of the community of the church than of individual persons. It, however, still compares religious life with life in the world and argues that the religious life is of higher value.

In the systematic description of the evangelical counsels, obedience plays a special role alongside poverty and celibacy. This is supported with a reference to the demand for self-denial in the call to discipleship found in Luke 9:23. For members of religious communities, self-denial is expressed by obedience to the rule and to the superiors of the order. Other rules may also be considered evangelical counsels, for example, the renunciation of revenge in Matt. 5:39ff. The individual accepts these evangelical counsels as rules for personal life through a voluntary act of self-obligation. Making such vows, therefore, is the final confirmation of the vocation to religious life.

It is characteristic for this approach to ethics that the individual person must make a basic choice. Will the God-pleasing life be lived in this world in obedience to God's Commandments or will it take the form of striving for perfect holiness *(status perfectionis)* in the religious life? It is true that this question assumes that someone has a special vocation to the religious life. This vocation, however, begins with the church's strong recommendation of the religious life as the more certain way to salvation. The Augsburg Confession argued that this recommendation leads people to believe that only monastics can achieve perfect holiness and thereby obscures God's Commandment. "For this is Christian perfection: that we fear God honestly with our whole hearts, and yet have sincere confidence, faith, and trust that for Christ's sake we have a gracious, merciful God; that we may and should ask and pray God for those things of which we have need, and confidently expect help from him in every affliction connected with our particular calling and station in life."[77] This differed from the late medieval two-stage approach to ethics in that it understood vocation primarily as the calling to live in the world.

The Roman Confutation rejected the arguments of the Augsburg Confession. It denied that the religious claim that they alone achieve perfect holiness "for those in these orders claim not for themselves a state of perfection, but only a state in which to acquire perfection—because their regulations are instruments of perfection and not perfection itself."[78] The Apology of the Augsburg Confession responded with the accurate observation that, if this were the case, then the life of farmers or artisans must be as perfectly holy as monastic life. For these occupations also assist in achieving perfection. "All men, whatever their calling, ought to seek perfection, that is, growth in the fear of God, in faith, in the love of their neighbor, and similar spiritual virtues."[79] At the end of the discussion, there are still two differing understandings of vocation and of the consequent difference in the value placed on life in the world. This is the real reason why the Reformers rejected the religious life. This rejection is directly related to the Reformation's basic decision and to its intentionally God-centered pattern of thinking.

There were also two different interpretations of the Scripture. As a result it was almost impossible to reach agreement. When the Roman Confutation quoted Matt. 19:29 as Christ's promise to those who chose the religious life and forsook all to follow him,[80] the Apology replied that there are two ways of leaving everything behind. One occurs "without a call, without a command of God; this Christ does not approve, for works which we have chosen are 'vain worship' (Matt. 15:9)." Jesus is obviously not speaking of a monastic flight from the world. He speaks about leaving wives and children. God, however, commands us not to forsake them. "The other kind of leaving is that which happens by a command of God, when a government or a tyranny forces us either to leave or to deny the Gospel. Here we have the command rather to bear the injury, to let property, wife, and children, even life itself, be taken from us."[81]

The presupposition is that no one is to choose their own way of following Christ. Although it clearly recognized that special life styles are possible, the Augsburg Confession also specified that they should be required of us by external events. We should not choose some special activity because we think that it is more spiritual or a better way of serving God. That is a useless service of God. God does not require it, rather we choose it for ourselves. The situation is completely different when we cannot avoid doing something special. That is the way of discipleship. We walk it when we are certain of Christ's command and promise. On this basis, monastic vows and the self-chosen religious life are rejected for two reasons. First, people who are unable to live chastely while celibate cannot be forbidden to marry. For God's command is, "Because of fornication let every man have his own wife."[82] Second, human vows and obligations cannot invalidate God's commandment. If such vows have been made, we are released from them by the command to marry. Indeed, those who made these vows as a way of choosing their own service of God have acted contrary to God's Commandment. They are not only free, but are therefore obligated not to keep vows made for that reason.

Divine Guidance in Worldly Life

The basic Reformation principle for rejecting the religious life as a self-chosen and self-designed service of God was "A good and perfect kind of life is one which has God's command in its favor."[83] This presupposed that the orders of worldly life are defined on the basis of Scripture: Marriage, the household and human work in general, the relationship of parents to their children, government which has the special tasks of maintaining justice and preserving peace, as well as the office of the ministry, of preaching and hearing the Word. These forms of life were contrasted with self-chosen religious works, whether they are the religious communities of the church with their ceremonies and fasting or the religious life as a self-chosen life style. These religious works have overshadowed God's Commandments. They have claimed to represent a perfect and spiritual life style. As a result, many have preferred them to God's commandments and to being active in one's vocation in the world, "the administration of public affairs, the administration of the household, married life, and the rearing of children."[84] Everyone naturally chooses the kind of life that is considered good and holy.

The very fact that religious life is claimed to have special value as a more God-pleasing life style has to have a disturbing effect on life in the world. The Reformation protested against this. It did not permit the consciences of those who live according to God's Commandment and plan to be disturbed by those who praise a self-chosen holiness.

> The common people, hearing the state of celibacy praised above all measure, draw many harmful conclusions from such false exaltation of monastic life, for it follows that their consciences are troubled because they are married. When the common man hears that only mendicants are perfect, he is uncertain whether he can keep his possessions and engage in business without sin. When the people hear that it is only a counsel not to take revenge, it is natural that some should conclude that it is not sinful to take revenge outside of the exercise of their office. Still others think that it is not right for Christians, even in the government, to avenge wrong.[85]

The Reformation protested against the troubling of consciences that results from confusion about what God's will really is. Is the Commandment not to take revenge binding only on those who have accepted this duty or is it a general rule? Does it conflict with the government's administration of justice? The Reformation maintained the unity of saving faith and obedience to our vocation. Both together are necessary for Christian perfection.[86] Because we know that we are saved for Christ's sake, we know that we are in harmony with God and can fear and love God more than anything else. Being in harmony with God was interpreted to mean that we are then also in harmony with the world.

The Augsburg Confession interpreted the nature of human-being-in-the-world in terms of the idea of vocation. We have a definite place in the world. This means that God has called us to engage in the activities associated with this place. Christian perfection can be found only by staying in the place to which we have been called rather than by fleeing from the world into religious life. This presupposes that the world in which we find ourselves is itself under God's regulation and that it has been set in order by God. Goodness, the will of God to which we subject ourselves, does not need to enter first into this world. The world is neither immoral nor even morally neutral—as though it first had to be converted by the good works of good people into the kind of place in which we could realize our inherent selves. Our goodness as human beings is provided for by the Word of the gospel that forgives our sins. We can now let God worry about our being good and turning our attention to the tasks that confront us in the world. For this world it itself a world that is held together in God's commands. Therefore, anyone who does what is needed in the world thereby does God's will.

This understanding of Reformation ethics led to a strong affirmation of the world and its actual structures. That is not without its own problems, which result primarily from the fact that people sometimes hear only the affirmation and overhear the associated demand to live in such a way that the loving will of the Creator becomes apparent in the world. This takes place when we live in response to God's command. Only when the affirmation of the world and the demand that we live in it in obedience to God's command are heard together can we recognize the validity of Article XVI of the Augsburg Confession. This article is titled "civil governments" (or, in the Latin, "civil affairs"). In terms of its content, this is a very problematical article. It must be understood in the larger context of the Reformation's ethics. One of its problems is that Melanchthon wrote this article in a very defensive way. The Reformers wanted to deny that they had anything to do with people who were disturbing the orders of secular life and appealing to the gospel in support of what they were doing. Some of these were not members of religious communities, but the main group was the Anabaptists. Because of the concern to reject them, Article XVI almost completely suppressed the very necessary critical analysis of the structures of secular life.

Article XVI did close with a reference to Acts 5:29 (the so-called *clausula Petri*): "But when the commands of the civil authority cannot be obeyed without sin, we must obey God rather than men."[87] There was, however, no clear description of any sin that the government might command and the Christian would be required to refuse to obey. The Reformers would probably have used

126

the example of a sin against the first table of the Decalogue (the first three of the Commandments dealing with religious life)—assuming that this would follow the general pattern of the Augsburg Confession.

Article XVI began by describing the structures that give order to life in the secular world as having been created by God. For this reason, Christians do not sin simply by living in this world and doing what is necessary to live. Specific examples are given: the administration of justice according to existing law, executing the death penalty, waging war, taking oaths, possessing property, married life, etc. The Anabaptists were condemned because they assert that some of these cannot be done by Christians. The second section of the articles also condemned "those who place the perfection of the Gospel not in the fear of God and in faith but in forsaking civil duties."[88] The German text of this article specifically spoke of "forsaking of house and home, wife and child, and the renunciation of such activities."

These condemnations could have been read as applying to those who valued the religious life more highly than life in this world. The Roman Confutation, however, did not comment on this point and therefore seems to have read this as a rejection only of the Anabaptists. In Article XVI itself, the basis for this condemnation was, however, quite problematical. It asserted, "The Gospel does not teach an outward and temporal but an inward and eternal mode of existence and righteousness of the heart. The Gospel does not overthrow civil authority, the state, and marriage."[89] The Latin text was briefer: "The Gospel teaches an eternal righteousness of the heart, but it does not destroy the state or the family." This statement is problematical because it seems to distinguish between religiosity as an inner realm and life in the world as an external realm. That might be possible as long as both were held together in God's command and promise. It is, however, easy to see the gospel as related to the inner realm and the affirmation of the world as related to the external realm. It would be a critical error to think of these two parts of a unified whole as being separated from each other. Such a separation would result in the loss of an important eschatological element of the scriptural gospel. This eschatological awareness enables Christians both to maintain an eschatological distance from and thereby to avoid identification with this world and to maintain an eschatological perspective on life in this world.

This eschatological perspective seems to have been lost in the Apology which more strongly emphasized the affirmation of this world. The Apology described a false accusation made against the early Christians that the gospel would destroy secular order. Melanchthon responded that Lutherans know that "the Gospel does not legislate for the civil estate but is the forgiveness of sins and the beginning of eternal life in the hearts of believers. It not only approves governments but subjects us to them, just as we are necessarily subjected to the laws of the seasons and to the change of winter and summer as ordinances of God."[90] In this passage, the actuality of the secular world is so closely identified with God's ordering of the world that it is hardly possible to distinguish the two. From here, it was only a short distance to the kind of Lutheran theology that uncritically affirmed the world. We still encounter the manifestations of this kind of theology in the present as well as in the recent history of Lutheranism. The Reformation's positive affirmation of the secular order is valid, but it is valid only if the critical element in this affirmation is explicitly emphasized. This critical element asks whether and to what extent the secular order is an expression of love.[91]

Article XVI of the Augsburg Confession did not simply affirm the orders of this world. Even when Melanchthon distinguished the inner realm in which the gospel works righteousness from the external, temporal nature of life in this world, he immediately focused on the way in which life should be lived. For the gospel does not overthrow the orders of this world but rather "requires that all these be kept as true orders of God and that everyone, each according to his own calling, manifest Christian love and genuine good works in his satuation of life."[92] The Latin text said it more briefly: The Gospel requires "the exercise of love in these ordinances." Only then do the orders of this world function as God's orders. This is, however, possible because the person who acts in love fulfills God's will. Such love is the way in which God works creatively through people.[93] This meant that the ordered structures of this world are not God's orders simply because they exist. Rather, that correspondence must be demonstrated on the basis of their meeting the criterion of love.

It is not easy to apply this pattern of Reformation thinking to our contemporary situation. On the one hand, such an application easily turns into an uncritical affirmation of the world and of its autonomy. On the other hand, the attempt to avoid that danger leads to a purely negative critical analysis that cannot accept this world as God's world but rather asserts that we ourselves must make it a good world by what we do. The good world then becomes a human creation. If we always look at the world from the perspective of the gospel, however, our critical awareness of the problems in the world will not lead us to forget to affirm it. This perspective will in turn facilitate our own living and working in the context of this world. In any case, no discussion of these problems should fail to refer to this perspective.

The Confident Life

The Reformation tried to liberate secular life from the ongoing disturbance of Christians' relationship to the secular world that resulted from the late medieval assertion that the religious life and religious good works were more valuable than secular life and works. In contrast, the ethical teaching of the Reformers tried to create the certainty that we can live life as God wills it to be lived by living actively in this world. This instruction was experienced as a liberation. The Reformers properly prided themselves on having helped people to live more confidently through recognizing the value of life in this world. "Our theologians have explained this whole matter of political affairs so clearly that many good men involved in politics and in business have testified how they were helped after the theories of the monks had troubled them and put them in doubt whether the Gospel permitted such public and private business."[94]

It is not advisable to describe this confidence as the certainty or the confidence of a good conscience. That language should be reserved for the conscience that has been comforted by the gospel. The good conscience is created by receiving the gospel. When we speak of living confidently in this world, however, we are speaking of acting confidently. These two, receiving the gospel and acting in the world, should not be confused. We must be very clear about the sequence. The confidence that results from receiving the gospel precedes the confident active life and makes it possible. Thus the Augsburg Confession constantly repeated: Fearing and trusting God in faith are the presupposition for the activity in which we realize our own vocation.

This relationship between receiving and acting must be further developed is such a way that we become clear about its theoretical context. For example, more attention needs to be given to the distinction between authority in the church and in the world as a basic factor in the teachings of the Reformation.[95] The specifically political dimension of this could be described in terms of the so-called doctrine of the two kingdoms. The state is free to exercise its authority under law without the interference of the church. The church is free to carry out its specific task of proclaiming the gospel. At this point, we become aware of the particular ethical dimension involved in the distinction between the spiritual and the secular.

In this context, it becomes clear that neither Luther nor later Lutheran theologians provided the basis for an adequate systematic statement of this doctrine of the two kingdoms. It was not really a systematically developed doctrine but rather a way of discussing issues. Obviously, it is important to note that the ethical and the political dimensions of the doctrine of the two kingdoms must always be considered simultaneously. For the certainty of a confident conscience depends on the church adequately fulfilling its task of preaching the gospel. And confident action in the political realm—for example, in the administration of the state's legal system—depends in turn on the certainty that such activity is commanded by and a service of the same God who for Christ's sake justifies sinners through faith.

Confident action in this world can be accompanied by religious certainty only if we are convinced that we are doing God's will in this world. How can we gain this confidence? Naturally, we can always teach people that their activity in this world fulfills God's will. We can instruct them about how God's creative will is carried out through their living service to other people. The question, however, is whether this is an adequate basis for maintaining the confidence of religious certainty. There is nothing about these actions that in any way specially identifies them as God-pleasing or Christian acts. The question was specifically raised by the Roman Confutation when it asserted that anything that Turks and Tartars do cannot be considered the highest Christian work.[96] That is still quite a convincing argument and shakes our confidence that secular work is really religious work.

At this point, we will find it helpful to think about the Reformation's reference to the cross that is laid on each Christian. We become certain that our activity in this world is a good religious work whenever this activity takes the form of bearing the cross. The Reformers were no strangers to life. They knew what life is really like and were well acquainted with human sinfulness and selfishness. It is true that God uses even this selfishness and narcissism to do God's work in this world. Life must go on. And if people will not voluntarily live their lives in a way that supports life, then there may be no other solution than to force them to do so. That is the task of the state and of all secular authority, for example, the economic system's *(Haushalt)* requirement that we engage in productive work. It is, however, quite a different matter that our efforts to live in this world as God created it and to love people often result in failure. This experience is particularly painful when we realize that God is not using our work to carry out God's loving and creative will, but rather that selfish human beings have taken over our work and exploited our well-intended efforts for their own corrupt purposes. It is not easy to live among such people and still be confident that God works creatively in what we do—even when we see just the opposite happening.

When we experience this radical uncertainty, we have reached the point at which we can gain religious certainty about the nature of our work in this world. We are then experiencing what the Reformers called "the cross." This experience of the cross is the way in which we experience the spiritual dimension of God's presence in the secular realm. Note carefully that this is not the usual pious interpretation of the cross. That more usual Lutheran interpretation is based on the separation of the two kingdoms and of the law from the gospel. The understanding of the cross proposed here remains completely within the context of the thinking of the Augsburg Confession and of the Apology. An extensive concordance study of the word "cross" in these two documents would demonstrate that. At present, it is important to note that the cross was disucssed in the context of those spiritual temptations, the *afflictiones* and *Anfechtungen,* which indicate that the time for faith has come. In this situation, we experience that our faith in the gospel becomes more certain and this in turn gives us the confidence that we need in order to go on living in this world an to overcome all our doubts about the value of the work that we do in carrying out our vocation. At this point, the distinction between the spiritual and the secular disappears. We experience both as a single unity. "With regard to the mortifying of the body and the discipline of the flesh we teach exactly what we said in the Confession [AC, XXVI:33–39], that the cross and the troubles with which God disciplines us effect a genuine and not a counterfeit mortification. When this comes, we must obey God's will, as Paul says (Rom. 12:1), 'Present your bodies as a sacrifice.' This is the spiritual exercise of fear and faith."[97]

In this kind of experience, the confident life receives the certainty that permits it to do what needs to be done in any case, because it knows that in so doing it will encounter God. This is no theoretical certainty about the doctrine of God's two kingdoms. Such theoretical certainty has its place in theological discussion and in that context is an important argument for the holiness of life in this world. Such theoretical certainty is, however, not yet the kind of experience that comes from living. As is the case with faith, there is also an appropriate time for us to gain confident certainty about life. The right time for this is the time when we are experiencing the cross. This is the time when the person bearing the cross experiences the unity of God's spiritual and secular governments. This is how the Reformation's approach to ethics was tied into the Reformation's basic decision that God alone saves people. Even when we are called to be active participants in life, we receive the certainty that God is near and will use our doing of this work in order to focus our attention once again on the experience of salvation as something that we can only receive.

6

Luther's Writings
in the Book of Concord

This chapter deals with those writings of Luther that were included in the Book of Concord. It will neither summarize the essence of Luther's theology on the basis of these writings nor will it compare and contrast Luther's style of presenting the basic decision of the Reformation with Melanchthon's style on the basis of the writings of each that were included in the Book of Concord. Rather, we are concerned with identifying the confession itself and using it as our guide to understanding the gospel. In pursuing this task, the special character of Luther's confessional writings included in the Book of Concord—the Smalcald Articles, the Large Catechism, and the Small Catechism—will sometimes be noted. In so doing, the purpose will not be to describe Luther's theology but rather to understand the confession. This is the constant focus of attention in this whole book. This task, however, will require us to pay attention to the unique nature of each of the confessional writings. It will also require us to understand the content of each writing in a way that is appropriate to its unique character.

THE SMALCALD ARTICLES

The Development and the Nature
of the Smalcald Articles

The Smalcald Articles defined the controversy with late medieval theology in a much sharper way than the Augsburg Confession had, in terms of the substance of the issues as well as of the literary style.[1] This was certainly due in part to the personal character of Luther, who was much less willing to compromise for the sake of unity than Melanchthon was. It was also partly due to the fact that the split in the church was even deeper in 1537 than it had been in 1530. The character of these articles, however, was primarily determined by the purpose for which they were written.

The Lutherans had as part of their political strategy insisted that a general council be called to resolve the religious controversy. At the same time, they were well aware that they did not want to submit themselves to the judgment of a council that was under papal leadership. In the summer of 1536, Pope Paul III called a council to meet in Mantua in the spring of 1537. This is the council that, after many changes in schedule and place of meeting, finally met in Trent in December 1545. On December 11, 1536, the Elector of Saxony asked Luther to draft a list of items that were negotiable for the sake of peace and of items on which no compromise was possible. Luther went to work without delay. His draft was discussed by a conference of theologians in Wittenberg at the end of December and a few changes made. The representatives of the Smalcald League met in Smalcald in February 1537 but did not officially adopt the articles. The controversy on the Lord's Supper with the southern Germans had been resolved through the adoption of the Wittenberg Concord in 1536.[2] A new outbreak of this theological controversy was to be avoided. Luther's articles were signed by the great majority of the theologians who were present in Smalcald. In the summer of 1538, Luther published an expanded version of these articles. It is this version that was included in the Book of Concord of 1580.

In the preface to this printed edition,[3] Luther reported that the articles were developed in preparation for the proposed council. He expressed his opinion that it would not be a free council. The Roman Curia was too afraid of that happening. He was therefore taking the opportunity to publish these articles as his own confession. He could no longer defend himself against the twisting of his meaning, against the lies and malicious slanders. The devil himself is behind these attacks. The preface closes with a prayer to Christ: "Dear Lord Jesus Christ, assemble a council of thine own, and by thy glorious advent deliver thy servants. The pope and his adherents are lost. They will have nothing to do with Thee. But help us, poor and wretched souls who cry unto Thee and earnestly seek Thee."[4] This shows Luther's frame of mind when these articles were written. Luther felt he was facing an opponent who was unwilling to change. "In the council we shall not be standing before the emperor or the secular authority, as at Augsburg, where we responded to a gracious summons and were given a kindly hearing, but we shall stand before the pope and the devil himself, who does not intend to give us a hearing but only to damn, murder, and drive us to idolatry. Consequently we ought not here kiss his feet or say, 'You are my gracious lord,' but we ought rather speak as the angel spoke to the devil in Zechariah, 'The Lord rebuke you, O Satan' (Zech. 3:2)."[5]

The articles were written in the style of an opinion. That is what the elector had requested. These articles, however, were also shaped by Luther's vehement polemic against the pope and the papacy. In addition, Luther included many personal affirmations of his own convictions and of his personal identification with the doctrines he was presenting. In discussing the mass, for example, he reported that the papal legate Campegio had told him during their meeting in Augsburg that he would rather be torn to pieces before he would give up the mass. Luther continued, "So by God's help I would suffer myself to be burned to ashes before I would allow a celebrant of the Mass and what he does to be considered equal or superior to my Saviour, Jesus Christ. Accordingly we are and remain eternally divided and opposed the one to the other."[6] Naturally, this did not permit Luther to consider any kind of negotiations. This was the tone of Luther's entire presentation. It left no room for the kind of compromise that the elector had asked him to consider. He therefore concluded with this statement: "These are the articles on which I must stand and on which I will stand . . . I do not know how I can change or concede anything in them. If anybody wishes to make some concessions, let him do so at the peril of his own conscience."[7]

There is no quick and easy way of understanding the Smalcald Articles. This due not only to the difficulty of their content and their polemical spirit, but also to the great difference in scope and importance of the various articles. It is possible, however, to identify a clear line of development in their structure that is related to their content. Luther divided the articles into three groups. Part I treated the "sublime articles of the divine majesty."[8] Luther reviewed some of the basic doctrines of the Trinity and of the person and work of Christ. He referred to the Apostles' and the Athanasian Creeds as his authorities. He then said that there is no need to discuss these articles because they were not involved in the present controversy.

Part II treated "the articles which pertain to the office and work of Jesus Christ, or to our redemption."[9] Obviously the article on justification through faith for Christ's sake had to be discussed in the section.[10] Luther also added three polemical articles dealing with the mass and the invocation of saints, monastic life, and the papacy. In these articles, he did not develop the position of the Reformation but rather critically analyzed the position of the late medieval church. Luther repeatedly referred to the relationship between these articles and the first and chief article dealing with Christ and faith. He concluded that the papal church was in contradiction to this article. Luther's line of argument in this section is sometimes questionable. This is reflected in the reservation stated by Melanchthon when he signed these articles: "I, PHILIP MELANCHTHON, regard the above articles as right and Christian. However, concerning the pope I hold that, if he would allow the Gospel, we, too, may concede to him that superiority over the bishops which he possesses by human right, . . ."[11] Melanchthon was obviously not entirely convinced by Luther's arguments against the pope.

Part III of the articles developed the specific theology of the Reformation. Luther said that these were "matters which we may discuss with learned and sensible men, or even among ourselves."[12] Even this positive statement is interrupted by polemical sections, such as "The False Repentance of the Papists."[13] In the version of these articles published in 1538, Luther added a section on the enthusiasts.[14] The last two articles contained purely polemical sections.[15] The conclusion of the articles was followed by an appendix discussing "the pope's bag of magic tricks" and all kinds of dedication services. Luther expressed only contempt for the latter.[16]

The style of Smalcald Articles was often very coarse and polemical. This makes it difficult to interpret it in a way that takes Luther's opponents' religious and theological position—as presented in this confessional writing—seriously. Undoubtedly Luther was matching the tone of the opponents' attacks on himself when he did not treat their position seriously but rather expressed only his contempt for and condemnation of them as the devil's tools and accessories. Ordinarily we overlook such statements and it is certainly good that we are able to look at things differently from the perspective of a later time. This does not mean, however, that we ought to avoid the sharpness of Luther's theological judgments. For these sharp judgments constituted the special significance of the Smalcald Articles in their context in the Book of Concord. In a way far superior to that of the Augsburg Confession and the Apology, the Smalcald Articles provide a systematic definition of the Reformation's basic decision. Because of this systematic development of this decision, the Smalcald Articles have special value for a theology of the Lutheran confessions.

Luther's Ranking of the Importance of the Articles

The systematic structure of the Smalcald Articles cannot be determined by examining the external form of these articles. Articles of widely differing length and importance follow one another without clear transitions, especially in Part III. Rather, we must examine the interrelationships on the basis that Luther asserts for various articles. He never explicitly stated the relationship of Part I to the total context of the Smalcald Articles. His concluding remark to this part seems to indicate that an extensive discussion was not necessary because these articles were not the subject of controversy. Luther, however, made a correction in his own manuscript that may indicate that these articles were not simply intended to affirm agreement on these points of doctrine. Luther originally wrote: "These articles are not matters of dispute or contention, for both parties believe and confess them [*dieselbigen gläuben und bekenned"]."* He at some time then crossed out "believe *(gläuben).*"[17] The implication of this change was to express implicitly Luther's private opinion that the opponents did not really believe what they confessed and taught. That may, of course, only reflect the coarseness of the polemic. At the very least, the correction meant that the faith described in Parts I and II cannot be subdivided. It is possible really to believe in the God described in the doctrines of the Trinity and about the Incarnation only if the doctrines of Christ's person and saving work are also understood as the Reformation understood them.

This conclusion is very important for our question about the gospel—the question that underlies this whole book. Although we must clearly distinguish between the basic decision of the early church and its Trinitarian and christological doctrines on the one hand and the basic decision of the Reformation on the other hand, we cannot permit them to be separated from each other. If we really agree with the basic decision of the early church that God alone works our salvation, we cannot reject the Reformation's interpretation of the Scripture. If we affirm the one without affirming the other, our confession can only seem to be correct. The gospel is a unity. Therefore, when someone disagrees about the understanding of this gospel, we are compelled to ask whether they really agree with us in accepting the traditional teachings of the early church. This is the case even if the question about the gospel on which there is disagreement is a question that arises in the contemporary discussion and was not previously raised in the church.

In this context, Luther's distinction between Parts II and III is particularly significant. Although Luther granted that the dogmatic issues listed in Part II could be discussed at a council, Luther actually saw no room for negotiation on these points at any future council. Such discussion would have to be limited to the interrelationships of these doctrines. In any case, Luther felt that the basic decision of the Reformation expressed in these doctrines and the reformation of the church carried out on the basis of this decision were simply not subject to discussion. Luther described these issues as the "articles which pertain to the office and work of Jesus Christ, or to our redemption."[18] The work of Jesus Christ and our redemption are one and the same. Since both belong together, nothing that human beings do, whether it is the work of the church or the work of Christians, can force its way between this work of Christ and those who have been redeemed by it. The only thing that can even be named as coming between the Christian and Christ is faith. Faith, however, joins us together with Christ. The Christ for us and this faith that joins us together with him are the center of the Reformation's gospel.[19]

This is the way in which Luther ranked the articles according to their importance. This fact obligates us, whenever we attempt to understand the gospel as the Reformation did, to relate everything to this center and to interpret it on this basis.

Luther himself did this very explicitly when he began his discussion of those doctrines in which the late medieval church contradicted this central teaching of the faith. This understanding of the mass "must be regarded as the greatest and most horrible abomination because it runs into direct and violent conflict with this fundamental article. Yet, above and beyond all others, it has been the supreme and most precious of the papal idolatries, for it is held that this sacrifice or work of the Mass (even when offered by an evil scoundrel) delivers men from their sins, both here in this life and yonder in purgatory, although in reality this can and must be done by the Lamb of God alone, as has been stated above."[20] Obviously this polemic can be countered with the reminder that Luther has overlooked the fact that the sacrifice of the mass is indissolubly joined to the sacrifice of Christ. This counterargument loses its power, however, when this relationship is compared to the relationship of the work of Christ and redemption that is established in faith. There is no room in this faith for the mediation of the church and its priests—regardless of whether their relationship to Christ is emphasized or recedes into the background. The only possibility that remains is to celebrate and administer the sacrament in conformity to its institution, which clearly reveals that it is God who graciously turns to people and never people who take the initiative in turning to God.[21]

As soon as Christ's institution of the sacrament is perverted and God's work in people becomes people's own work that they present to God, however, the gate is opened wide for every kind of religious activity to be offered to God. That is what Luther meant when he enumerated other late medieval practices that compete with redemption through Christ: "Besides, this dragon's tail— that is, the Mass—has brought forth a brood of vermin and the poison of manifold idolatries."[22] Luther mentioned purgatory and referred us to the fact that the sacrament was almost always celebrated for the dead, even though Christ had instituted the sacrament only for the living. Then he mentioned other things that were done on behalf of the dead. That kind of thing is, he said, simply not permissible. Pilgrimages and brotherhoods were also common methods of doing good works on behalf of one another.[23] The reverence of relics and, finally, indulgences were also discussed. Even though Luther did not always clearly indicate how these were related to the sacrifice of the mass, he always asserted that these abuses expressed a misunderstanding of the "chief article." "For the merits of Christ are obtained by grace, through faith, without our work or pennies. They are offered to us without our money or merit, not by the power of the pope but by the preaching of God's word."[24]

Luther extensively analyzed the sacrifice of the mass and religious works. This detailed analysis was followed by a brief article on "chapters and monasteries." Originally, these had been established as educational institutions. If they no longer served this purpose, they should be torn down. That would be a better solution "than to preserve them with their blasphemous services, invented by men, which claim to be superior to the ordinary Christian life and to the offices and callings established by God. All this, too, is in conflict with the first, fundamental article concerning redemption in Jesus Christ."[25] Part III then asserted that monastic vows are not binding. "Whoever takes the vows of monastic life believes that he is entering upon a mode of life that is better than that of the ordinary Christian and proposes by means of his work to help not only himself but also others to get to heaven. This is to deny Christ."[26] Once again Luther was concerned about denial of the Reformation's basic decision based on the chief article. Luther did not describe what he affirmed except for referring to "the offices and callings established by God."[27]

Luther's third negative statement of a doctrine—the fourth in the series of those articles not subject to negotiation under any circumstances—described the papacy. "The pope is not the head of all Christendom by divine right or according to God's Word . . . [but] only the bishop and pastor of the churches in Rome."[28] Luther acknowledged that the pope was also the secular ruler of some who had become his subjects through their own choice or through the legitimate action of secular authority. Although Luther was willing to recognize the pope's status in "secular government, where God sometimes permits much good to come to a people through a tyrant or scoundrel," he described the papal claim to primacy as based on "purely diabolical transactions and deeds . . . which contribute to the destruction of the entire holy Christian church (in so far as this lies in his power) and come into conflict with the first, fundamental article which is concerned with redemption in Jesus Christ."[29] Luther then explicitly named the papacy's claim that obedience to the pope is necessary to salvation. He also held the pope responsible for the practices and conditions in the church that he had named in previous articles, for the "Masses, purgatory, monastic life, and human works and services."[30]

In this section Luther also came to terms with the argument that the church needs to have a head in order to preserve its unity. Luther agreed that the pope—if he did not claim to be the head of the church by divine right—could be elected to this position. (This agreed with Melanchthon's reservation in signing the Smalcald Articles.) Luther thought that such an election would not help the situation. For if the pope were to try to exercise his absolute authority without being able to claim a divine right, more divisions and sects would inevitably result. "Consequently the church cannot be better governed and maintained than by having all of us live under one head, Christ, and by having all the bishops equal in office (however they may differ in gifts) and diligently joined together in unity of doctrine, faith, sacraments, prayer, and works of love."[31]

Although Luther's polemic was, at this point, unrestrained, his charges against the pope were basically correct. The direct relationship of faith to Christ and the freedom granted by the gospel were inconsistent with the papacy's demand for obedience. For the papacy did not demand that Christians obey Christ in the gospel but rather be obedient to the institution of the papacy itself. It is for this reason that Luther—in the section on enthusiasm which he added to the published edition of the Smalcald Articles—labeled the papacy as "nothing but enthusiasm" and spoke of the pope in conjunction with Müntzer and the other enthusiasts.[32] The enthusiasts, Luther said, thought they had received the gift of the Spirit and therefore enjoyed a direct relationship to God that permitted them to pass judgment on the Scripture and on the gospel. This sense of lordship destroys the fellowship of the children of God. It is the nature of this fellowship that we recognize one another as brothers and sisters in Christ. This mutual recognition is expressed in the process of hearing the Scripture together and making necessary decisions on the basis of our agreement about Christ's will for us. This agreement must be constantly reworked and reconfirmed. If this process is replaced by the decision of the minister—whether the minister claims to have the spirit because of personal charisma or because of respect for the office of the ministry—a lordship has been established which abrogates the freedom to believe. This freedom is then replaced by obedience to the will of the minister as the custodian of the Spirit. The common quest for the will of Christ as this is made known to us in Scripture is in practice then replaced by submission to the will of the minister. This is the basis of Luther's identification of the ways in which the papacy and enthusiasm contradicted the basic decision of the Reformation.

The articles of Part III of the Smalcald Articles are ranked differently than Parts I and II. In Part II, the Reformation's basic decision is designated as the "chief article." On the basis of this basic decision, Luther demonstrated why certain elements of the late medieval church could not be tolerated. In contrast, Part III developed those teachings that are presupposed by and follow from the Reformation's basic decision. Luther said that these articles might be discussed. He certainly did not mean to say that these matters could be decided in any way people wanted to. Luther's final conclusion was he did not know of anything in any of the articles that might be changed or conceded to the opponents.[33] At the same he expressed willingness to discuss the articles in Part III in terms of their basis, their interrelationship, and their clear and logical formulation. That is what Luther was thinking of when he said that these articles could be discussed "with learned and sensible men, or even among ourselves."[34]

Although it is not necessary to discuss the details of Part III, it is useful to analyze its basic systematic structure. The Reformation's basic decision stands in the center. This decision has immediate implications for the form of the church which must allow room for the word of Christ. It presupposes agreement with the early church and its basic decision. It requires us to rethink every doctrine in whole and in part on the basis of this basic decision. As important and unalterable as this doctrine is: The Reformation's basic decision does not require the church to make its confession *(status confessionis)* for the sake of the teaching. Rather such a confession is required whenever it is necessary to resist any and all expressions of the church's life that contradict Christ. That is, in any case, the way that Luther described it in the Smalcald Articles.

THE SMALL AND THE LARGE CATECHISMS

The Catechism as an Elementary Handbook of Doctrine

The Formula of Concord explained the inclusion of Luther's catechisms in the Book of Concord on the basis of the needs of the laity. "Since these important matters also concern ordinary people and laymen who for their eternal salvation must as Christians know the difference between true and false doctrine, we declare our unanimous adherence to Dr. Luther's Small and Large Catechisms."[35] The Formula of Concord then recognized that Luther's catechisms were widely distributed. In writing these catechisms, however, Luther had not intended them to be used by the laity, but rather by pastors. In the preface to the Small Catechism, Luther referred to the need for religious instruction that he became aware of as a visitor. Religious ignorance was especially great in the country and the pastors themselves were unable to teach. Luther suggested that they use the Small Catechism as the basis for their teaching.[36] The Large Catechism, which was based on Luther's own catechetical preaching, was also intended to provide a basis for such catechism instruction.

In the prefaces to the catechisms, Luther explained what a catechism is and how it was to be used. A catechism is not primarily a book. (We commonly use the term in this sense when we speak, for example, of "a Protestant catechism for adults.") Rather, catechism is training in a certain body of knowledge. In the early church, this was the Creed and the Lord's Prayer. The Middle Ages added the Decalogue. The expansion of this material to include instruction about the sacraments of Baptism and the Lord's Supper was an innovation made at the time of the Reformation. It prevailed particularly because of the pattern set by Luther's catechisms. Luther himself described the first three chief parts as a summary of the Scripture. "Under no circumstances should a person be tolerated if he is so rude and unruly that he refuses to learn these three parts in which everything contained in Scripture is comprehended in short, plain, and simple terms."[37] The Epitome of the Formula of Concord echoed this theme when it described the catechisms as "the layman's Bible" which "contain everything which Holy Scripture discusses at greater length and which a Christian must know for his salvation."[38] The Epitome was thinking of the chief parts of the catechism, not only of the texts but also of the Reformation's understanding of these texts as typified by Luther.

Training in the catechism was to take place in two steps. First, the texts were to be memorized. That happened as a result of constant repetition. Luther described his own practice: "I do as a child who is being taught the catechism. Every morning, and whenever else I have time, I read and recite word for word the Lord's Prayer, the Ten Commandments, the Creed, the Psalms, etc." Such familiarity with the text requires that it have a definite and unchanging form. For this reason, Luther emphasized this principle of catechism instruction:

> In the first place, the preacher should take the utmost care to avoid changes or variations in the text and wording of the Ten Commandments, the Creed, the Lord's Prayer, the sacraments, etc. On the contrary, he should adopt one form, adhere to it, and use it repeatedly year after year. Young and inexperienced people must be instructed on the basis of a uniform, fixed text and form. They are easily confused if a teacher employs one form now and another form—perhaps with the intention of making improvements—later on. In this way all the time and labor will be lost.[40]

Pastors and preachers are not the only ones who are responsible for this kind of training. Heads of households should also require their children and servants to memorize these parts of the catechism.

The second step in catechetical training is that of understanding. It is not enough to memorize the words. That is why "The young people should also attend preaching, especially at the time designated for the Catechism, so that they may hear it explained and may learn the meaning of every part. They will also be able to repeat what they have heard and give a good, correct answer when they are questioned, and thus the preaching will not be without benefit and fruit."[41] Luther thought that such understanding went beyond understanding a definite text such as that of the Small Catechism.[42] In any case, Luther recommended this to pastors who used the Small Catechism. After people had learned and mastered the interpretation of the individual chief parts, they could move on to a broader interpretation and gain a freer understanding of these texts in terms of their personal situations—Luther's Large Catechism is a good example of this kind of instruction.[43]

Catechetical instruction thus begins with a text that has a consistent wording. This text is interpreted and the student memorizes its meaning in fixed formulas. Only then, can and may the student attempt a freer interpretation that is no longer tied to the fixed text of a memorized interpretation. Such a freer interpretation always begins with and reorients itself to this memorized interpretation. Luther's Small Catechism is such a useful interpretation that can be memorized—theologians will find it especially useful as a basis for their understanding of the gospel.

Training in historical method enables us to use Luther's formulations even though their language is sometimes not directly relevant to our contemporary situation. We can memorize his interpretations of the chief parts without going through the cumbersome process of translating their meaning into a new text that might seem more closely related to contemporary life. This is especially true of Luther's interpretations of the Commandments and the Creed. Luther's formulas provide a particularly useful basis for a broader understanding. Memorizing these texts of the Small Catechism is sometimes experienced as an ascetic practice. Students of theology, in particular, will find this ascetic practice a useful element of theological study.

Luther's Large Catechism as Training in the Practice of Theology

Theology is here understood as theology in the narrow sense, as thinking and speaking about the doctrine of God. How to do this correctly is a question that constantly occupies the theologian who is expected to have mastered this task. Because we often have difficulty in thinking about God, we may avoid the task and speak about people, spiritual people, even good people, rather than speaking about God. We are more comfortable speaking about what we human beings can do and ought to do. In contrast, it seems old-fashioned to speak about God in this current situation. In fact, it is not at all easy to speak about God. It is especially difficult to do so on the basis of the presuppositions of modern thought—especially when we can only speak about God by explicitly contradicting these presuppositions. This means that theologians must be very knowledgeable about the presuppositions of contemporary thought. They must also be very aware that their thinking and self-understanding will be influenced by these presuppositions even when they explicitly reject them. Luther's Large Catechism was written in a different time and situation. For that reason, we cannot simply adopt it, imitate its language and vocabulary, and then assume that this ability to repeat it means that we have mastered the correct theory and practice of speaking about God. In spite of this, it is useful to know how Luther's Large Catechism spoke of God in its own historical context. Theologians will still find its text a useful resource. It is an example of how Luther spoke about God in his time and place. As such, it can help us understand the nature of our own task.

The Interpretation of the Decalogue

Luther's interpretation of the Decalogue, or the Ten Commandments, distinguishes between God and the world in reference to God's will. This distinction is the presupposition of everything else that we have to say about God. For whoever uses the term "God" does not mean "the world"—at least not in the context of biblical, Jewish-Christian discourse about God. Unlike metaphysical patterns of thought, this distinction between God and world remains a distinction in terms of human existence—at the level of the "heart," as Luther said. Metaphysical thought seeks to comprehend the being of God in terms both of God's differentiation from as well as of God's relation to the being of this world. The heart, however, asks about God because it needs a point at which it can anchor its trust. This is what Luther said in the explanation of the First Commandment. "A god is that to which we look for all good and in which we find refuge in every time of need."[44] Luther then went on to say that it is only faith and heartfelt trust that makes God and idols. That is not to be understood as meaning that the heart creates either the true God or false gods by projecting trust onto them. Luther was not quite that "modern," although Ludwig Feuerbach did try to claim Luther in support of his theory of religion.[45] Rather, Luther was concerned that the heart bestow its trust on the true God and not on a false god. "The purpose of this commandment, therefore, is to require true faith and confidence of the heart, and these fly straight to the one true God and cling to him alone."[46] The real art of speaking about God is to help people hit the mark in this way. Luther tried to achieve this "by citing some common examples of failure to observe this commandment."[47] Luther also tried to show where God is not present and the heart has therefore placed its trust in an idol. His first example was the false god Mammon, money and possessions. What did he mean? An abstract answer to such a catechism question would be: Money is every possibility that we have under our control, or at least think we have under our control. We think we can buy everything with money; we easily forget that not everything is for sale. Luther then carried the discussion one point further, beyond this reference to the abstract possibility that is under our control. Money is not only the only power that we have and trust, there is also "great learning, wisdom, power, prestige, family, and honor."[48] Religious resources were also named as false gods, for example, the worship of saints and deals with the devil. Specific possibilities of life were raised to the status of gods, as Luther illustrated in terms of classical mythology. "For example, the heathen who put their trust in power and dominion exalted Jupiter as their supreme God. Others who strove for riches, happiness, pleasure, and a life of ease venerated Hercules, Mercury, Venus, or others."[49] The most extreme form of such idolatry is the effort to gain heaven by presenting our good works to God. Luther did think that this latter example might be "a little too subtle to be understood by young pupils."[50]

This last observation may help us to go further. It describes the heart as trusting in its own freedom to do the good. We take our life and try to use it as though it were our own and to preserve it by our own powers. The will to live[51] then determines our life style; we use the possibilities of life in this world for our own purposes of gaining and preserving life. The heart clings to those things that it equates with life: possessions, power, pleasure, heaven. We spend our lives in making this world available to ourselves as a resource for this life. In so doing, we have trusted in a false god and have given this false god control over our own life and this world. This apparent freedom to do what we want to do creates the kind of God that we find useful and we arrange things in the world to reinforce the image of this false god. "Idolatry does not consist merely of erecting an image and praying to it. It is primarily in the heart, which pursues other things and seeks help and consolation from creatures, saints, or devils. It neither cares for God nor expects good things from him sufficiently to trust that he wants to help, nor does it believe that whatever good it receives comes from God."[52]

The heart trusts God when it completely trusts him as the one who is beyond our own control. "To have God, you see, does not mean to lay hands upon him, or put him into a purse, or shut him up in a chest. We lay hold of him when our heart embraces him and clings to him."[53] We find our life with God, who defines what life is and who alone makes life possible. This kind of life follows God's leading, accepts the world as it comes as God's will for us, and permits its activity to be caught up in God's activity. This is not the free will seeking to create its idol out of the world and seeking security in this world; rather, the heart now comes to terms with and accepts whatever God sends; it is this trust that gives us life in relation to God.

Luther was well aware that it is not easy to trust God in this way. He therefore underscored the statement of God's will in the First Commandment by referring to the threat and promise described in Exod. 5:6. Should it seem to happen otherwise and idolatry lead to a good and easy life, "we must grasp these words, even in the face of this apparent contradiction, and learn that they neither lie nor deceive but will yet prove to be true."[54] In this context, we differentiate God from the world in terms of God's will precisely when we deal with the world properly. This means seeking the life that comes from God and has been promised to us as a gift rather than the life that comes from this world. This commandment, with its threat and promise, assists us in doing this and, whatever we experience, focuses our attention on God. We thus learn to distinguish between the illusory world of idolatry that people create for themselves and the real world established by God. Thus trust passes through the world and clings to the God who is not this world.

Such trust is practiced through the Word. This theme is introduced by the Second Commandment, which does more than merely forbid the misuse of God's name, false oaths, and the effort to conceal our own naughty willing and acting behind God's name. Rather this commandment demands that we use God's name properly and teaches us to use God's name to oppose evil and as a source of good. Everything that is not from God but from the devil can be resisted in the name of God and we can give thanks in God's name for all the good that we experience from God. Luther thereby took the distinction that the First Commandment made in theory and applied it to our experience in this world. To do that, however, we need to be trained in the use of God's Word.

This was the theme of Luther's explanation of the Third Commandment. Luther did not overlook the fact that this commandment specifically commands us to rest in observance of the holy day. The right way to do this, Luther said, is to devote this day to the Word of God. Luther described this Word as "the true holy thing above all holy things."[55] We can never conclude that we have had too much of the Word of God *(acedia)*.[56] For the devil never stops trying to create unbelief in our hearts. He succeeds whenever the Word is not present, wherever the heart is idle and not engaged with the Word of God. Whenever the heart does work with this word, however, it produces fruit. "For these words are not idle or dead, but effective and living."[57] We can not keep the First Commandment, so to speak, "without hands." If we try, we become involved again in what we want and are able to do and end up incapable of doing anything. Our heart, which ought to trust God and not a false god, misses the mark whenever it aims at performing the good on the basis of its own inherent capacity—as the late medieval doctrine of the conscience as the *synteresis* (the infallible awareness of moral truth remaining after the Fall into sin and providing the basis for the moral judgments of the conscience) taught that it should. We can do that only through the activity of the Word of God and, therefore, we constantly need to study this Word. At this point, we never finish learning—neither the catechism nor the Scripture.

The First Commandment determined the basic character of the entire Decalogue as well as of the "first table" of the law. Similarly, Luther's explanation treated the Fourth Commandment as basic to all those commandments that refer to our relationship to our neighbor. It is obviously very difficult for us to work with the patriarchal relations that Luther taught were both the basis of this commandment and God's will. The first difficulty results from Luther's emphasis that we are commanded not only to love, but also to honor our parents. "Thus he [that is, God] distinguishes father and mother above all other persons on earth, and places them next to himself. For it is a much greater thing to honor than to love. Honor includes not only love but also deference, humility, and modesty, directed (so to speak) toward a message hidden within them."[58] It is God's will that we love our parents "however lowly, poor, feeble, and eccentric they may be."[59] Luther then reminded us of all the good that we have received from our parents and of the promise that accompanies this commandment. Luther continued his explanation by claiming that all other authority is derived and developed out of the authority of parents.[60] Ultimately all stations in life are established by the Fourth Commandment. "Thus we have three kinds of fathers presented in this commandment: fathers by blood, fathers of a household, and fathers of the nation. Besides these, there are also spiritual fathers . . . who govern and guide us by the Word of God."[61]

This explanation of the Fourth Commandment makes it very clear that Lutheran theology affirms the world as it finds it. This unavoidably creates difficulties for theology.[62] Luther himself, however, clearly distinguished between the norm of the commandment with its promise of good life and the nature of reality. He concluded that the difficulties in reality were caused by human disobedience. "We spurn favor and happiness; therefore, it is only fair that we have nothing but unhappiness without mercy. Somewhere on earth there still be some godly people, or else God would not grant us so many blessings! If it depended on our merits, we would not have a penny in the house or a straw in the field."[63]

The process of explaining the commandment in such a way that it becomes a rule for our own lives ought not stop at the point at which Luther made the partriarchal institutions of his time normative. As the analysis of the First Commandment indicated, we should act in trust in God and not shape our lives in terms of what we would like life to be. As a result, we are dependent on life as it is given to us. Our parents, through whom we have received life and whom we have neither chosen nor shaped, have generated us and raised us. They are typical of the fact that all of life is a given. We should recognize God's activity in this reality just as we recognize it in our being born again in faith. Respecting God's will in this life requires us to stay with this life and not to try to run away from it into some possibility of a seemingly better life that we have created for ourselves. This is what this commandment directs us to do. It assumes that the possibilities of our lives are given to us by God and it directs us to live the life that has been set before us. The promise is that good things will come to us from God if we thus do what God wills. "Do your duty, then, and leave it to God how we will support you and provide for all your wants."[64] We will understand God's will only by submitting ourselves to life as it has been given to us rather than by speaking a world that we have interpreted and made comfortable for ourselves in terms of the human possibilities that seem to be available to us.

The explanations of the rest of the Commandments show us how to do this. The good things of life, our own bodies, the spouse to whom we are married, our temporal possessions, honor and good name are all protected by these commandments. Luther interpreted these commandments not only in terms of what they forbid but also of what they require us to do. He was not sparing in his sharp criticism of contemporary conditions. The Ninth and Tenth Commandments are especially directed against the kind of activity that appears to be righteous and honorable. "Above all, God wants our hearts to be pure, even though as long as we live here we cannot reach that ideal. So this commandment remains, like all the rest, one that constantly accuses us and shows just how upright we really are in God's sight."[65]

In conclusion, Luther emphasized that, apart from these commandments, no work or person can be holy, or good, or pleasing to God. He once again summarized what it is that God wills. Actually we would have our hands full if we just did that. "But such works are not important or impressive in the eyes of the world. They are not unusual and pompous, restricted to special times, places, rites, and ceremonies, but are common, everyday domestic duties of one neighbor toward another, with no show about them."[66] For this reason Luther interpreted these works through which everyone fulfills God's commandment according to our vocation on the basis of the First Commandment. "Thus you see how the First Commandment is the chief source and fountainhead from which all the others proceed; again, to it they all return and upon it they depend, so that end and beginning are all linked and bound together."[67]

The Creed

Luther's discussion of the Creed in the catechisms was briefer than the discussion of the Ten Commandments.[68] It is not a detailed doctrine of God. Rather, it provides a pattern for speaking about God in a way that emphasizes the Creed's description of the relationship between God and the world. The Large Catechism focuses on this relationship in terms of God's gifts to us and emphasizes that the basic gift is always a personal relationship to God.[69]

Basically, we must distinguish between but not separate God and the world. If they were separated, there would be nothing for faith to trust. The opposite is true. God encounters us only in the world and through the events of this world. The Commandments, especially the First Commandment, require us to distinguish between our encounter with God and our encounter with the world. Only by making this distinction can we discern God's will. For the heart meets God in this world but must not make the world its false god by trying to reshape the world to match its own desires. The task of faith then is to perceive the real world as God has made it and simultaneously perceive that life has both its source and goal in God.

Luther briefly summarized the Creed in terms of the three persons of the godhead: "I believe in God the Father, who created me; I believe in God the Son, who redeemed me; I believe in the Holy Spirit, who sanctifies me."[70] Luther thus defined the nature of God in terms of God's gift of God together with God's gifts. Obviously, this is not a statement about God in metaphysical or ontological terms. Rather, this is the way in which God encounters faith. For this reason, it is the language of the confession of faith. Creation, redemption, and salvation are described as the individual works of three divine persons;[71] the individual statements of the Apostles' Creed are interpreted in terms of these works. This interpretation seeks to give full expression to God's love: "In these three articles God himself has revealed and opened to us the most profound depths of his fatherly heart, his sheer, unutterable love. He created us for this very purpose, to redeem and sanctify us. Moreover, having bestowed upon us everything in heaven and on earth, he has given us his Son and his Holy Spirit, through whom he brings us to himself."[72]

Luther described the difference between the Creed and the Commandments: the Commandments tell us what we ought to do but the Creed tells us what God does and gives.[73] This distinction is true only in a limited sense. On the one hand, the Commandments are concerned about the real presupposition of all successful living, the distinction between God and the world. On the other hand, this presupposition, as well as doing the Commandments, is possible only where *God* is present with these gifts. In faith, "we see that God gives himself completely to us, with all his gifts and his power, to help us keep the Ten Commandments: the Father gives us all creation, Christ all his works, the Holy Spirit all his gifts."[74] Life is God's gift and is preserved and made possible only by God's activity, by his creative power, by the light of the redemption, and the power of salvation. As a result of this activity of God, we are able to see our life in the eschatological perspective of God's will to save us.

The Lord's Prayer

In his introduction to the third chief part, Luther referred to God's commandment as the reason for us to pray. God wants us to honor his name by calling on it in prayer.[75] This commandment to pray is accompanied by the promise that none other than God will put words into our mouths and teach us how to pray: "God takes the initiative and puts into our mouths the very words we are to use. Thus we see how sincerely he is concerned over our needs, and we shall never doubt that our prayer pleases him and will assuredly be heard."[76] Luther followed this with a polemic against all those prayers that are understood as good works, prayers that do not intend to receive something from God but rather to give something to him. The Lord's Prayer is quite different. It is a catalogue of human needs drawn up by God so that we would know what to ask God for any time we need help.

This viewpoint was determinative for Luther's explanation of the Lord's Prayer: Each petition focuses our attention on a particular aspect of human need in which we should call on God for help. This does not mean that God's gracious response, in which faith trusts, is under human control. To avoid this misunderstanding, we must continue to practice the distinction between God and the world in terms of God's will. Everything that we encounter in life, all that life gives to us and demands from us, must be understood in terms of God. That does not simply happen automatically. If we do not remain confidently relaxed and attentive, we will fail to recognize God. Prayer is this kind of relaxed attention to God. God teaches us to remain confidently relaxed and attentive. When we are confidently relaxed in prayer, we do not seek our own way out of a situation and thereby miss what it is that God has done for us; rather, in prayer we recognize that we obey God merely by praying. Our attention is thereby focused on our need and we are all the more ready and able to seek and expect God's help and to recognize that help when it comes. It is this help from God that meets each need and continues to lead us along the way of life.

"Observe that in these [first] three petitions interests which concern God himself have been very simply expressed, yet we have prayed in our own behalf. What we pray for concerns only ourselves when we ask that what otherwise must be done without us may also be done in us."[77] God's name is hallowed wherever our teaching and life is focused on God. That is why we pray that the gospel may be rightly taught in a world that is "full of sects and false teachers, all of whom wear the holy name as a cloak and warrant for their devilish doctrine."[78]

The kingdom of God is present everywhere where Christ has redeemed us from the power of the devil and rules in our hearts through the Holy Spirit who enlightens and strengthens us in faith. Luther spoke both of the kingdom that is already present and the kingdom that is still to come: "God's kingdom comes to us in two ways: first, it comes here, in time, through the Word and faith, and secondly, in eternity, it comes through the final revelation. Now, we pray for both of these, that it may come to those who are not yet in it, and that it may come by daily growth here and in eternal life hereafter to us who have attained it."[79] Luther emphasized that the prayer for the kingdom is no small prayer. God, however, desires the honor of our bringing such great petitions.

The prayer that God's will be done is a prayer that God's name be hallowed and the kingdom of Christ be established among us. For we are attacked by the devil and by our own flesh. We do not simply "have" either God or a successful life. "For where God's Word is preached, accepted or believed, and bears fruit, there the blessed holy cross will not be far away."[80] This is precisely the time when we need prayer as a protection against the will of the devil and world, so that evil will not triumph because God has preserved us.

The fourth petition includes everything that we need for the support of our physical life. Luther especially focused on the social conditions of life, community, peace, and order. These are constantly threatened and we cannot live without them.

The fifth petition is concerned with life, that even with God's Word and blessing, cannot be lived without sin. "This should serve God's purpose to break our pride and keep us humble."[81] It is important to note that Luther described something that Christians do as a source of certainty. The fact that we forgive others is "a sign along with the promise" that we are forgiven.[82]

In explaining the sixth petition, Luther categorized temptations into three groups: from the flesh, from the world, and from the devil. The young "are tempted chiefly by the flesh," older people through the world, and strong Christians who are concerned with spiritual matters are especially tempted by the devil.[83] A review of the Commandments and the Creed will help us understand what Luther meant: The heart becomes uncertain in such temptation and no longer finds God. Luther also thought that experiencing such temptation would not harm anyone. "We cannot be harmed by the mere feeling of temptation as long as it is contrary to our will and we would prefer to be rid of it.

If we did not feel it, it could not be called a temptation."[84] This means that the heart that experiences spiritual temptation is preserved through its prayers which also keep it focused on God.

Luther understood the seventh petition as a summary of our needs. He interpreted the Greek text to mean "deliver or keep us from the Evil One, or from the Wicked One," that is, from the devil.[85] The task here is to rid ourselves of all corruption in our hearts and all its results so that we may gain life by rightly distinguishing between God and the world.

Although the first three chief parts read so differently and are interpreted by Luther in such divergent ways, all three together lead us to the goal of God-centered thinking that was characteristic of the Reformation. In so doing, they refer in many different ways both to the nearness of God in our lives to the difficulty and possibility of finding God. The preceding brief summary is not an exhaustive treatment but merely encourages regular study of the catechisms as a theological discipline.

No attempt has been made to explore the chief parts dealing with Baptism and the Sacrament of the Altar. Luther emphasized the commandment and promise contained in the words associated with each sacrament. Each sacrament is to be administered according to God's will and contains a promise. The imperative admonition to administer the sacraments was understood as directly related to the indicative promise of the gospel.

7

The Interpretation and Tradition of the Reformation's Basic Decision in the Formula of Concord

The Formula of Concord was not only a religious but also a political document.[1] This was the source of a basic problem: The Formula of Concord was written on the basis of the problematic decision to consolidate the Lutheran confessional identity by finally and absolutely distinguishing Lutheranism from Calvinism. That is one, but not the only problem that we need to consider as we critically evaluate the text of this last document of the age of Lutheran confessionalism. In addition, we must observe how the Formula of Concord itself clearly demonstrates the difficulty of transmitting the Reformation's basic decision in the form of a clearly formulated doctrinal statement.

Thus our study of the Formula of Concord may help us better understand the problems that arise from the effort to formulate the tradition of the gospel in terms of a theological doctrine. Unquestionably, the Formula of Concord was the result of a long and extensive effort to arrive at doctrinal agreement. This already gives it a high rank among the documents of Lutheran theology. It did succeed in preventing the disintegration of Lutheranism into small church bodies with varying doctrinal traditions. The agreement that was necessary to achieve this purpose was reached without making compromises with the truth—as the authors of the Formula of Concord understood it.

On the other hand, it was very difficult for the Formula of Concord to distinguish theological scholastic opinion from the gospel that the church is obligated to preach. This is why we so often find the exhaustively detailed discussions of the Solid Declaration tiresome. The authors were aware of this themselves and therefore preceded it with a shorter summary, the Epitome. The Epitome basically listed the statements that were accepted and those that were rejected. These series of statements attempted to define the church's teaching in the smallest details.

The issues discussed and decided in the Formula of Concord were certainly very serious issues. We also quickly become aware, however, that the individual points of controversy are isolated issues and that they are of quite different degrees of importance. Only Article IX, Christ's Descent into Hell, was written with an appropriately light touch. The Formula of Concord is not characterized by a clear vision of how various doctrines are related to one another. Rather, the individual points that were discussed were determined by the often-unrelated theological controversies of the 1550s and 1560s. Although the resolutions of specific problems were often well worked out, it is still not possible to integrate them into a clear and comprehensive view of the entire document. Every effort was made to decide an issue as Luther would have and his writings were frequently quoted. The Formula of Concord, however, still did not succeed in completely rejecting a human-centered way of thinking. Precisely because each point of doctrine was discussed in isolation from others, the human being always became the center of attention. Instead of describing God's activity in people, human conditions and situations were described.

Precisely because we are concerned to appropriate the Reformation's basic decision as the basis of our own thinking, we need to analyze the Formula of Concord critically. Such careful analysis will demonstrate the problems resulting from the effort to pass the Reformation's basic decision from one generation to the next in the form of a detailed theological doctrine. It is true that the concept of the *corpus doctrinae* reminds us that every generation must restate doctrine—even though once stated in terms of a prescribed exemplary doctrinal statement—in a new form. It was difficult for the Formula of Concord to follow through on this insight because preaching and theological thought are so closely related. If theological thought tries to be clear both in its terms and its contents, it will create a comprehensive statement of teaching and work it out in its finest details. The Formula of Concord did this and, in the process, emphasized the function of the Scripture as the norm of teaching. Of course, this emphasis on the Scripture can also result from its use as the source of the preaching of the gospel. The Scripture will then become the source of the vital power of such preaching. The Formula of Concord, however, was too interested in passing judgment on true and false teaching. As a result, the primary function of the Scripture as such a source of preaching was not clearly defined. The corresponding form of interpreting and applying the Scripture was also less clearly emphasized than it needed to be for the good of theological work.[2]

The Formula of Concord, at least partially, exemplified the kinds of problems in understanding traditional theological doctrine that usually still arise today among people who value traditional teaching. That is at least partially true of the German tradition. For that reason, every attempt to understand the doctrinal tradition of the Reformation in that way will effectively discredit every form of doctrinal commitment. Even this book—because it attempts to present a theology of the Lutheran confessions that will assist people in making the theology of these confessions their own and apply it to their lives will have this result. Therefore, our critical analysis of the Formula of Concord is not intended simply to devalue the theological achievement that the Formula of Concord represents. Rather, we must be critical of the Formual of Concord because the current necessary controversy about the validity of the confession requires such a critical attitude. We, however, may not therefore abandon the definition of accepting the Formula of Concord to those who misunderstand it in a fundamentalistic sense. Rather, we must take responsibility for encouraging the acceptance of the Formula of Concord in the context of a critical and even historical-critical approach to theology.

The following discussion basically follows the structure of the Formula of Concord. Articles I and II deal with the doctrines about human beings, III through VI matters related to the doctrine of salvation, and Articles VII–IX reflect the controversies with Calvinism or, sometimes, Crypto-Calvinism. Article XI is included in this group, and is therefore discussed out of order. Article X treats the last issue, that of the adiaphora.

ANTHROPOLOGICAL DEFINITIONS

The God-centered thinking of the Reformation required certain conclusions in anthropology—a term used here in its theological sense, as the theological doctrine of human persons.[3] The human person is defined through what God does to and with a particular person. The human person cannot—as Roman Catholic theology attempts to do—be described as an independent counterpart in relation to God. For this reason, the doctrine of human persons must be formulated as a doctrine of sin. Sin cannot be described as a condition of the human person, but rather as a distortion of the relationship to God. This focused the controversy between these two confessional positions in a very concentrated way on the issue of the freedom of the will.

Any theology that is defined by the Reformation must reject the position of the Council of Trent on this point. Trent ascribed to people a residual ability to turn to grace by their own power, or at least to cooperate with or reject the prevenient grace that God gives and which offers this decision to people and awaits their response. The Formula of Concord, however, interpreted the assertion that God works all in all in its literal sense. This is the reason why the relationship to God that is destroyed by sin can be reestablished in the new relationship of faith. This way of thinking never permits the conclusion that sinners become the focus of theological discussion and definitions—neither in terms of human ability nor of inability to participate in the process of salvation. For the decisive definition of the human being is that God's work justifies the sinner. The theological controversies between the followers of Philip Melanchthon (the Philipists) and the "super-orthodox" Lutherans (the Gnesio-Lutherans) resulted, however, in a discussion of the nature of the sinner in abstraction from God's saving work. As a result, the course of the discussion led the Formula of Concord involuntarily into, or at least close to, the kind of human-centered thinking that it was trying to reject.

Original Sin

The controversies about original sin, which were dealt with in Article I of the Formula of Concord, must be understood in the context of the so-called synergistic controversies. This is also the case with the discussion of the problem of the freedom of the will, which Article II attempted to decide. If it is clearly the case that a human being can reject God's call to faith and thus incur the personal guilt of unbelief, then it would seem that the reverse is also true: Positive response to grace must be considered one of the causes of salvation alongside the Word through which God calls us and the Spirit who works faith. That at least was the argument of the Synergists. Obviously, they were walking a dangerous path that could quickly lead to the distortion of the Reformation's basic decision. In opposing this synergism, the Formula of Concord used the doctrine of sin in order to develop fully the presuppositions about the nature of human persons that underlay the Reformation's basic decision. As long as these presuppositions about the nature of human beings are only theological in nature, this is an acceptable procedure. The Formula of Concord, however, then went on to ask inappropriate questions about the nature of people.

Matthias Flacius Illyricus had been particularly active in opposing the synergistic doctrine. His emphasis on the sinfulness of human beings was entirely acceptable in the context of Reformation theology. That emphasis also provided the basis for demonstrating that the human person is absolutely unable to cooperate in conversion. Lazarus Spengler put his theological position into the form of a hymn, which not only influenced people's thinking at the time of the controversy and was explicitly approved by the Formula of Concord, but is also still sung in Lutheran churches in Germany and in the United States.[4]

Flacius, however, was trapped into asserting that original sin is not only something that is true about human beings—an "accident," in the scholastic terminology of the time—but rather the very nature—"substance"—of the sinful self. The substance of the sinful human being is therefore no longer formed through the image of God but has rather been transformed into the image of Satan. Sin has thereby become the substantial form (substantia formalis) or the formal substance (forma substantialis) of the human being. Form was understood as the previously determined possibility of determining the nature of matter (materia) as real existence (substantia). The terminology itself was ultimately unusable for this purpose, especially since there was no commonly accepted understanding of its detailed meanings. It was the sixteenth-century version of Aristotelian ontology that divided the characteristics of being into two categories: those that exist independently *(substantia)* and those that exist as variations *(accidens)* of an independent being. *Forma* and *materia* were similar sixteenth-century concepts of Aristotelian ontology and causality. *Materia* was unformed matter that only became a specific being or substance through the operation of the formal cause.

What Flacius really wanted to say was that no real human person can be thought of as being without sin. He was obviously thinking of fallen human beings, not of the theoretical possibility of human being itself as it would have if there were no salvation history, no Fall into sin and no redemption.

Flacius's statements were, however, not acceptable in terms of his usage of the concepts then used in scholastic metaphysics—the technical terms substance and accident, matter and form. His contemporaries misunderstood him as though he were speaking about sin as a condition of human beings rather than as the disturbed or destroyed relationship to God. The fact is that Flacius himself could not long avoid his fatal dilemma. Faith in God the Creator affirms that only God can create being and that every substance is God's creation. What can Flacius's assertion that human beings are sinners in their very substance and that sin detemines their real being have meant? It was necessary to assume that *God* had created human beings as sinners, or, had transformed them into sinful beings. The only possible alternative was to say that Satan had done this and thereby to ascribe creative power to Satan. Naturally, neither Flacius nor any of his supporters thought of saying anything of the kind, for both assertions are ultimately absurd. Having once asserted that original sin is the substance of human beings, however, such absurdities could not be avoided. That does not mean that Flacius's synergistic opponents were right in their efforts to reduce sin that people at least had the capacity either to reject or accept salvation. They said that original sin is only an accident, a merely accidental condition in which human beings find themselves.

The Formula of Concord attempted to clarify and decide the controversy. It also could not avoid the basic dilemma, however. The system of ontological thought with its distinction of substance and accidence as two basic categories was too powerful. Article I on original sin clearly identified the issue and rejected every Pelagian effort to minimize the nature of sin.[5] At the same time, it refused to approve of any Manichaean thinking.[6] It was simply not possible to distinguish between human nature and sin in such ways. "We are not able to point out and expose the nature by itself and original sin by itself as two manifestly separate things, nevertheless . . . [these] are not one and the same thing."[7] The task was to separate human nature from sin in terms of theological thought. This distinction was supported by a respectable collection of arguments. This distinction is demanded by the fact that the triune God has worked to save people. As Creator, God created human nature but not sin. In terms of redemption, the Son of God assumed human nature, but not sin, in order to redeem us. Human nature is sanctified, but not sin. And the resurrection and eternal life is promised to the human person but not to sin. And it does make sense that human nature and sinful nature must be distinguished from each other even though the human nature of the sinner cannot be described in a way that does not involve the reality of sin.

The Formula of Concord did not consider this an adequate basis for asserting that it is necessary to distinguish human nature and sin. It, too, wants to find more exact concepts. There was no way of avoiding that since its very purpose was to clarify theological terminology. In doing so, however, the Formula of Concord should have differentiated more carefully between the language of theological reflection and the language of the church's preaching. The latter is not technical theological language but rather has strong affective overtones. Described in theological language, the doctrine of original sin should, for example, have been stated quite differently than in the chorale of Lazarus Spengler that was referred to earlier. Luther also frequently used language that was not permissible as a technical definition of doctrine.

As a result, the Formula of Concord did try to distinguish the various languages that were used. On the basis of clear and precise observations, the various linguistic frames of reference were identified. In order to avoid arguing about words, it was necessary to pay attention to words that are spelled the same but have different meanings. "Thus in the statement, 'God creates man's nature,' the word 'nature' means man's essence, body, and soul. But in the statement, 'It is the serpent's nature to bite and poison,' the term 'nature' means—as it often does—a disposition or characteristic. It is in this latter sense that Luther writes that sin and sinning are man's disposition and nature." The Smalcald Articles likewise describe original sin as the deep corruption of our nature. "Sometimes, however, the term is applied in a wider sense to include the concrete person or subject (that is, man himself with the body and soul in which sin is and inheres) because through sin man is corrupted, poisoned, and sinful. Thus Luther could say, 'Your birth, your nature, your entire essence is sin, that is, sinful and unclean.' "[8]

The Formula of Concord correctly observed that this is a completely different usage of language than in scholastic metaphysics. It should have gone on to conclude: We must distinguish between the strict meaning of the language of scholastic metaphysics with its carefully defined terms and the language of preaching with its affective overtones. This conclusion was not drawn, however—even though preachers were advised to avoid burdening the "simple church," that is, the assembled congregation with sermons using the Latin words *substantia* and *accidens*.

That did not really overcome the tiresome problem of this terminology. It was the source of the dilemma that the Formula of Concord was now trying to overcome. Once the categorical distinction between substance and accident had been applied to the facts underlying the doctrine of original sin, there was no other alternative than to describe original sin as an "accident." This terminology, however, seems to have the effect of rendering sin harmless. The Formula of Concord does not wish to do that under any circumstances. Yet, it cannot prevail against the apparent truth of the categorical distinction and must "answer simply and roundly that original sin is not a substance but an accident."[9]

That, however, was not the final answer. Rather the Formula of Concord in fact retracted the metaphysical terminology. For there is "no philosopher, no papist, no sophist, indeed, no human reason, be it ever so keen, can give the right answer" to the question "What kind of accident is original sin?"[10] The answer to the question is given only by Holy Scripture. The Scripture bears witness to the depth and the inexpressible damage done by original sin. "Thus the term 'accident' does not in any way minimize original sin if the term is explained in harmony with the Word of God."[11] What, however, did this procedure of the Formula of Concord mean for the question under discussion? Was this not really an admission that the terminology used to describe the reality underlying the doctrine of original sin was not very useful in clarifying the problem it was intended to solve? The categorical distinction must be immediately clarified in the context of biblical language and style of thinking. The Bible does not use this distinction at all. Ought we, therefore, not go further in our conclusion than the Formula of Concord did? The categorical distinction between substance and accident is not useful in discussing original sin in the proclamation of the Word in sermons; it is also not useful in technical theological discussions. If that had been recognized, it would have been easier to overcome the Formula of Concord's discussion of the problem as an isolated issue and discuss it in the context of Reformation teaching.

The Experience of the Self and the Theological Interpretation of the Freedom of the Will

Extending the discussion of the doctrine of sin in terms of its content, we ask whether people are free to do what is good? Is it even possible to speak of such a freedom? In what sense can we speak of it? The traditional answers that Reformation theology gave to these questions were wide open to human-centered thinking. It is not at all hard to understand how the older Melanchthon could adopt the synergistic form of teaching that lead to the controversy. As a pedagogue and a teacher, he was tempted to construct a theory of the human being on the basis of the question as to how the gospel is taught and received by people. Such a theory easily becomes a very questionable matter.

The most obvious example of this fact is the controversy about nature and grace that was carried on by Emil Brunner and Karl Barth.[12] The issue in this

157

modern controversy was natural theology rather than free will, the explicit issue at the time of the Reformation. The development of these controversies revealed, however, that both were concerned with the same theme, the question about the nature of the human person as involved in the process of being saved. Brunner attempted to develop this doctrine of the human person with reference to the actual process of salvation. He described the human being as a responsible person able to answer for itself. This was admittedly only a purely formal capacity. As Barth's critical response demonstrated through a point-for-point analysis, however, Brunner's assertion that the human person is capable of being addressed (Ansprechbarkeit) inevitably lead to more substantial assertions. As Brunner himself said, "Only a being that can be addressed is responsible, for it alone can make decisions. Only a being that can be addressed is capable of sin. But in sinning, while being responsible, it somehow or other knows of its sin. This knowledge of sin is a necessary presupposition of the understanding the divine message of grace."[13]

Obviously, Brunner did not intend this as a repudiation of the Reformation's understanding of the gospel. Rather, it was his intention to express this gospel fully. When he asserted, however, the necessary conditions of God's working in people and described the theologian as trying to reach an understanding with these people "as an intellectual and conceptual work of preparation, which clears obstacles out of the way of proclamation,"[14] he stated an understanding of sin which—contrary to his intentions—no longer agreed with the Reformation. He described human being as having some capacity for the good, even though this capacity was severely damaged. Thus the goodness of God because the goodness of the human being. Given this basis, Brunner could not avoid a synergistic pattern of thought.

Luther had good reasons from the Scripture and from experience to argue against the freedom of the will. He most clearly formulated his position in the book that he considered one of his most valuable works, *The Bondage of the Will* (1525). This position did not in any way prevent him from appealing to the human will. He did so, for example, in explaining the Commandments in the catechisms. He stated that fulfilling the Commandments leads to a good life, whereas despising them leads to unhappiness. In passages like this, Luther apparently affirmed the freedom of the will. He seemed to take it for granted here just as he did when he interpreted the words of institution in the sacraments as both command and promise and appealed to people to receive the sacraments in obedience to God's command.

It was at this point that Melanchthon assumed the validity of a theological theory about the nature of the human being as the basis of this appeal to the human will. Naturally, Melanchthon also said that the human being is not free to choose the good. At the same time, however, the will of the human being who is the subject of the action is also involved in the action. The theological theory must take that into account. Thus in the final version (1559) of his handbook of doctrine *(Loci praecipui theologici)*, this theory read: "If we base our doctrine on the word, there are three causes of good works, the word of God, the Holy Spirit, and the human will which assents to and does not resist the will of God. The human will is able to tear out the word of God, just as Saul did. However, if the mind hears and responds without resisting and without giving in to unbelief, but rather tries with the help of the Holy Spirit to accept the word, the will is most certainly not merely a passive observer *[non est otiosa]*."[15]

Many reasons could be adduced in support of such a theory. One is the self-experience of religious personalities who experience that even their wills swing back and forth between belief and unbelief until they bring the pendulum to a halt through a conscious decision. It is, of course, true that the time is not always right for such a decision. The person whose mind is at rest *(homo otiosus)*[16] can only imagine that a decision has been made—without really having decided. Alongside such self-experience, the imperative proclamation of the gospel, that is, with the command to believe it, can be adduced in support of Melanchthon's theory. Is it meaningful to command a person to believe the gospel if that person is completely unable to respond to the command? Finally, and this is the main basis of this theory, the doctrine of the bondage of the will must not be permitted to create the impression that the human person is released from the demands that God's Word and will make of us. We are in danger of using our lack of freedom as an excuse for doing whatever we happen to want to do at the time. Melanchthon was a pedagogue and whoever wishes to teach people must assume that they are teachable and have the capacity to change and to learn. Even more than that, the teacher who ascribes this capacity to people must also be able to demonstrate that they actually have it.

Melanchthon's theological followers attempted to establish this position as the normative Lutheran position. Those who did not agree were vehement in their opposition. They knew very well that the Reformation tradition excluded every kind of synergism, no matter how weakly it was defined. Even those who explicitly denied that people were able to keep God's Commandments, or really fear, love, and trust in him by their powers, still asserted that the human person "nevertheless still has so much of his natural powers prior to his conversion that he can to some extent prepare himself for grace and give his assent to it, though weakly, but that without the gift of the Holy Spirit he could accomplish nothing with these powers but would succumb in the conflict."[17] It was theologically necessary to reject this position clearly. Therefore, the Formula of Concord taught: "We believe that in spiritual and divine things the intellect, heart, and will of unregenerated man cannot by any native or natural powers in any way understand, believe, accept, imagine, will, begin, accomplish, do, effect, or cooperate, but that man is entirely and completely dead and corrupted as far as anythng good is concerned."[18] Although this formulation clearly and unambiguously rejected every form of synergism, it still made two significant limitations. First, it restricted its statement to "spiritual and divine things"; second, it spoke only of the unregenerated person. Both of these limitations were common in the Reformation's traditional teaching. It is precisely these limitations, however, that indicate the problems inherent in this style of thinking.

By thus differentiating the various relationships, the Formula of Concord undoubtedly recognized an important element of the theological doctrine of the human person. They recognized that the human person cannot be theologically understood as an unchangeable being, but only in terms of the history of the relationship to God. Four states were described: "(1) before the Fall, (2) after the Fall, (3) after regeneration, (4) after the resurrection of the flesh."[19] Then, however, the discussion of human freedom was restricted to the point of time in which conversion or rebirth occurs. As a result, it creates the impression that the event in which the human person is brought to faith through God's activity is a once-for-all event that can be part of our past. Once rebirth is in the past, the human person is again free in spiritual matters.

This is another variation of the problems associated with human-centered thinking. This human-centered thinking is not simply rejected by referring to the formula of "at one and the same time righteous and a sinner" ("simul iustus et peccator"). That can basically happen only through the affirmation that God's working all in all produces the salvation of people. Is it possible, however, to reconcile this statement with the Formula of Concord's differentiation of four states. As soon as rebirth is no longer hidden in God's activity, but is rather understood as a new capacity of the human person, the Reformation's pattern of teaching is in great difficulty. It is not accidental that the pattern of the four states was first developed in the theology of Augustinian scholasticism. Once rebirth was understood as liberation to do the good, then the good which the reborn Christian does must be related to this believing person's freedom and ability. Then, however, justification as God's action and salvation as human action are separated in a way that constitutes a fatal error for Reformation theology. At this point, we stand before an unresolved problem of the Lutheran understanding of salvation.[20] Thus the Formula of Concord's attempt to solve the problem by restricting it to one of the four states led theology back into a deeper awareness of the same problem.

Even the Formula of Concord's attempted solution was of questionable validity. We must definitely recognize that the authors of the Formula of Concord did not attempt to bypass either the pedagogical or the even more serious pastoral problems associated with the doctrine of the bondage of the will. These problems arise even when the question is limited to the bondage of the unregenerate in spiritual matters. How can people be dealt with who hear that they contribute absolutely nothing to their conversion and proceed to draw the greatest possible variety of conclusions? Some become enthusiasts, others Epicureans, who refuse to engage in any Christian activity such as praying or reading and meditating on the Word. Either they think that God will forcibly convert them against their will if God wants to do that or will pour the spirit into them without Word and Sacrament so that they will be able to feel their conversion by themselves. On the other hand, anxious hearts can fall into doubt and despair—even if they are elect and the Holy Spirit is active in them—because they do not experience a strong burning faith and heartfelt obedience but rather weakness, anxiety, and misery.[21] These two groups of people are sometimes made up of the same people whose feelings swing back and forth because they are rooted in the gospel.

Over against such behavior, the Formula of Concord referred to the gospel, the spoken Word and the sacraments. For God's work in people does not take place without means. This again becomes problematic because the human speaking and hearing that mediate God's activity are not firmly bound to the work of God. Rather speaking and hearing are seen as an independent process that is experienced as being under the control of the people involved. That, however, left the back door open to the synergism that had been driven out the front with such emotion. God has instituted the preaching of repentance and forgiveness as a tool of the Holy Spirit through which people are converted and become willing and able to do what is good. Thus anyone who wants to be saved should listen to this preaching. That is something people are able to do. This is dealt with by introducing the distinction between external or worldly and spiritual matters: "The person who is not yet converted to God and regenerated can hear and read this Word externally because . . . even after the Fall man still has something of a free will in these external matters, so that he can go to church, listen to the sermon, or not listen to it.[22] It is true that this statement is followed by a strong emphasis on God's activity through the Word. The question is, however, whether this shows too much consideration for the understandable desire of the pedagogue and pastor for a theological basis for their activity.

It is not clear to what extent this solution was really different from the position of the Council of Trent.[23] The Formula of Concord asserted that people have the freedom to respond to the invitation to help themselves to God's offer of grace by using the means of grace. Obviously, this did not assume that the Word is effective simply because it has been spoken and heard (ex opere operato). Human speaking and hearing of the Word only creates faith when the time is right and God uses it for this purpose. The authors of the Formula of Concord knew that very well. For this reason, they were also careful not to make God's working dependent on human experience. "We should not and cannot pass judgment on the Holy Spirit's presence, operations, and gifts merely on the basis of our feeling, how and when we perceive it in our hearts.

On the contrary, because the Holy Spirit's activity often is hidden, and happens under cover of great weakness, we should be certain, because of and on the basis of his promise, that the Word which is heard and preached is an office and work of the Holy Spirit, whereby he assuredly is potent and active in our hearts (II Cor. 2:14ff.)."[24] On the one hand, this description of the effectiveness of the Word clearly expressed Reformation thought. On the other hand, the problem that lies in this assertion of human freedom to do the good must be noted with equal clarity. The authors of the Formula of Concord would say that they had protected themselves from this danger by distinguishing those external matters, in which people have freedom, from the spiritual matters, in which we have absolutely no freedom. In fact, however, the argument inevitably led to a form of synergism that is as close to being identical with the Tridentine solution of this problem as one egg is to another. That was not the intention. Once the question had been asked in this way, however, the only possible solution was this or something very similar.

DECISIONS ABOUT
THE SAVIOR AND SALVATION

The first two articles of the Formula of Concord dealing with the nature of the human being have already revealed a basic set of problems. The unified view of God's working, which had been the background of individual statements in the early confessional writings, was very difficult to preserve. The *corpus doctrinae* was in danger of losing its head and its heart. This resulted in unclear statements that created an ambiguous context for all doctrines. That was certainly not intended. We must also remember that these theologians of the second and third generations of the Reformation had been well trained in focusing their statements of doctrine so that they would be useful weapons of theological controversy (polemics). It is quite probable that this made it especially difficult for them to look beyond the individual doctrines to the totality of the gospel. It is precisely this discussion of individual points of doctrine in isolation from one another that makes it so difficult to integrate the Formula of Concord into our own theological position. Perhaps, however, the difficult work of coming to terms with it will prove rewarding—if only because it requires us to maintain a unified view of the gospel. If the Formula of Concord helps us to do that, it will assist us to a better understanding and awareness of the unique nature of the Reformation's confession than the Augsburg Confession did with its series of individual articles. For it is not the individual points of doctrine that are of decisive significance but rather the total picture. Once we have gained such a comprehensive view, we will be able to evaluate critically any statement of an individual doctrine, whether offered by the Formula of Concord or by someone else.

Christ as the Righteousness of Faith

Andreas Osiander was a leading theologian of the Reformation in Nürnberg. He accepted a call to Königsberg in order to avoid being subjected to the effects of the Interim of 1548.[25] During his work in this new location, he unleashed a vehement controversy on the doctrine of justification that for a time absorbed the total attention of Lutheran theology. Osiander attempted—and did so in a way that was always related to the basic starting point of the Reformation—to describe Christ as the righteousness of faith. The difficulty was that he did so in a way that separated Christ's historical work of redemption from the Christ who is present and working in the hearts of believers at any given time.

Osiander taught that the historical work of reconciliation is the content of the gospel and the presupposition of God's gracious gift of salvation to people. He said, however, that salvation does not consist in the imputation of the historical work of Christ to believers as that which makes them righteous through faith. Rather, when God's Word is received in faith, the eternal Son of God personally enters into believers and becomes their righteousness. The person who has thus become righteous through the indwelling of God is also able to do righteous works. Osiander was concerned to combine this emphasis on the effects of justification with an emphasis on the ethical dimension of obedience. This meant the history of Jesus Christ was relegated to the past as the presupposition of a process that constantly goes on in the present. Because it could be repeated at any time, justification was seen as a direct and timeless relationship to the eternal God. The righteousness of God that is present in the believer is God's essential righteousness. Through faith, Christ the true Son of God is present and motivates the believer to do what is right. In this view, the history of Jesus Christ is only the presupposition for the event of salvation. Salvation takes place through the indwelling of the Word of God in the believers. Christ's presence makes them really righteous and enables them to do what is right.

If we evaluate this Osiandrian style of teaching in terms of a God-centered approach to theology based on the Reformation's basic decision, we find serious deficiencies. It separated the objective side of salvation related to the person and work of Christ from the subjective side related to the work of the Holy Spirit. The problem does not lie in the fact that Osiander spoke of the Son or Word of God rather than of the Spirit. It was traditional, however, to speak of God's dwelling in people and effective presence in believers as the work of the Holy Spirit. The fact that Osiander ascribed this to Christ as the Son or Word of God alerts us to a more basic abridgment. At the time, both the Philipists, the followers of Melanchthon, and the Gnesio-Lutherans were united in their rejection of Osiander's position; and they were certainly right.

Once again, however, the Formula of Concord's polemical style of thinking narrowed the perspective on the problem. The Formula of Concord defined the basic issue in the controversy: Is "Christ our righteousness only according to his human nature"? Or, is Christ our righteousness according to both his divine and his human nature "by his perfect obedience"?[26] Choosing the latter alternative meant affirming that the righteousness of faith is and remains outside the believer. Faith trusts the history and obedience of Jesus Christ that is preached in the gospel. The righteousness of faith is, and remains, an alien righteousness that belongs to the believer because God has imputed it to faith. Justification is not understood as effective justification that results in the believer's own righteousness—this was Osiander's position—but rather as a forensic, imputative process. The human being is really a sinner but is declared to be righteous in God's sight on the basis of Christ's righteousness.

What did the Formula of Concord understand the righteousness of Christ to be? This righteousness of Christ was his perfect obedience of God. Christ was not obligated to this obedience but rather acted voluntarily.

> Since Christ is not only man, but God and man in one undivided person, he was as little under the law—since he is the Lord of the law—as he was obligated to suffer and die for his person. Therefore his obedience consists not only in his suffering and dying, but also in his spontaneous subjection to the law in our stead and his keeping of the law in so perfect a fashion that, reckoning it to us as righteousness, God forgives us our sins, accounts us holy and righteous, and saves us forever on account of this entire obedience which, by doing and suffering, in life and in death, Christ rendered for us to his heavenly Father.[27]

This righteousness is distributed in the gospel and appropriated in faith.

The Formula of Concord divided the historical Christ's work of obedience into the passive obedience of suffering and the active obedience of fulfilling the law. Not only did his suffering and dying make the forgiveness of sins possible; his fulfilling of the law is the basis on which actual righteousness is imputed to believers. This style of teaching preserved an essential element of the Reformation's basic decision. Those who are righteous through faith trust in Christ as the basic form of their life without reference to whether they themselves are righteous or unrighteous. Given this doctrine of justification, however, it was very difficult to speak of the way in which the Holy Spirit renews the life of the believer.

The forensic doctrine of justification, as represented by the Formula of Concord, thus needed to separate the righteousness of faith from the righteousness of good works. In contrast, Osiander was able to emphasize unity on this very point: The indwelling of the Word of God in people both makes them righteous and motivates them to do what is right. Forensic justification had to think of these separately and that resulted in the remarkable distinction between the imputed righteousness of faith and incipient righteousness of the believer's own new obedience. "It is indeed correct to say that believers who through faith in Christ have been justified possess in this life, first, the reckoned righteousness of faith and, second, also the inchoate righteousness of the new obedience or of good works."[28]

This way of speaking was not a problem as long as it remained clear that this new obedience is as much the work of the Holy Spirit in people as faith itself is. It is for this reason that the incipient renewal is accepted by God as God's own work. As Melanchthon said in the Apology of the Augsburg Confession, "this incipient keeping of the law does not justify, because it is accepted only on account of faith."[29] The actions of the person who is righteous through faith are good because they are done in faith. They never replace or produce this faith. The Formula of Concord committed a fatal error, however, when it argued: "Because this inchoate righteousness or renewal in us is imperfect and impure in this life on account of the flesh, no one can therewith and thereby stand before the tribunal of God. Only the righteousness of the obedience, passion, and death of Christ which is reckoned to faith can stand before God's tribunal."[30] The net effect was to make the perfect work of Christ a substitute for the inadequate work of the believer.

As a result, the Formula of Concord described the new obedience as God's work but did so ambiguously. This is related to its discussion of the freedom of the will and the narrow focus of God's activity in the process of salvation on the point of justification or of rebirth.[31] By doing that, the Formula of Concord assumed the burden of the almost-irresolvable problem of distinguishing justification and sanctification. Justification was now described as coming from outside the believer through the gospel. Faith receives the righteousness of the gospel. This is accompanied by a process of sanctification or renewal that is based on the capacity to do the good which the Spirit has given to the regenerate believer. The idea is that the believer will become an observably better person. The Formula of Concord was very conscious that this could raise serious questions about the certainty of salvation. It therefore insisted that this process of sanctification must be clearly distinguished from justification. It always follows justification and is never the condition that makes justification possible. On the other hand, it can never be separated from justification. Justifying faith can never coexist with an evil intention.[32]

All this revealed a basic problem in the Formula of Concord. Since the love that flows out of faith was described in terms of the new obedience of the human person, good works became something that the regenerate person both can and must produce. Now it was no longer possible to divide the doctrine of the person and work of Christ (Christology) so cleanly from the doctrine of salvation (soteriology) as the Formula of Concord intended when it rejected their confusion in Osiander's teaching. The result is that a new form of legalism was created. Theological thinking was more dominated by the idea that the believer owes obedience to God than that God works in the believer.

The actual presence of this danger was revealed by the way in which the Formula of Concord subordinated the gospel to the law and made the gospel one way of fulfilling the law. God wills obedience; people are to obey God's will as revealed in the law. Jesus Christ obeyed this will through his free and perfect obedience. He is therefore the righteousness that is imputed to faith, the righteousness in which the believer can and should trust. Simultaneously the Holy Spirit is working against the opposition of our flesh to create at least the beginning of the obedience we owe to God.

Certainly, the Formula of Concord's statement of the doctrine is not simply to be rejected as false or as contrary to the Reformation. As soon as the controversy on the necessity of good works began, however—we will discuss that in the next section—it became clear how much had been gambled and lost: the picture of God as working to give goodness to his creation through human activity. God was no longer seen as such an always-active God working on behalf of people but rather was now seen as the God who demands and receives obedience.

Apparently no one noticed that this was happening. The law had assumed the dominant position of the gospel, contrary to the basic decision of the Reformation. "Since . . . it is the obedience of the entire person, therefore it is a perfect satisfaction and reconciliation of the human race, since it satisfied the eternal and immutable righteousness of God revealed in the law. This obedience is our righteousness which avails before God and is revealed in the Gospel, upon which faith depends before God."[33] Did this mean there really is some other righteousness of God that is superior to the righteousness revealed in the gospel (Rom. 1:16–17)? Is this other, superior righteousness really the eternal righteousness of God revealed in the law? This would no longer be the righteousness that comes "from faith to faith" but rather would consist in some perfect obedience to the law that so satisfies God that he is willing to impute this righteousness to faith through the gospel.

The paradox of this whole development is that this kind of thinking introduced human-centered thinking into the doctrine of the person and work of Christ. The Father and the incarnate Son were now thought of as being related to each other in such a way that the Father demanded obedience and the Son obeyed. Of course, the Son obeyed voluntarily because he himself had the right to demand rather than to present the required obedience. This idea was not invented either by the authors of the Formula of Concord or by the supporters of Osiander's doctrine of justification. The ideas that Christ brought a satisfaction to God for human guilt and that his suffering and dying were meritorious because he was not obligated to endure them are both common ideas of Western theology. Precisely that, however, reinforces the observation that the Formula of Concord was unable to preserve adequately the picture of God as working through the gospel. If failed to do so precisely at the point at which it discussed the basis of justification in the person and work of Christ.

The Necessity of Good Works

The basic question about human nature during the age of the Reformation was the question as to whether people were free to do the good. Agreement could have been reached that people ought to do the good and that God's gracious gift makes it possible for them to do the good. Agreement could not have been reached about the way in which God makes this possible. The ideas were too completely different. The late medieval and Roman Catholic approach was to describe grace as strengthening people's will to live, a will that was already seeking salvation by its own power. What grace does is to give this salvation-seeking human spirit insight into the nature of the good that is being sought and into the way in which this knowledge can be used to lead the will. The will is then able to control the passions of the flesh and do those good works that God has commanded to be done in daily life.

Roman Catholics thus described the will to live as being the exact opposite of what the Reformers thought it really was. The Reformers thought that it was necessary for this will to live to be turned away from its sinful efforts to realize itself and to find a new orientation in faith in God's activity. The gospel reshapes the human will and establishes it on a new basis. In this new form, the will to live fits into the kind of human-being-in the-world defined by God's activity and expresses its new orientation to the God-willed good works that we encounter in the doing and suffering that comes to us in the unavoidable realities of life. The following statement made by Melanchthon belongs in this context, "Good works should and must be done, not that we are to rely on them to earn grace but that we may do God's will and glorify him."[34] Melanchthon based this on the fact that faith holds to the forgiveness of sins and to grace. This faith receives the Spirit, who renews the heart. As Melanchthon said, this renewal creates new affects in the heart and these, in turn, produce good works. This described the way in which the sinful will to live is converted through the Holy Spirit who is given in faith. It is this Spirit that reorients our actual lives to God and enables us to do what is good.

The question as to how good works were the necessary result of such faith produced the passionate controversy that Article IV of the Formula of Concord attempted to resolve: Are good works really necessary to salvation, not as its basis but as its necessary result? There is no question that this was a problematic formulation, even though it could be derived from the connection between faith and love, that is, between receiving and acting in the new pattern of life established by God. The problem was that it was almost impossible to protect this formulation from being distorted to mean that the hope of salvation is the motivation for doing good works. That would, however, immediately presuppose an interpretation of the human freedom to do good that would locate this freedom in the will to live or the desire to be saved. When that happened, this freedom could not express itself externally in the liberated will to live. The Formula of Concord undoubtedly made the right choice between these alternatives when it rejected this statement of the alternatives as inadequate: Good works are necessary, but they are not necessary to salvation. The proposal that this issue should be dealt with by defining good works as harmful to salvation was nonsensical. That statement could be made only if a particular hypothetical situation were assumed: Good works would be harmful to salvation if the person doing them thought that these works would merit salvation.

Of course, the Formula of Concord did not settle the matter simply by rejecting the proposition that good works are necessary to salvation. In developing the basic issues in the controversy, the Formula of Concord proposed a second alternative. The question of the relationship of human freedom to the necessity of good works was raised. This, in turn, led to the real question. Are we to think of believers as coerced to do good works in the same way that "the law forces men to do good works"? Or is this necessity only an example of "the immutable order which obligates and binds all men to be obedient to God"?[35] What is the nature of the freedom from the law that only believers enjoy? This question was discussed in Article VI, The Third Function of the Law. It was already raised in this article, however, and the confusing way in which the question was raised made it very difficult to find a satisfactory answer.

The way in which the question was raised was so confusing because the good that needs to be done was no longer firmly rooted in God's working in this world understood as a world ordered by God's command. If the world had been understood in this way, it would also have been clear that living in this world is all that we need to require us to do what will support life. Instead, the Formula of Concord attempted to base human willing and acting on an abstract concept of God's will, the arbitrary will of the Creator that the creature is obligated to obey. Asking the question in that way made it appear that human freedom is threatened by coercion and force. It made it seem that God's activity was this threat to human freedom. The reality is, however, that God's freedom alone initiated this freedom and made it possible. It is simply not the case that there is a freedom located somewhere in the human being that we call the liberated or freed will.[36] As a result, there is no basis for thinking of such a human will as being free or able to choose to do God's will for some other reason than that it is compelled or coerced or motivated by social pressures or the need for approval. That was the position the Formula of Concord decided in favor of when it specified that faith could not possibly coexist with the human intent of remaining in sin. On the contrary, good works are necessary to faith. "Here, however, it is necessary to keep a distinction in mind, namely, that when the word 'necessary' is used in this context, it is not to be understood as implying compulsion but only as referring to the order of God's immutable will, whose debtors we are, as his commandment indicates when it enjoins the creature to obey its Creator."[37]

In taking that position, the Formula of Concord had undoubtedly made a choice in favor of the freedom of the believer from the law. In making it in this way, however, the authors of the Formula of Concord also repressed their awareness of the liveliness of God's will—which had been the special characteristic of Luther's interpretation. In his explanation of the First Commandment, Luther had described God as giving "the mother breasts and milk for her infant."[38] When a mother nurses her crying infant, is she acting in response to a compelling necessity or is she being coerced through the commandment? It is a taken-for-granted act of life in which something that needed to be done in any case is done as a good work.

In the course of the theological controversies, the theologians seem to have lost their awareness of the activity of God as the context of human good works. As a result, human freedom was seen in correlation to the will of God revealed in the law and thus became an independent topic of theology. This in turn made it necessary to emphasize the ethical dimension of good works not only in opposition to the Roman Catholic position but also to some Lutherans who asserted that good works are necessary to salvation. The authors of the Formula of Concord were rightly unwilling to confuse the discussion of justification and sanctification with the question of good works. The result, however, was that good works were now totally described as works done by the free will acting in obedience to God's will and law. Beyond this, they emphasized that the ethical element of good works is an independent factor. "Especially in these last times, it is just as necessary to exhort people to Christian discipline and good works, and to remind them how necessary it is that they exercise themselves in good works as an evidence of their faith and their gratitude toward God, as it is to warn against mingling good works in the article of justification. Such an Epicurean dream concerning faith can damn people as much as a papistic and Pharisaic confidence in one's own works and merit."[39]

That emphasis would have been correct if this statement had no larger context. Given the intention, however, to preserve the God-centered thinking of the Reformation, it was really necessary to describe good works in quite a different way. The Formula of Concord chose its way because it seemed the only alternative, once the polemical rejection of the necessity of good works for salvation had led them to describe good works in terms of human freedom. That left no other possibility of preserving even partial continuity with the Reformation's pattern of thought than the statement from the Epitome quoted at the end of the previous paragraph.

Everything would have been much easier if the Formula of Concord had discussed good works as motivated by love for the neighbor rather than by God's Commandments in the law. They would still have asserted that good works are necessary. This necessity, however, would have been the necessity of life itself. Life is, by its very nature, lived actively. As a result, the question would not have been asked in terms of the necessity of acting but rather in terms of identifying the good actions that support life.

Once again, we have seen how the Formula of Concord permitted faith and good works to become separated from each other because they were no longer thought of in the context of a unified understanding of God's activity. That context was replaced by a human-centered understanding of human freedom. Activity was no long understood in terms of its function in the world—a view that would preserve the spontaneity of good works as actions taken in support of life. Instead, good works became self-conscious acts of the believer done in order to confirm the reality of faith. People were told that they should do good works in order to demonstrate their faith and their gratitude toward God! As common as that understanding of the motivation to do good works is among Christians, it demonstrated just how far the authors of the Formula of Concord had strayed from the God-centered pattern of thought that had characterized the Reformation.

Law and Gospel

Articles V and VI of the Formula of Concord were intended to preserve the Reformation's basic decision and its concentrated focus on God's activity by using the distinction between law and gospel, a basic principle of Luther's theology. Once again, however, the same kinds of difficulties developed as had appeared in the discussion of the necessity of good works. The being of the human person that was saved was understood in terms of the inner life of the soul in its relationship to God. That is admittedly not totally different from Luther's understanding; however, Luther thought of the human person in the God-defined context of human life. For him, this world always remained God's world in the sense that people always encounter God in this world. This is especially true of God's law as it is available to us in the structures of this world, because these structures are determined by God's command and make the activity of love possible. In contrast, the Formula of Concord described the inner life of the soul as encountering God in the proclamation of law and gospel.

This was a very limited viewpoint. It had far-reaching effects on the restatement of the Reformation's basic decision. It resulted in the separation of salvation from the world and described an independent world that can be brought into relationship to God only with great difficulty. In addition, the inner life of the soul was focused on salvation in such a way that it was also difficult to maintain the relationship between the salvation that has been received and human activity. The theological descriptions of the necessity of good works clearly revealed this. We who participate in the realities of life of the contemporary church have not succeeded any better than the authors of the Formula of Concord did. Our criticism of them must also take the form of our own self-criticism.

The controversy underlying Article V of the Formula of Concord dealing with law and gospel arose from the question: Is the gospel not only a preaching of grace but also a preaching of repentance? After all, the gospel condemns unbelief as the worst sin of all. This argument could be supported by reference to the fact that the real knowledge of sin results from the revelation of God's wrath for sin in the suffering and dying of Christ. The Formula of Concord did not dispute this.[40] At the same time, the Formula of Concord was very clear about the necessity of rejecting Antinomianism. The preaching of repentance and the condemnation of sin are the function of the law and are exactly the opposite of the gospel. Luther himself—and the Formula of Concord was trying to preserve his position—had vehemently rejected the Antinomian ideas of Johann Agricola. Luther knew that the Antinomian position separated the reality of the world as defined and interpreted by the law from the preaching of repentance and faith. The Antinomians had said that the law belongs in the city hall and not in the pulpit. They failed to recognize that we sinners are led to repentance by our relationship to the world. We try to use the world for our own purposes. Our will to live tries to control the course of life itself.[41] The preaching of the law confronts this self-serving will to live. It reminds sinners of the life that they should have served and at the same time reminds them of God who leads and preserves our lives. The law as preached by Luther draws us out of our self-chosen world of appearances and does so in such a way that it focuses our attention both on God's grace in the gospel and on the task of doing good works in the real world that has been structured by God's command. Because the law shows us the world as a world structured through God's will and directs us to live our lives in this will of God, we cannot be Antinomians who abandon the world to its own devices without the preaching of God's will.

The Formula of Concord tried to preserve this tradition. Its authors understood that law and gospel belong together precisely because they are so strictly distinguished. All oversimplifications—such as the equation of the law with the Old Testament and the New Testament with the gospel—must be avoided. The distinction of law and gospel is properly used as a hermeneutical principle "which serves the purpose that the Word of God may be rightly divided and the writings of the holy prophets and apostles may be explained and understood correctly."[42]

This discussion of the preaching of law and gospel was a discussion of repentance and faith. This means that it applied the Reformation's basic decision to the work of the office of the ministry. As a result, it is necessary for us to be especially careful to clarify our concepts and to avoid ambiguities. For example, the term "gospel" is sometimes used in a broader and at other times in a strict way. Used in its broader sense, the gospel describes the life

171

and teaching of Jesus Christ. In this sense, the gospel includes the interpretation of the law and the preaching of repentance as well as the promise of the forgiveness of sins in faith in Christ. In its strict sense, however, the gospel is only the preaching of grace. In a corresponding manner, the term "repentance" can be understood in a broader sense and includes the whole process of conversion. Repentance can also be understood in the strict sense as the knowledge of sin produced by the law and the accompanying sorrow for our sins. This repentance can only lead to salvation if the gospel adds faith to this sorrow. Similarly, Christ was seen not merely as the herald of the gospel but rather as the authoritative spiritual interpreter of the law. The Formula of Concord referred to Matthew 5 and Romans 7.[43] The same was said of the Holy Spirit. "Therefore the Spirit of Christ must not only comfort but, through the office of the law, must also convince the world of sin. Thus, even in the New Testament, he must perform what the prophet calls 'a strange deed' (that is, to rebuke) until he comes to his own work (that is, to comfort ant to preach about grace)."[44]

This is the accusing function *(usus elenchticus)* of the law. It is the law condemning the sinner of being sinful. This emphasis is necessary in any discussion of the relationship of the preached law to the gospel. Yet, the statements of the Formula of Concord were in danger of overlooking the fact that the law is effective in this function only when preached at the right time. Instead, the Formula of Concord taught and confessed "that, strictly speaking, the law is a divine doctrine which reveals the righteousness and immutable will of God, shows how man ought to be disposed in his nature, thoughts, words, and deeds in order to be pleasing and acceptable to God, and threatens the transgressors of the law with God's wrath and temporal and eternal punishment."[45]

This general statement was correct—as correct as it was irrelevant to the discussion of the relationship between God's working through law and gospel on the one hand and repentance and faith on the other. For persons whose consciences are at rest *(homo otiosus)* will gladly agree and then use the law to demonstrate that they are pleasing to God. In an effort to prevent this, the Formula of Concord quoted one of Luther's theses from a disputation against the Antinomians. " 'Everything that rebukes sin is and belongs to the law, the proper function of which is to condemn sin and to lead to a knowledge of sin' (Rom. 3:20; 7:7)."[46] Since unbelief is at the root of all the sins rebuked by the law, the law also condemns unbelief.

Such a definition of the accusing function of the law is, however, hardly adequate to explain the way in which the law grabs hold of us at the time of temptation when we experience the terrors of conscience. The problem is that the Formula of Concord described the law in terms of its effect on the inner life of the soul without clarifying the way in which it is mediated through the situation in which we find ourselves. As a result the accusing function itself became the subject and focus of theological teaching about the law. We see what sort of problem this created when the gospel was defined primarily in terms of its effect. "For everything which comforts and which offers the mercy and grace of God to transgressors of the law strictly speaking is, and is called, the Gospel, a good and joyful message that God wills not to punish sins but to forgive them for Christ's sake."[47]

All of that is quite correct and can be said within the limits of the Reformation's basic decision. At the same time, however, we may not ignore the fact that defining the gospel in terms of its effects, in terms of the manner and way in which it is received by the individual person, led to other difficulties. As important a task of theology as the distinction of law and gospel is, we must also emphasize that God through God's Word both terrifies and comforts the conscience at the right time. Any theologian who is at all skilled in distinguishing law and gospel knows that this distinction does not depend on the skill of the theologian but rather on God's working. That means the law and gospel ought not to be distinguished on the basis of their effects but rather that the gospel's message about the person and work of Christ should be the object in which faith trusts. Once that content has been learned, the Word can work both repentance and faith at the proper time.

The controversy about the third function of the law *(tertius usus legis)*[48] can be dealt with very briefly. One side maintained the thesis that the believer is no longer under the law but rather that believers, under the guidance of the Holy Spirit, do good works without needing to think about it and without needing the guidance of a written law. Their opponents agreed that God's Spirit motivates believers to do the will of God. "Nevertheless the Holy Spirit uses the written law on them to instruct them, and thereby even true believers learn to serve God not according to their own notions but according to his written law and Word, which is a certain rule and norm for achieving a godly life and behavior in accord with God's eternal and immutable will."[49] The Formula of Concord agreed with the latter position. This is the right position because faith is not a condition in which the believer is and can now remain. Rather, the believer always needs the working of the law that shows us our willful attempts at self-realization and reorients us to God's will.

In order to take this position, the Formula of Concord had to modify the understanding of the law established in Article V. This function of the law can obviously not be defined in terms of the law's function of accusing sinners. Here the law is the good will of God that is to be fulfilled. Instruction in doing what is right cannot take place without reference to the good will of God as described in the written law. Otherwise the question about what the good is will be answered in terms of the more or less pious feelings and thoughts of the individual person, who will always look for the easiest way. Melanchthon had already made that clear in Article IV of the Apology of the Augsburg Confession. The written law, however, must be combined with Spirit-filled persons who interpret this written law in their actions and relationships. Only then is God's will really done. This means that the law is needed because, but never merely because, believers always remain sinners who willfully seek to satisfy their desire for self-realization—and do so especially when certain of being in a state of grace. "For the Old Adam, like an unmanageable and recalcitrant donkey, is still a part of them and must be coerced into the obedience of Christ, not only with the instruction, admonition, urging, and threatening of the law, but frequently also with the club of punishments and miseries, until the flesh of sin is put off entirely and man is completely renewed in the resurrection."[50] The law, therefore, is not only the threatening demand for obedience that coerces the rebellious flesh into obeying. The law is also a guide to doing good works. This is the new form that the law assumes in relation to faith. "But the believer without any coercion and with a willing spirit, in so far as he is reborn, does what no threat of the law could ever have wrung from him."[51]

DEFINITIONS OF THE DIFFERENCES BETWEEN LUTHERAN AND CALVINIST TEACHINGS

The unification of Lutheranism achieved by the adoption of the Book of Concord was purchased at the price of drawing the boundaries with Calvinism. I have already referred to the religious and political sacrifices that were made in this process. Theological problems also resulted. Lutherans were required to resort to very problematical doctrinal constructions in the effort to resolve their differences. Many of these could hardly be described as derived from the Reformation's basic decision. As was the case in the previous sections of this chapter, it will again be necessary to evaluate critically these sections of the Formula of Concord that defined differences with Calvinism. This will involve the topics of the Lord's Supper, the person and work of Christ, and predestination. The first two were of particular importance in the unification of Lutherans. For there were many Lutherans who had endorsed "crypto-Calvinist" teachings, teachings that were intended to provide a basis on which these Lutherans and Calvinists could agree with each other. In the doctrine of predestination, however, the differences were so clearly defined that there was no parallel controversy within Lutheranism.

The Doctrine of the Lord's Supper

The Formula of Concord intended to define the doctrine of the Lord's Supper so clearly that it would never again be possible for crypto-Calvinist formulations to be considered Lutheran. That required doing more than simply restoring the original form of Lutheran teaching. The proper definition of terms would obviously not be adequate. Of course, there were crass Sacramentarians who set forth in clear German words what they believe in their hearts, namely, that in the Holy Supper only bread and wine are present, distributed, and received orally. Others, however, are subtle Sacramentarians, the most harmful kind, who in part talk our language very plausibly and claim to believe a true presence of the true, essential, and living body and blood of Christ in the Holy Supper but assert that this takes place spiritually by faith. But under this plausible terminology they really retain the former crass opinion that in the Holy Supper nothing but bread and wine are present and received with the mouth.[52]

The Formula of Concord attempted to clarify the Augsburg Confession's teaching about the Lord's Supper by analyzing the controversies about this doctrine since the early years of the Reformation and, on this basis, tried to establish a basic continuity in the Lutheran understanding of the Lord's Supper. It was particularly difficult to fit the Wittenberg Concord of 1536 into this scheme.[53] This was the agreement that had made it possible for the southern Germans to join the Smalcald League. The Formula of Concord first quoted the key sections of the Wittenberg Concord.[54] Then it asserted that the Sacramentarians had misinterpreted the text of the Wittenberg Concord "to their own advantage, namely, that the body of Christ, together with all his benefits, is distributed with the bread in precisely the same way as with the Word of the Gospel, and that sacramental union is intended to mean nothing more than the spiritual presence of the body of the Lord Christ through faith."[55] The Smalcald Articles, however, had "stopped up every subterfuge and loop-hole" by specifying that "the bread and the wine in the Supper are the true body and blood of Jesus Christ which are given and received not only by godly but also by wicked Christians."[56] Additional statements about the Lord's Supper made by Luther were then extensively quoted. This was done on the basis of the very problematical assumption that "Luther is rightly to be regarded as the most eminent teacher of the churches which adhere to the Augsburg Confession" and that his teachings are the norm for understanding the meaning of the Augsburg Confession.[57] Not only was that unfair to Melanchthon who had written the Augsburg Confession. It also, for all practical purposes, subordinated a document subscribed by the churches to the authority of Luther as a teacher of the church. The church's confessional document should, however, have been recognized as providing room for a wider range of theological opinion than Luther's personal approach to the doctrine, which was stated in unusually polemical terms. There was good reason for the Solid Declaration's reference to "Dr. Luther's doctrinal and polemical writings."[58]

In defining the boundaries separating Lutheranism from Calvinism, the Formula of Concord adopted a sacramentalism that at least created problems for the coordination and identification of Word and Sacrament. The Lutheran concern was clear. Faith does not make the sacrament valid as a sacrament as little as faith makes the preached gospel into the Word of God. The opposite is the case. The Holy Spirit creates faith through the gospel. Similarly, the sacrament demonstrates its effectiveness because faith can depend on the gift that God or Christ gives through the sacrament. The Sacramentarians could also apparently say that much. For example, Calvin also said that everything that Christ has done for us through his incarnation, death, and resurrection comes down to us: "It remains for all this to be applied to us. That is done through the gospel but more clearly through the Sacred Supper, where he offers himself with all his benefits to us, and we receive him by faith."[59]

This meant that the Formula of Concord needed to say more and say it more clearly in order to prevent the Sacramentarians from adopting the teaching—for everyone knew that they were saying something different even if they used the same words. This is how Lutheran Sacramentalism developed. This is why the Lutherans found it necessary to go beyond the Reformation's coordination of Word and Sacrament as two ways of distributing the same gospel. It is most remarkable that this Sacramentalism expressed itself only in the doctrine and not in the use of the sacrament. For this reason, it produced exactly the opposite effect of what it intended: it made faith part of the constitutive nature of the sacrament. More exactly, the worthy celebration and saving reception of the sacrament were made dependent on correct teaching about the sacrament and belief in this teaching.

Apparently, the authors of the Formula of Concord found it necessary to introduce new categories into the conversation in order to clarify the issues in the controversy. Thus they spoke of a twofold eating of Christ, of a spiritual and a sacramental eating. The spiritual eating was based on the Scriptural language in John 6—and the Lutherans neither would nor could dispute its reality. This spiritual eating occurs through faith and there was no controversy about its necessity. The Formula of Concord was completely within the limits of the Reformation's definition of the gospel when it described spiritual eating as occurring "in no other way than with the spirit and faith, in the preaching and contemplation of the Gospel as well as in the Lord's Supper. It is intrinsically useful, salutary, and necessary to salvation for all Christians at all times. Without the spiritual participation, even the sacramental or oral eating in the Supper is not only not salutary but actually pernicious and damning."[60]

It was quite another matter that the Formula of Concord separated this spiritual eating from the oral and sacramental eating. "Believers receive it as a certain pledge and assurance that their sins are truly forgiven, that Christ dwells and is efficacious in them; unbelievers receive it orally, too, but to their judgment and damnation."[61] This was not only the fatal error of reversing the relationship between the sacrament and faith. The authors of the Formula of Concord compounded the problem with their tortuous analysis of the words of institution as they attempted to prove their point against the clear meaning of the biblical text.

This is what Christ's words of institution say, when at table and during supper he handed his disciples natural bread and natural wine, which he called his true body and blood, and said therewith, "Eat and drink." Under the circumstances this command can only be understood as referring precisely to oral eating and drinking—not, however, in a coarse, carnal, Capernaitic manner, but in a supernatural, incomprehensible manner. But Christ adds another command, and in addition to the oral eating he ordains the spiritual eating, when said, "Do this in remembrance of me." In these words he required faith.[62]

The reasons given by the Formula of Concord itself clearly demonstrate that the distinction itself cannot be proved on the basis of the meaning of the words of institution.

It was equally problematical of the Formula of Concord to make the presence of Jesus Christ dependent on the natural elements of the sacrament in a very special way. This was not the personal union of the natures that was described in Christology but rather a very unique sacramental union. This could, however, be conceptualized only if the physical body of Christ were thought of as being present. To accomplish this, the Formula of Concord adopted metaphysical distinctions from Luther's treatise on the Lord's Supper of 1528.[63] These were all distinctions in the various ways in which Christ's body could be present in a certain place. First, the Formula of Concord described the usual way in which a body occupies a particular place *(localiter esse)*. This was the natural form of Christ's presence during his life on earth and will characterize his coming again in glory. Second, the Formula of Concord described a mode of presence in a particular place that does not occupy space. That is the way in which the soul is thought of as being present in the body. Christ was present in this way after the resurrection when he left the grave and entered closed doors. Reference was also made to his birth of a virgin *(diffinitive esse)*. Christ's body is also present in the sacramental elements in this way. Third, as a result of the personal union with the deity, the earthly body also participates in the divine omnipresence *(repletive esse)*. This will be discussed in the following section on Christology.

What did such a metaphysical description of the presence of Christ contribute to the understanding of the gospel? The fact is that it dissolved the relationship between the sacrament and its historical basis in the passion of Christ. The Formula of Concord had insisted on maintaining this relationship when it rejected Osiander's metaphysical understanding of Christ as the righteousness of faith. Now it was in danger of letting it slip away. The place of the remembered history discussed in the words of institution was taken by the heavenly something present in the sacramental elements. In the Apology of the Augsburg Confession, Melanchthon had explained the proper use of the sacrament in terms of remembering the historical facts and had emphasized that this remembering is more than evoking a set of ideas. "The remembrance of Christ is not the vain celebration of a show or a celebration for the sake of example. . . . It is rather the remembrance of Christ's blessings and the acceptance of them by faith, so that they make us alive."[64] The Apology, in explaining the article on the Lord's Supper that had been accepted by the Roman Confutation, defended the traditional opinion accepted throughout the church when it said, "In the Lord's Supper the body and blood of Christ are truly and substantially present and are truly offered with those things that are seen, bread and wine. We are talking about the presence of the living Christ, knowing that 'death no longer has dominion over him.' "[65]

At the time of the Formula of Concord, however, the reference to the presence of the living Christ and his benefits was no longer sufficient to distinguish the Lutheran teaching from the false teaching of the Sacramentarians. Rather, these false teachers now used similar statements to conceal their error.[66] The Formula of Concord, therefore, could contradict their error only by asserting that a holy something was distributed in the sacrament. And this holy something became a terrifying something. The comforting presence of the Savior had effectively been converted into an automaton, a slot machine that under the right conditions paid off in judgment and damnation.

> We believe, teach, and confess that not only the genuine believers and those who are worthy but also the unworthy and the unbelievers receive the true body and blood of Christ; but if they are not converted and do not repent, they receive them not to life and salvation but to their judgment and condemnation.
> For although they reject Christ as a redeemer, they must accept him even contrary to their will as a strict judge. He is just as much present to exercise and manifest his judgment on unrepentant guests as he is to work life and salvation in the hearts of believing and worthy guests.[67]

This was just the opposite of the Reformation's assertion that faith is created through the gospel in Word and Sacrament. Instead, the Formula of Concord here said that this faith must already be present if the sacrament is to be received as a worthy gift. The intention was to exclude faith as a constitutive element of the sacrament and define the sacrament as objectively as possible. The final result, however, was exactly the opposite of the intention.

Christology

Both Lutherans and Calvinists accepted the decrees of the Council of Chalcedon as the frame of reference for developing their doctrines of the person and work of Christ. The development of Lutheran teaching almost destroyed the frame. The controversy about the person and work of Christ resulted from the disagreement about the presence of Christ in the Lord's Supper. Certainly, this presence was asserted because of the statements of Scripture—as the parties to the controversy understood them. This understanding could not remain isolated, however; rather it had to be related to other doctrines such as the statement of the creeds that Christ "is seated at the right hand of the Father" and even to an axiom of metaphysics asserting that every body occupies a definite space ("omne corpus est in loco"). The axiom described the nature of bodies. Whatever does not occupy a definite space cannot be a body.

Accepting this axiom as true, Calvinistic teaching described the resurrected Christ as bodily present in heaven, out somewhere beyond the sphere of the fixed stars (the so-called *coelum empyreum*). The image seemed to be obvious, but it also concealed a difficult problem. For the deity joined in a personal union *(unio hypostatica)* to the now-glorified body of Christ could not be limited to being in this one heavenly place as the body was. Otherwise the deity's personal union with the humanity would have robbed the deity of its omnipresence. This problem was a major subject of concern—first of all, naturally, because of the controversy with the Lutherans. The extent of that concern was indicated by the extensive discussion of this question in the Heidelberg Catechism. This catechism concluded that Christ, according to his human nature, is no longer present on earth. According to his deity, majesty, grace, and Spirit, he never leaves us. The question (# 48) and answer were put in this way: "But are not the two natures in Christ separated from each other in this way, if the humanity is not wherever the divinity is? Not at all; for since divinity is incomprehensible and everywhere present, it must follow that the divinity is indeed beyond the bounds of the humanity which it has assumed and is nonetheless ever in that humanity as well, and remains personally united to it."[68] This meant, however, that the deity of Christ had to be thought of apart from its personal union with the humanity. Lutherans used a Latin term to designate this way of thinking: the *Extra Calvinisticum.* Lutherans accused this position of not taking the personal union of the deity and the humanity of Christ seriously.

The Formula of Concord raised these objections and did so on the basis of extensive quotations from Luther. In the first controversy about the Lord's Supper, Luther had developed his understanding of the relationship between his doctrine of the Lord's Supper and of the person and work of Christ. Article VIII of the Formula of Concord quoted this material extensively and basically agreed with it. Luther had tried to demonstrate that Christ according to his humanity is present in the Lord's Supper. His theological speculations on this point led him to assert that since the deity and the humanity had been inseparably and eternally united in the person who is both God and human, we may not think of the deity of Christ without also thinking of his humanity. Since the deity is omnipresent, the humanity must also be omnipresent. This was called the doctrine of ubiquity.[69]

Such an assertion of the omnipresence of Christ according to his humanity required closer definition in order to prevent a conflict with the decrees of the Council of Chalcedon that forbade any ideas about the personal union of the natures that mix them with or change them into each other. Theological statements must distinguish matters that are unified for faith. The human nature as such does not acquire the divine attributes. The person of Christ is, however, so united with the deity that it shares in that which essentially belongs to the other nature. Similarly, the deity which as such is not able to suffer shared in the sufferings of the divine-human person. In this way, the humanity shared in the majesty of the deity—because this majesty belonged to the divine-human person.

There ideas of Luther were adopted by Article VIII of the Formula of Concord. A certain imbalance was unmistakably still present, however. The authors of the Formula of Concord were reluctant to adopt Luther's fully developed doctrine of ubiquity as the standard of Lutheran theology—even though two of them, the Württemberg theologians Johannes Brenz and Jakob Andreä, personally held and had further developed this doctrine. Instead they accepted Martin Chemnitz's proposal of an ubivolipresence *(Ubivolipräsenz)*. This term meant that Christ can choose to be present according to his humanity wherever he wills. There was no intention of coarsely thinking of the humanity of Christ as stretched out to cover all the space in heaven and earth. "Without transforming or destroying his true human nature, Christ's omnipotence and wisdom can readily provide that through his divine omnipotence Christ can be present with his body, which he has placed at the right hand of the majesty and power of God, wherever he desires and especially where he has promised his presence in his Word, as in the Holy Communion."[70]

The limitation did not really correspond to the Formula of Concord's pattern of speculation. If the humanity of Christ really participates in the omnipresence of the divine-human person, we clearly must think of it doing so in the same way that we think of the divine omnipresence. Since God is not present only where he wills to be but rather is omnipresent in the sense that he is in everything that exists, nondivine beings can be present only where God is present. Wherever God was not present, the possibility of being would be so negated that it is impossible even to imagine anything existing under that condition. As a result the idea of Christ's ubivolipresence more clearly reveals the inadequacy of the Formula of Concord's speculation about the presence of Christ in the Lord's Supper than the unmodified doctrine of ubiquity ever would have.

In fact, Luther had already developed his doctrine of ubiquity by asserting the saving significance of Christ's presence according to his human nature even apart from the Lord's Supper. The Formula of Concord affirmed this line of thinking. The sinful human being is never confronted by God's "unveiled deity, which to us poor sinners is like a consuming fire on dry stubble, . . . but that he, he, the man who has spoken with them, who has tasted every tribulation in his assumed human nature, and who can therefore sympathize with us as with men and his brethren, he wills to be with us in all our troubles also according to that nature by which he is our brother and we are flesh of his flesh."[71] This religious concern obviously extended beyond the sacramental presence of Christ in the Lord's Supper and was not well served by a doctrine of a mere ubivolipresence. The idea of ubiquity was needed for this purpose. The omnipresence of Christ according to his human nature was, however, asserted in only one passage of the Formula of Concord.[72] This incongruence clearly revealed that the Formula of Concord was a compromise document and that its authors were willing to abandon some clear statements for the sake of unity.

Since the Formula of Concord intended to present a comprehensive statement of doctrine, it was necessary to integrate these theological statements about the nature of Christ's presence into the larger context of the doctrine of the person and work of Christ. The Formula of Concord did this through its doctrine of the communication of attributes or properties *(communicatio idiomatum)*. It is important to remember that these attributes can be described only in terms of analogies and not directly. Three kinds or so-called genera (the Latin plural of genus) were distinguished. These three were, communication of the attributes as: a form of speaking about Christ *(genus idiomaticum)*, as a form of Christ's working *(genus apotelesmaticum)*, and as a description of the reality of Christ's person *(genus maiestaticum)*.[73]

The first genus, the *genus idiomaticum*, was introduced in the early church. The Formula of Concord, however, felt it was a dangerous way of speaking because it gave the Sacramentarians the opportunity to conceal their pernicious errors. This way of speaking ascribed factors that were the unique characteristics of one of the natures to the whole person. This, in turn, then made it possible to ascribe a characteristic of one nature to the other nature. One example is the description of Mary as the Mother of God.

The second genus, the *genus apotelesmaticum*, described Christ's manner of working: "The person does not act *in, with, through, or according to* one nature only, but *in, according to, with,* and *through* both natures, or as the Council of Chalcedon declares, each nature according to its own properties acts in communion with the other. Thus Christ is our mediator, redeemer, king, high priest, head, shepherd, and so forth, not only according to one nature only, either the divine or the human, but according to both natures."[74] The reference to the Council of Chalcedon is a reference to the letter of Pope Leo approved by the council. The Formula of Concord's statement really went against the grain of that document.[75]

The point that was really at issue in the controversy was the third genus, the *genus maiestaticum*, the communication of the attributes as modes of being. The Formula of Concord needed to set limitations on this concept from the very start of its presentation. The being of the deity does not grow or expand as a result of its sharing the attributes of the human nature. God is unchangeable. As a result, although the first two genera of the communication of attributes could be described as a mutual exchange, this genus can be described only as one-sided. The divine attributes are shared with the human nature of Christ as the result of this nature's personal union with the deity.[76]

These assertions were supported by references to the Scriptures, especially to texts which speak of the exaltation of the resurrected Christ. That, however, clearly reveals the basic problem of this style of teaching. Its ideas are imposing because of their very audaciousness, but they offer no assistance in thinking about the earthly Jesus. The communication of attributes did not take place after the exaltation of Christ but rather in the personal union of the two natures in the incarnation. The Formula of Concord tried to get around this by assuming that the earthly Jesus either hid the divine majesty or emptied himself of it. "Hence also the human nature has, after the resurrection from the dead, its exaltation above all creatures in heaven and on earth. This is precisely that he has laid aside completely and entirely the form of a servant (without, however, laying aside the human nature, which he retains throughout eternity) and has been installed in the complete exercise and use of the divine majesty according to the assumed human nature."[77]

This was all problematical for a number of reasons. Not only did the Formula of Concord introduce the artificial construction of an emptying, that is, of an only occasional and secret use of the divine majesty by the earthly Jesus, in order to maintain a very limited harmony with the gospel stories. It was also necessary to twist the text on which the emptying was based, Phil. 2:7. In the text itself, the subject of the emptying is not the incarnate but rather the preexistent Christ. Once again, the contradiction between the Formula of Concord's dogmatic construction and the Scriptural passages cited in its support show how the polemical orientation forcibly separated the Formula of Concord's teaching from its basis in Scripture.

Predestination

There was, at the time the Formula of Concord was written, no controversy about the doctrine of predestination among Lutherans. Unlike the doctrines of the Lord's Supper and of the person and work of Christ, there was no need to fear a Calvinist infiltration of the doctrine of predestination. The Formula of Concord's statements were intended to prevent future controversies and therefore lacked the controversial tone of other articles. The doctrine itself was presented in a moderate, pastoral manner that attempted to show that predestination is really a comforting idea.

At this point, the Formula of Concord was closer to Melanchthon than to Luther. Luther's *Bondage of the Will,* which contained many coarse predestinarian as well as almost deterministic statements, was not approved. In withholding its approval, the Formula of Concord also failed to endorse Luther's theology in this volume, a style of theology that clearly expressed the God-centered approach of the Reformation. As a result, Article XI of the Formula of Concord, "Eternal Foreknowledge and Divine Election," was another stage on the slide to human-centered thinking. This slippery slope was the basic characteristic of the Formula of Concord's attempt to interpret and preserve the Reformation's basic decision.

The Formula of Concord began the discussion of predestination by distinguishing between God's eternal foreknowledge and the eternal election of God's children to salvation. Foreknowledge (*praescientia* or *praevisio*) applies to everything that happens, whether good or evil. God must, of course, be described as remaining free of the evil, which God foreknows but does not forewill. Evil events are not due to God's gracious will but rather to the evil, perverse will of the devil and of human beings. God's foreknowledge participates in this evil through preserving the structures of creation in spite of the evil, setting limits and restrictions on the evil, and preventing and punishing it—as God wills.[78] Thus God is not involved in the evil actions of people as though he caused them. In contrast, "God's eternal election . . . not only foresees and foreknows the salvation of the elect, but by God's gracious will and pleasure in Christ Jesus it is also a cause which creates, effects, helps, and furthers our salvation and whatever pertains to it."[79]

By thus distinguishing foreknowledge and predestination, the Formula of Concord established an area in which God works salvation that is distinct from the ordinary processes of this world. This distinction makes us certain of God's saving activity. This certainty should not be threatened by speculating about God's hidden will. Rather the principle is established that predestination has not been correctly understood when people respond to it with impenitence or despair.[80] The Formula of Concord carefully stated that the preaching of both repentance and the promise of the gospel are universal, that is, both are addressed to all people. This call through the gospel should be taken seriously, "for the Word through which we are called is a ministry of the Spirit."[81] This meant that those who are called believe by the power of the Spirit and are certain that God will also complete the good work that God has begun in them. The believer can be certain of being called by God. For if the reason why "many are called, but few are chosen" could be found in God's choice, we would be saying "that God . . . contradicts himself."[82] Christ instituted the sacraments as another basis of the believers' certainty that God wills their salvation. "He has attached [the sacraments] as a seal of the promise . . . by which he confirms it to every believer individually."[83] God has also decided "that he would harden, reject, and condemn all" who reject the Word and resist the Holy Spirit. Such people do not despise the Word as a result of God's foreknowledge but rather because of their "own perverse will."[84]

The Formula of Concord thus presented the doctrine of predestination as a comforting doctrine. It confirms the article on justification for it shows that our salvation is based in God's will to save. This will was established long ago and thus is not dependent on any kind of human merit. It makes us certain we are saved because it demonstrates that God was personally concerned about each elect individual even before the world was created. It is a comfort in times of the cross and of temptation because it guarantees that everything will come out all right in the end and thus awakens hope. Finally, it teaches that the true church of the elect "shall exist and remain against all the 'gates of Hades' (Matt. 16:18)."[85]

This definition of predestination as election in Christ gives God the proper honor. At the same time, however, "this doctrine never occasions either despondency or a riotous and dissolute life. This does not exclude any repentant sinner but invites and calls all poor, burdened, and heavy-laden sinners to repentance, to a knowledge of their sins, and to faith in Christ and promises them the Holy Spirit to cleanse and renew them. This doctrine gives sorrowful and tempted people the permanently abiding comfort of knowing that their salvation does not rest in their own hands . . . [but] in the gracious election of God."[86]

This concentrated focus on the gospel is very impressive. In spite of this fact, this approach to the doctrine had its problems. These became evident in the stated criterion for the right teaching of predestination. "The true understanding or the right use of the teaching of God's eternal foreknowledge will in no way cause or support either impenitence or despair."[87] We have already identified this same problem in the Formula of Concord's definition of the distinction between law and gospel. In both cases, decisions were made about the teaching of a doctrine on the basis of observing the effect of this teaching. Then the teaching was adjusted in order to avoid negative effects. Obviously, there was no intention of doing this at the cost of faithfulness to the Scripture. Thus Article XI of the Solid Declaration presented a rich variety of biblical passages that support its understanding of predestination. When the Formula of Concord distinguished between foreknowledge and predestination, however, it followed the path of freeing God from the burden of unbelief and placing this burden on human beings. Did the Formula of Concord really succeed in establishing that only salvation and faith depend on God's election, so that election is always gracious election? Calvin asserted that it was thoughtless and childish to affirm election to salvation but to refuse to admit that God has rejected anyone, "since election itself could not stand except as set over against reprobation."[88] Calvin's strict doctrine of predestination was intended to prevent the God-centered thought of the Reformation from sliding off into human-centered thinking.[89] The Formula of Concord's doctrine of predestination was certainly not able to serve that purpose.

FREEDOM IN CHURCH ORDER

Article X of the Formula of Concord was titled "The Ecclesiastical Rites that Are Called Adiaphora or Things Indifferent." It too deserves critical analysis. The reforms of the life of the church that were carried out on the basis of the

Reformation's basic decision often resulted in significant and permanent changes in the form of the church.[90] The second half of the sixteenth century was characterized by theological discussions that increasingly focused on individual points of doctrine that were considered in isolation from the whole of doctrine. This period was also characterized by the Reformation's introduction and implementation of regulations for the life of the church. These regulations were, of course, issued by the governmental bureaucracies and we ought not imagine that anything like our modern ideas of freedom and self-determination were involved.[91] The principle was maintained, however, that ecclesiastical ceremonies and religious practices could not be required at the cost of the freedom to believe. This was the kernel of the gospel: Christian freedom could not be subjected to the church's law as it had been under the papacy. In this respect, the Formula of Concord faithfully preserved and transmitted the heritage of the Reformation. Thus our appraisal of Article X will confirm what was already said in our interpretation of the Augsburg Confession and of Luther's Smalcald Articles: The form of the church is inseparably joined to the Reformation's basic decision. It is not merely doctrine, but primarily the life of the church that witnesses to the gospel as the Reformation understood it.

At the time the Formula of Concord was written, the expression of this freedom to believe was threatened in the life of the church. Otherwise, no explicit statement about these issues would have been needed. People had learned otherwise in the struggle for the freedom of the gospel. The threat had come from the Interim. The Interim was a law of the empire that was intended to regulate the life of the church in the interim (hence its name) until the council—already in session at Trent—would arrive at a final reform and restructuring of the church. The first interim was issued by Emperor Charles V in 1548 after he had militarily defeated the Smalcald League. Since it was issued in Augsburg, it was called the Augsburg Interim.[92]

The Augsburg Interim was originally intended to be binding on all the estates of the empire, including those who supported the papacy. These latter, however, claimed and received exemption on the basis that the essential elements of the Catholic order of the church had not been violated in their territories. As a result, the Augsburg Interim became a special law applying only to Protestants. This Interim required Protestants to teach about justification in ways that were more in harmony with late medieval theology. It also required Protestant territories to reinstate the authority of the bishops who supported the papacy. Furthermore, the late medieval liturgies and all the usual ceremonies, as practiced before the Reformation, were to be reinstated. Clergy were also to wear clerical garb and liturgical vestments in the medieval style.

The Leipzig Interim was something different from the Augsburg Interim.[93] It was a special version of the Augsburg Interim written for the benefit of Duke Moritz (Maurice) of (Albertine) Saxony. Although the Reformation had been introduced in his territories, Moritz fought on the side of the emperor and against Electoral (Ernestine) Saxony. As his reward, the emperor gave him the title and office of elector, extensive sections of Ernestine Saxon territory, including the city and University of Wittenberg, and promised him—at least, Moritz said he had—that the life of the church in his territories need not be changed until after the council.

On the basis of the latter promise, the newly appointed Elector of Saxony negotiated a special form of the Augsburg Interim that protected his territories—including the University of Wittenberg—from the worst require-ments of the Augsburg Interim. This agreement was called the Leipzig Interim. It had been negotiated with the cooperation of the leading theologians of the university, particularly of Melanchthon, and went into effect late in 1548. Its general character was to follow the demands of the Augsburg Interim wherever possible, that is, in matters related to the life of the church but not in teaching. The negotiators on the side of the Reformation said that matters related to the life and order of the church were *adiaphora*. This was a Greek term used to say that Scripture neither commanded nor forbade practices related to the life of the church. Such matters could therefore be regulated according to human judgment and preference. These Lutherans therefore felt that concessions could be made and reforms undone as the papal party demanded. It is really difficult to know what they should have done. Was it not better for a Lutheran pastor to include a few papally advocated ceremonies in his celebration of the mass, for example, to wear liturgical vestments, than to be forced to completely abandon his congregation. The congregation might then not be cared for at all or might even be assigned a priest who was loyal to the papacy. We can understand why these kinds of arguments for submitting to the Interim convinced many.

Article X of the Formula of Concord agreed with the opponents of the Interim. The freedom of the gospel is threatened whenever certain rites and ceremonies are claimed to be necessary and are therefore forced on the church. Things which are, in and of themselves, matters of personal prefer-ence take on a new quality when they are required as necessary. In such a situ-ation, all are required to take a confessional stand *(in statu confessionis)* and there are no adiaphora. First, the chief article of justification is threatened whenever a religious ceremony is made a legal requirement and people are forced to participate. This creates a new law that must be kept as a condition of salvation. Second, the adoption of such required ceremonies disturbs the conscience of the people of the church, because they are often more aware of the liturgical ritual than of the teaching. They could begin to think that the Lutheran churches had not merely accepted a few external changes but had totally capitulated to the papacy. The conclusion of Article X was that obeying the Interim's demand for changes in adiaphora was a violation of conscience.

> We should avoid as forbidden by God, ceremonies which are basically contrary to the Word of God, even though they go under the name and guise of external adiaphora. . . . Nor do we include among truly free adiaphora or things indifferent those ceremonies which give or (to avoid persecution) are designed to give the impression that our religion does not differ greatly from that of the papists, . . . or that a return to the papacy and an apostasy from the pure doctrine of the Gospel and from true religion has taken place or will allegedly result little by little from these ceremonies.[94]

The Augsburg Interim was often administered with a heavy hand, particularly in southern Germany. The authors of the Formula of Concord spoke out of bitter experience when they wrote:

> We believe, teach, and confess that at a time of confession, as when enemies of the Word of God desire to suppress the pure doctrine of the holy Gospel, the entire community of God, yes, every individual Christian, and especially the ministers of the Word as the leaders of the community of God, are obligated to confess openly, not only by words but also through their deeds and actions, the true doctrine and all that pertains to it, according to the Word of God. In such a case we should not yield to adversaries even in matters of indifference, nor should we tolerate the imposition of such ceremonies on us by adversaries in order to undermine the genuine worship of God and to introduce and confirm their idolatry by force or chicanery.[95]

The Interim did not long remain in effect. A group of princes under the leadership of Moritz of Saxony conspired against Emperor Charles V. In 1552 they forced him to sign the Treaty of Passau, which granted toleration to the Protestants. This toleration was confirmed in the Religious Peace of Augsburg of 1555.[96] Still, the experience of the Interim had helped to clarify the basic principle, that is, freedom to believe is a principle of the Lutheran confession. Such freedom can never be restricted to the internal life of the believer. Rather, it basically defines both the form of the church as well as the confession of Christians. Nothing in that Christian confession may or can be compromised.

8

Christian Confession

Up to this point, we have focused on the task of critically interpreting the Lutheran confessional writings in terms of whether they were valid expressions of the Lutheran confession at the time in which they were written and therefore valid parts of the Lutheran confessional tradition. Now we must ask whether these confessional writings are valid witnesses of the confession in the present time. This evaluation must be made both of the basic decisions of both the ancient church—as formulated in the liturgical creeds—and of the Reformation—as formulated in the Lutheran confessional writings. Do the results support the claim that these confessional writings still represent the Christian confession?

The idea of a *corpus doctrinae* was useful in its time.[1] The development of this concept by the Formula of Concord, however, revealed weaknesses that cannot possibly be ignored. As a result, this idea cannot simply be transferred to and applied in our contemporary situation. On the one hand, it would be possible to achieve considerable agreement about the role of the confessional writings in the right interpretation of Scripture—especially among the adherents of the traditional Lutheran position. At the same time, however, this claim of the confessional writings have been effectively negated by the results of the historical-critical study of the Scriptures. The most obvious result is that commentaries no longer give reliable clues to the confessional tradition of their authors. There is even a commentary on the New Testament that is being produced by a team of Protestant and Roman Catholic scholars.[2]

Does this mean that biblical scholarship is no longer concerned about the truth? In any case, the fact that the traditional differences between the confessional churches have not yet been reconciled no longer seems to be of decisive significance for the results of the scholarly interpretation of Scripture.[3] At the same time, the confession and loyalty to the confession have become more significant in our understanding of the church. It is increasingly taken for granted that a church will identify itself in reference to an already existing confession (Bekenntniskirche) or describe itself as a "confessing church" (Bekennende Kirche) in which the confession is an ongoing process.

These developments require further attention. In Germany, this emphasis developed as a result of the struggle against the false teachings of the so-called German Christians (Deutsche Christen), whose platform called for formation of a single organization of all the Protestant territorial churches. They succeeded in this purpose when the German Evangelical Church (Deutsche Evangelische Kirche) was organized in 1933[4] The larger decisions that confronted the German Protestant churches as a result of the formation of this body was briefly stated and responded to in the Theological Declaration Concerning the Present Situation of the German Evangelical Church adopted by the Barmen Synod, May 29–31, 1934.[5] The extent to which this decision has already been adopted or still awaits such a positive reception cannot be accurately determined. In any case, it appears that the ecclesiastical and theological perspectives of that declaration have been superseded. And it has not been received by many other churches an an ecumenical confession.[6]

The Barmen Declaration has been regarded as documenting a break with the whole development of theology that reached its high point in the Geman Christians. Opposition to this position was especially strong from 1919 to 1950. Many supporters of Barmen considered Friedrich Schleiermacher to have been the theological heresiarch of a whole theological movement that had produced the German Christians as its most typical product. In recent years, however, Schleiermacher has again become increasingly popular. These are very superficial indicators. They do not demonstrate that the basic issue that the Barmen Decalaration responded to has been resolved. After 1945, the German territorial churched experienced new popularity—due in part to people's experiences in the struggle for the integrity of the church (Kirchenkampf) under the National Socialist government. Paradoxically, it may be that this new popularity of the church has negatively influenced the acceptance of the Barmen Declaration. It is quite possible that situation of the church will change again and the question will return in differnent forms. Only then will it become clear whether the Barmen Declaration has had any significance for the churches as they move further into the post-Constantinian Age. Since we cannot predict what those future developments might be, we must focus on the present situation.

Since the first assembly of the "Confessional Movement: No Other Gospel" in Dortmund in 1966,[7] we have continually heard the assertion that today is a time that demands confession, a time when the church is in a new struggle for its integrity *(Kirchenkampf)*. Is that really true? Is it the case that a secularized church and a modernistic theology must be called to order by this "confessing congregation" *(Bekennende Gemeinde)*? The other possibility is that these are ultimately insignificant controversies and that the real situation demanding confession *(status confessionis)* lies elsewhere and is to be found in the area of ethical action rather than teaching. The 1968 Assembly of the World Council of Churches in Uppsala, Sweden, introduced the concept of "ethical heresy." That possibility must be taken seriously.[8]

We must ask whether contemporary confession in response to new challenges can be based on a previous confession that has since become part of the church's tradition. An alternative is to say that the fronts on which the church fights today run perpendicular to the boundaries of the confessional churches that resulted from the Reformation. Perhaps these battle lines can even be described as not being in any relationship to those confessional churches. As concerned as we may be to agree with the basic decisions expressed in the church's tradition, we must still be ready to respond to new challenges. The confession is not some kind of fortress into which either the church or individual believers can withdraw in order to survive the storms of our age with as little damage as possible. The confession together with the Scripture points the way that we must go during this time. Decisions may have been made in the past with the primary purpose of preserving enduring truth against new errors that might develop in the future. For example, the early church defended itself against the heretics' lust for new ideas. The Reformation understood itself as returning to the original truth, the truth that the papal church had abandoned. The Reformation's opponents, the advocates of late medieval theology, rejected such a simplified picture of what was happening. They in turn reversed the Reformers' accusation and labeled the Reformers as really being the heretics who were always itching for something new.

At the time of the Formula of Concord the controversies were primarily controversies among the Lutherans themselves. This enabled them to describe their task as the restoration of a previously existing integrity of the church in terms of the new common slogan, "Back to Luther." The same common historical viewpoint has led to the designation of the German Christians of the 1930s as the highest and terminal point in a historical process of apostasy from Christianity. The current fundamentalist confessional movement in German Protestantism also looks at history in this same way.

This assumption that the process of confession is a return to a previously existing condition of truth and integrity is a very oversimplified view. We cannot allow ourselves to slip into this kind of thinking—especially not because the challenges of our present historical situation require us to reexamine this assumption carefully. On the contrary, we need to consider carefully whether even this common self-understanding of confession can still be taken for granted or must be revised. By asking this question intentionally, we will remain in the mainstream of the basic decision-making process and fulfill the specific task that the Lord of the church and of the ages has given to us as the present context of our life.

FROM THE PRUSSIAN UNION
TO THE LEUENBERG AGREEMENT

Emperor Theodosius issued a decree in 380 making the orthodoxy of the Nicene Creed the standard of citizenship in the Roman Empire. As a result, the confession has—until very recent times—also been a legal requirement. This was a mjaor reason why the religious schism of the sixteenth century was experienced as a political problem. The attempt to restore the unity of the church by military action failed. The reality of the schism was, however, recognized by the Religious Peace of Augsburg of 1555, which provided a legal basis for the coexistence of the Lutheran and Roman Catholic churches,[9] and by the Peace of Westphalia in 1648, which recognized the Calvinist churches as also meeting the constitutional requirements of the empire. No one, however, even thought of the possibility that either a territory or an individual person could exist within the framework of the empire without having an explicit confessional identity.

Although this legal structure was maintained until 1919, the implications of confessional commitment were more and more loosely interpreted. The Enlightenment was critical of all political and social institutions, but it was particularly critical of the churches. It raised the question as to whether individuals could be compelled to change their own religious views in order to conform to the confessional documents that determined the religious indentity of the territory in which they lived. The first solution was to distinguish between the publicly practiced religion of the state and the personal practice of each individual's personal religion. This was only a temporary solution. It preserved the traditional understanding of the relationship between church and state, however. Then the Congress of Vienna in 1815 did the previously unthinkable. In amalgamating many German states into a few large territories it not only disregarded the differences between Protestants and Roman Catholics but also between Lutherans and Reformed. This also made it possible for people to move from one territory to another without having to consider whether they would be required to change their religious affiliation. The result is that all of the confessional churches were represented in all the territories.

The Prussian Union and the Development
of Confessionalism

Given the spirit of the time at the beginning of the nineteenth century, it was almost inevitable that an attempt would be made to unify the separated Protestant confessional churches. The occasion was provided by the celebration of the Reformation jubilee in 1817. This union took different forms in individual territories. Since Prussia was the leading Prostestant member of the German Confederation *(Deutscher Bund)*, the form of the union in the Prussian territories was especially influential on other territories. On September 27, 1817, Friedrich Wilhelm III, king of Prussia, called on the Protestant churches to unite—but stopped short of commanding them to do so. After enumerating the benefits of such a union, he said: "No obstacle which has its source in the nature of the matter remains, as soon as both parties seriously and honestly desire such union in the true Christian spirit. In that spirit they will worthily express the thanks which we owe divine Providence for the invaluable blessing of the Reformation."

The king, however, promised to respect the decision of the churches. "But no matter how strongly I desire the Reformed and Lutheran churches in my territories to share my well-grounded conviction, I respect their rights and freedom and have no intention of forcing anything upon them by my decree and decision. But this union will have genuine worth only if neither pressure nor indifference have a part in it, if it comes clearly out of the freedom of individual conviction, and if it is not only a union according to the outward form but has its roots and vitality in the unity of hearts according to genuine Biblical principles."

The king then announced his intention of setting a personal example for such a union. "In this spirit I intend to celebrate the centennial of the Reformation by uniting the present Reformed and Lutheran court and garrison congregations in Potsdam into one 'Evangelical,' that is, Prostestant[10] Christian congregation—and to receive the Holy Supper with them. I hope likewise that this my example will have a good effect on all the Protestant congregations in my territories and may be universally followed in spirit and in truth." The details of the union were left "to the wise leadership of the consistories, to the pious zeal of the clergy, and to their synods."[11]

The hoped-for Union church based on the consensus of the churches did not fully materialize. A large group of Lutherans in Silesia refused to introduce the new liturgical forms that symbolized the Union. Even more significant was the fact that even those territories and congregations that entered the Union without protest in fact continued to emphasize their Lutheran or Reformed character. The net result was that Protestantism in Prussia presented an even more complex mixture of confessional churches. Alongside those congregations that continued to function as Lutheran and Reformed congregations, there were now "united" congregations. Some of these united congregations had adapted their liturgy in response to the summons and example of the king; others were newly formed congregations. All three of these types were held together in a so-called administrative union. In other territories, however, such as Hessen-Nassau, Baden, the Palatinate *(Rheinpfalz)*, the union was fully established. The confessional stand of the churches in the Old Prussian territories was never clarified, however. That created serious legal and theological problems for these churches during the struggle to preserve the integrity of the church *(Kirchenkampf)* in 1933 and the following years.

It is very hard to discover any single factor that was characteristic of the reorganization of the German Protestant churches in the nineteenth century. In any case, there was a common process of undoing the influence of rationalism in both theology and the church. The "Awakening" *(Erweckung)* played a significant role in this process. Many persons experienced their own personal conversion as they were meditating on or listening to the Scripture. That often resulted in a kind of churchmanship that returned to the traditional teachings of the confessional writings—in spite of the fact that these teachings seemed to many to have become obsolete.

That was not always the case, however. Many who participated in the Awakening were supporters of the Union church. Those who adopted a confessional position as a result of their awakening found the Lutheran confessional tradition to be most attractive. Awakened Lutherans reported that they were surprised by the discovery that their own personal experiences confirmed the statements of the Lutheran confessional writings.

The following statement by Gottfried Thomasius (1802–75; pastor in Nürnberg and, after 1842, professor of theology in Erlangen) was characteristic:

Thus we *were* Lutherans even before we ourselves knew it. We were Lutherans in fact, without having given much thought to the particular confessional position of our church and to the confessional differences which separate it from others. We did not even really know these differences exactly. We read the symbolical books of the church as witnesses of sound doctrine for the clarification and strengthening of our knowledge of salvation; we did not worry very much about their symbolical significance. As soon, however, as we began to ask questions about the way which God had led us, or about the witnesses from which our faith had grown, or about the historical roots of our contemporary situation in the church's past, we became conscious that we stood in the center of Lutheranism. We realized that our Christian saving faith was the Lutheran, as, in fact, the Lutheran Church neither is nor wants to be anything else than the witness to the one, Christian, saving truth; its confession, nothing else than the pure Scriptural confession of the Gospel, which is centered in the free grace of God in Christ. Going out from this center, in which we ourselves have found salvation, we, with Scripture in hand, read and lived ourselves deeper into that confession and with joy recognized therein—or, if you prefer, in its basic principles—the expression of our own conviction of faith. From then on, to value them [that is, the confessional writings] highly and to confess our agreement with them became itself a matter of faith and of conscience. We blessed the church for this; we were glad that we belonged to it. *Thus we became Lutherans, freely, from within.*[12]

The way which led from personal awakening to loyalty to a confessional church, from Scripture and experience to the confession and to the church was in itself characteristic of the Awakening. It was even more significant that this process provided a new basis for validating the confession. It is far more important to understand this new basis for valuing and respecting the confession than to focus on the confessional writings themselves—as we would, for example, were we to explore whether and to what extent there was actual agreement with the statements made by the traditional confessional writings. The experience of faith recognized itself as having been described by the confession. Thus the experience of faith demonstrated the relevancy of the confession while, at the same time, the continuity with the confessional tradition confirmed the experience of faith. As a result, those who had experienced their own personal awakening could now assert that their personal experience of faith was the norm of Christian experience. What they had experienced as "awakening" consisted in coming to the knowledge of sin, repentance, conversion, and being accepted by God for Christ's sake. In other words, they had experienced the gospel of the free grace of God that was the central focus of the Reformation's understanding of the gospel. This demonstrated that they were united with and stood in continuity with the fathers of the church. As a result, people like Thomasius could describe their submission to the church's confession without giving the appearance of being in bondage to a heteronomous authority. This was true even though their personal experience of faith had by no means confirmed all of the traditional statements of the church's confessional writings. For them, the confession was not an alien law of faith imposed by ecclesiastical authority but rather the expression of their own personal experience.

At the same time, this personal identification with the church's confession required them to distinguish their position from that of the Union church and of modernism. For since the confession is constitutive of the church itself, anyone who is not prepared to affirm this confession should draw the necessary conclusion and leave the church. This position expressed the then-popular understanding of the church as a voluntary association. The church as a legal corporation was understood as a voluntary association and the standard of membership was agreement with its constitution. In the church, this constitution was defined by the church's confession. It is important to note that this understanding of the church can hardly be reconciled with the specifically Lutheran confession, which defines membership in the church in quite a different way. As a matter of fact, this desired unity of all members of the church in making the same confession was never achieved in the church. The closest that the church ever came to this was to develop a common confessional consciousness; but this was found more among the clergy than among all members of the church.

The Confession as the Constitutive Basis of the Church

By the beginning of the twentieth century, the distinctive differences among the Protestant confessional churches were obscured by the conflicts between conservative (*positive*) and liberal theology and churchmanship. After World War I, however, new interest in the confession developed. As a result of the dissolution of the state church and the government's resignation of the exercise of episcopal functions, the territorial churches were required to reconstitute themselves as independent corporations. Those groups in the church that were more conservative took this opportunity to establish the confession as the spiritual basis of these newly formed churches. This is still the usual form of the constitutions of the churches. In addition, the renaissance in Luther studies on the one hand, and the emergence of dialectical theology on the other, led to a rethinking of the Reformation's tradition. All this focused attention on the confession. For example, the four-hundredth anniversary of the presentation of the Augsburg Confession was observed with a new edition of the text of the confessional writings of the Evangelical-Lutheran church.

Herman Kapler, president of the German Evangelical Church Federation, wrote a preface to this volume in which he said: "May this new work be a delight to students of theology and to pastors. May it strengthen the joy which the churches of the Protestant Reformation find in affirming their Confession, as the motto of the Augsburg Confession said: 'I will also speak of they testimonies before kings, and shall not be put to shame.' [Psalm 119:46]."[13] It is worth noting that Hermann Kapler was also president of the Evangelical Church of the Old Prussian Union.

In 1933, a flood of confessions and statements that were similar to confessions were produced.[14] The atmosphere at that time was unusually emotionally loaded. This appears to have stimulated readiness to public expression of personal theological and/or religious convictions. Many also thought the new political situation demanded not merely a new church but also a new confession. These acts of confession in opposition to and support of the German Chrisitan movement at first found no adequate form of expression that could serve as the basis of a general consensus. The situation was too confused and the ideas still too fuzzy for that to happen. Thus the Pastors' Emergency League (*Pfarrernotbund*), working from August to almost the end of 1933 produced the "Bethel Confession."[15] The basic theme of this statement was: "The confession of the fathers and of the confessing congregation." It did not become a rallying point nor did it clarify and focus the issues—possibly because it was too detailed and attempted to integrate more viewpoints than was then possible.[16]

On July 14, 1933, the constitution of the newly formed German Evangelical Church (*Deutsche Evangelische Kirche;* frequently referred to as the *Reichskirche*) was proclaimed. It made no contribution to the question of the confession. Article 1 established: "The inviolable foundation of the German Evangelical church in the gospel of Jesus Christ, as testified to us in the Holy Scriptures and brought to light again in the confessions [that is, confessional writings] *[Bekenntnisse]* of the Reformation. The full powers which the church needs for her mission are thereby determined and limited."[17]

Article 2 continued the spiritual independence of the territorial churches and particularly referred to their differing confessional affiliations. "The *Landeskirchen* [that is, the territorial churches] remain independent in confession and worship." This statement became a very important factor in the controversies about the nature of the church that were then already developing. The German Christians had hoped to use the organization of the German Evangelical Church as an opportunity to diminish the intentional affiliation of the territorial churches in southern Germany with their confessional churches. The result would have been one Protestant Union Church. "We are fighting for a union of the twenty-nine Churches included in the 'German Evangelical Federation of Churches' into one evangelical State Church."[18] The controversies with the German Christians, however, soon clearly revealed the legal significance of these territorial churches, affiliation with a confessional church. The confession of these churches proved itself no empty formula but rather was the dynamic definition of their nature as church. At first it seemed that the major issues in the formation of the German Evangelical Church were focused on who would be its presiding bishop, the so-called *Reichsbishof.* As soon as it became clear, however, that the cost of establishing the German Evangelical Church as the Protestant Church of the Empire *(Reichskirche)* would be nothing less than the gospel itself, the question of confession became the central issue.

In response to this situation, some members of the new German Evangelical Church therefore assembled from May 29 to 31, 1934 in Barmen(-Gemarke) and designated themselves as a "Confessing Synod" *(Bekenntnissynode)* of the German Evangelical Church. Acting in this capacity, they debated and unanimously adopted a series of resolutions including the Theological Declaration. In anaylzing the details of this declaration, it is important to emphasize that this declaration for some time served as a rallying point and helped to clarify the issues. This successful use of the declaration is probably at least partially due to the fact that it was a controversial document. Its authors intentionally avoided speaking of a "confession," although given its form, this "declaration" was really a "confession." The authors knew, however, that confessional churches became nervous at the very mention of a "union confession." Such a "union confession" would have merged Lutherans and Reformed into a single church and thereby overcome the separation that had existed since the sixteenth-century Reformation. The Theological Declaration of Barmen had no intention of providing such a "union confession." This heritage of the separation of the confessional churches of the Reformation would become a significant burden in the later development of the "Confession Church," which dated its beginning to the adoption of the Barmen Declaration.

In 1934, however, the Barmen Declaration left this question open. "As members of the Lutheran, Reformed, and United Churches we may and must speak with one voice in this matter today. Precisely because we want to be and to remain faithful to our various Confessions, we may not keep silent, since we believe that we have been given a common message to utter in a time of common need and temptation. We commend to God what this may mean for the interrelations of the Confessional Churches."[19] The inherent difficulty of this position immediately becomes obvious when we try to reconcile this description of the problem resulting from the variety of confessional churches *(Bekenntniskirchen)* with Barmen's introduction to its theses, which were really presented as confessional statements. "In view of the errors of the 'German Christians' of the present Reich Church government which are devastating the Church and are also thereby breaking up the unity of the German Evangelical Church, we confess the following evangelical truths."

Only those who had, by the power of the gospel, constituted themselves as the true church and excluded false teaching from their midst could speak in that way. Hans Asmussen had commented on this in the lecture in which he presented the text of the Declaration to the synod.

> The question arises as to how we conceive of our confessional fellowship and co-operation in the future. To that question we can only answer that we do not know, and we are not so bold as to trespass upon God's government of the world. We look upon our confessional fellowship as something that God has brought about, and not we. Far from achieving an approximation of the Confessions, our theology has developed, rather, in the direction of a growing, day-by-day consciousness of our own Confessional stand. Since God has granted us this great and goodly fellowship, may he see to it what may come of it further! We trust him to bring it to a glorious fruition.[20]

That was all very edifying. It was, however, not an adequate response to the issues—especially in terms of the later development of the Confessing Church. Even today the territorial churches are associated in the Evangelical Church in Germany in way that leaves unresolved the difficult question as to whether this is a church or a federation of churches. As legally constituted, it is a federation of churches; in the thinking of its members and of the public, however, it is a church.

Questions related to theology and ecclesiastical law cannot be explored in depth at this point; however, some problems must be noted. What is the church in the strict sense *(ecclesia particularis)*? Is it the gathering of people in which the universal church is manifest? Or is it the ecclesiastical organizations that we call territorial churches *(Landeskirchen)*? Or is it the federations of these territorial churches in the organizations that we call the United Evangelical Lutheran Church in Germany or the Evangelical Church in Germany? Or is the church the community of those who come together now and then to hear the gospel and to celebrate the sacrament? What is the confession of this church, however it is defined? Is it the confessional position of the organization as described in its constitution or is it the actual act of making a confession that takes place in worship or even in declaration of a synod, such as Barmen was? If the latter, does such a synod define itself in terms of a true confessional statement—regardless of the personal confession of its members?

The theological discussion cannot be limited to this list of alternatives. The churchs experiences under Hitler, however, clearly demonstrated that the organized church and its confessional stance are not merely an external frame of reference which are given—or not given—content by the confessing of the community that actually lives within this organization. The relationship is much closer than that: It is the assembled congregation and its act of confession that legitimates the organization. It may be, of course, that the organization is not validated but rather subjected to criticism. This latter will be the case whenever the ecclesiastical organization and the congregations within it that hear and confess the gospel come to the parting of the ways. Then the false ecclesiastical organization is opposed by the true organization: As Dietrich Bonhoeffer so pointedly put it: "The boundaries of the church are the boundaries of salvation. All who knowingly separate themselves from the Confessing Church in Germany, serarate themselves for salvation. They thereby make their own meek confession. All who knowingly separate the question of membership in the Confessing Church from the question about salvation, simply do not comprehend that the struggle in which the Confessing Church is engaged is the struggle for their personal salvation."[21]

The Way to Agreement

For all the problems, however, Barmen moved the church a step further in the search for unity among the Reformation churches. It could, for example, now be taken for granted that the differences between the organizations of the German churches adhering to varying confessional positions did not necessarily have to be equated with the difference between the true and the false church. This was true even though Lutheran confessionalists continue to be concerned about whether they will lose their own confessional identity in any Union church. At present, this confessional identity actually consists primarily in the stable organizational structure of a particular confessionally defined territorial church. In contrast, the members of these churches are both in fact and in terms of ecclesiastical law simply Protestants. This fact is most clearly demonstrated by the so-called moving-truck conversions: Individuals moving from the territory of one territorial church to the territory of another automatically become members of the new territorial church—regardless of any prior affiliation with a confessional church. They may avoid this only through filing an explicit statement that they wish to become members of a congregation of their previous confessional church.

Since 1945 a number of doctrinal conversations on various levels have attempted to resolve the differences separating the Protestant churches. Finally the Leuenberg Agreement (Concord) was widely accepted. This concord was not a Union confession that might replace or transcend the confessional differences that developed during the Reformation. Rather it was an agreement on doctrine intended to make fellowship between differing confessional traditions possible. "In the view of the Reformation . . . agreement in the right teaching of the gospel, and in the right administration of the sacraments, is the necessary and sufficient prerequisite for the true unity of the church. It is from these Reformation criteria that the participating churches derive their view of church fellowship as set out below.[22] From the very beginning, the standard of agreement was defined in terms of Article VII of the Augsburg Confession. At the same time, the authors were clearly aware of their historical distance from the Reformation. From this prespective they recognized that they shared more of the dynamic that prevailed at the beginning of the Reformation than was recognized in the sixteenth-century controversies. At the same time, they also recognized that the churches' experience in the twentieth century had taught them "to distinguish between the fundamental witness of the Reformation confessions of faith and their historically-conditioned thought forms."[23]

Following this introductory section, there are a series of doctrinal paragraphs under two larger headings: "The Common Understanding of the Gospel" and "Accord in Respect of the Doctrinal Condemnations of the Reformation Era."[24] Given the intention of this document to provide the basis for a consensus, we ought not expect to find very precise formulations of doctrine. The Agreement's understanding of the gospel is based in the doctrine of the person and work of Christ and views the Reformation's doctrine of justification as the expression of the gospel of Jesus Christ. The Scriptures are the "fundamental witness to the gospel." "It is the task of the church to spread this gospel by the spoken word in preaching, by individual counselling, and by baptism and the Lord's Supper."[25]

The differences between the confessional churches that, since the time of the Reformation, made church fellowship impossible and occasioned mutual condemnation were related to the doctrines of the Lord's Supper, the person and work of Christ, and predestination. As a result, these three doctrines were explicitly discussed in the third section of the Agreement. Of course, all kinds of deficiencies can be identified in the restatements of these doctrines—as well as in the statements about the gospel in the second section. If these statements of the Leuenberg Agreement had been intended to serve as a norm of contemporary teaching and proclamation, such critical observations would be very much in place. These statements, however, were intended to document that consensus on the points at issue in the controversies at the time of the Reformation. Given this purpose, these doctrinal formulations really did fulfill their purpose of presenting obsolete differences as really obsolete. "Wherever these statements are accepted, the condemnations of the Reformation confessions in respect of the Lord's Supper, christology, and predestination are inapplicable to the doctrinal position. This does not mean that the condemnations pronounced by the Reformation fathers are irrelevant; but they are no longer an obstacle to church fellowship."[26]

On the basis of these arguments, church fellowship was declared among the churches that subscribed to this Agreement. "In the sense intended in this Agreement, church fellowship means that, on the basis of the consensus they have reached in their understanding of the gospel, churches with different confessional positions accord each other fellowship in word and sacrament, and strive for the fullest possible cooperation in witness and service to the world."[27] The meaning of such fellowship was more precisely stated. These churches "accord each other table [altar] and pulpit fellowship; this includes the mutual recognition of ordination and the freedom to provide for intercelebration."[28] The Agreement then went on to recognize that such fellowship only becomes a reality in "witness and service" and "common theological study." These in turn will lead to the realization of fellowship in these churches' organizational structures and in ecumenical relationships.

In view of the actually existing commonality of the Protestant churches in Germany, this declaration of church fellowship was certainly long overdue. The action of declaring fellowship was well considered. Actual differences were not simply ignored, but rather doctrinal issues were worked through as carefully as possible under the circumstances. More than this was not needed. In view of fact that this fellowship had been so carefully gained, it was absolutely necessary to continue to affirm that all parties preserved their own traditions as confessional churches. Otherwise, the result would have been a superficial sameness that would have sacrificed both the specific character of the Reformation's confession and the continuity of these confessional churches to the Reformation.

This simultaneous affirmation of the present reality of fellowship and of continuity with the Reformation must be constantly reexamined. It is not only the present theology and teaching of the churches that needs to be critically reexamined; rather, the detailed formulations of the basic decision of the Reformation, as these appear in the various confessional writings, need to be constantly reevaluated. In that process, the partners of this fellowship will be able to use their affiliation with a confessional church as a resource in the necessary and ongoing search for the meaning of the gospel. Under these circumstances, the traditional, legally established confessional position of the individual churches can lead to a relevant witness to the gospel and to the confession of the assembled community of the church. Confessional traditions will then not be a burden but rather will prove to be a help in deciding how to respond to new challenges.

WAS BARMEN A NEW BASIC DECISION?

Some fifty years after the adoption of the Barmen Declaration of 1934, we can still do little more than raise the question. As of yet, the Declaration has not been effectively adopted by the churches. In view of the desolate condition of theology and proclamation in our churches, it is even difficult to know what such reception might mean.

Perhaps it will be helpful to turn the latter question around. We would then ask: Is it possible that this present desolate condition is in some way related to the fact that the Barmen Declaration has not been received? The answer to this question is yes. Theology is still involved in chewing the cud of questions raised in the nineteenth century and in attempting to resolve them with the assistance of techniques of the humanistic disciplines. Theologians even adopt the goals and purposes of these disciplines in order to find meaning for the life and work of the church. If our associations with other Christians through-out the world would not occasionally create a draft of fresh air in our churches, we would remain completely preoccupied with solving the tradi-tional problems, defending the ancient battle lines, and answering the same old questions. All that may quickly change, however. When it does, it will have been to our advantage if at least a few of us have been awake enough to know what the challenges of the current age really are. This is one contribu-tion of an analysis of the Barmen Declaration—even though its meaning cannot be here explored in detail.[29] It is necessary, however, to indicate the larger perspectives developed in the Barmen Declaration that can be useful to us—particularly useful in understanding the difficulties of appealing to Barmen in the contemporary church.

Was Barmen a Rejection of Modern Protestant Theology?

Karl Barth's assertion in his brief historical commentary on the first sentence of the Theological Declaration of Barmen correctly emphasized that the issue was "the fact of the unique validity of Jesus Christ as the Word of God spoken to us for life and death. The repudiation of natural theology was only the self-evident reverse side of this notice."[30] Both sides of the controversy about Barmen focused, however, on the slogan of "natural theology." This term evoked emotional reactions. The same was true of the question as to how much of modern theology was rejected by the Barmen Declaration. Had it rejected the entire two previous centuries of modern Protestant thinking and church life or had it only rejected the position of German Christians—which all who were sympathetic to Barmen could easily see was theologically cha-otic, ecclesiastically unbearable, and generally impossible?

The authors of the Barmen Declaration clearly had been thinking about the first possibility. Asmussen made that very clear in his lecture introducing the Theological Declaration—a lecture that was then explicity adopted by the synod together with the Declaration itself. The first section of the Declaration included the following thesis: "We reject the false doctrine, as though the Church could and would have to acknowledge as a source of its proclamation, apart from and besides this one Word of God, still other events and powers, figures and truths, as God's revelation."[31] Asmussen explained the meaning of this:

> For the sake of our Lord Jesus Christ we may not become weary of stressing repeatedly that it is false doctrine when other authorities are set up for the Church beside the incarnate Word in Christ and the Word proclaimed in him. That is what is happening today. The demand is constantly and everlastingly being made upon the Church and its members to acknowledge the events of the year 1933 as binding for its proclamation and exposition of Scripture, and as demanding obedience alongside Holy Scripture and over and beyond its claim. When we protest against this, we do not do so as members of our people in opposition to the recent history of the nation, not as citizens against the new State, nor as subjects against the civil magistrate. We are raising a protest against the same phenomenon that has been slowly preparing the way for the devastation of the Chruch for more than two hundred years. For it is only a relative difference whether beside Holy Scripture in the Church historical events or reason, culture, aesthetic feelings, progress, or other powers and figures are said to be binding claims upon the Church.[32]

Barth seconded this interpretation when he wrote: "What the 'German Christians' wanted and did was obviously along a line which had . . . been acknowledged and trodden by the Church of the whole world: the line of the Enlightenment and Pietism, of Schleiermacher, Richard Rothe and Ritschl. And there were so many parallels to it in England and America, in Holland and Switzerland. . . . The German Christians were contradicted by the contradiction of the whole development at whose end they stood. . . . The protest was without doubt directed against Schleiermacher and Ritschl. The protest was directed against the basic tendencies of the whole 18th and 19th centuries. . . ."[33]

If we are not willing to adopt the historical perspective of Barth and Asmussen, the meaning of the Barmen Declaration is reduced to the rejection of the German Christians at that time. Today almost no one will dispute that this rejection was necessary. This general agreement is, however, due at least as much to the fact that the state that the German Christians served came to a catastrophic end in 1945 as it is to the theological reasons that were given as a reason for opposing the German Christians in 1933 and 1934. There were significant reasons for the church to become involved with this National Socialist government—at least as long as its policies were successful and its unjust character had not become as apparent as it since has.

I cannot accept the position that the Barmen Declaration was simply an episode in the controversy with the German Christians and that this controversy is now over. At the same time, I think that the relevance of Barmen in its historical perspective is more complex than the ongoing dispute about the meaning of the Barmen Declaration has yet revealed. It is quite clear that there was no straight line leading from modern Protestant theology (Neuprotestantismus) to the German Christians—contrary to the assertions of Asmussen and Barth that there was such a line—and that they were not the high point of its development. It is absolutely clear that the slogan "natural theology" was not the right term—unless very carefully defined—to designate the position that Barmen rightly rejected in 1934. As a result, the church today is not bound in its confession to reject this whole concept of "natural theology."

Asmussen, in his address at Barmen, said: "We are raising a protest against the same phenomenon that has been slowly preparing the way for the devastation of the Church for more than two hundred years."[34] That can hardly be the real meaning of Barmen. If it were, it is hard to understand how it could have become the symbol around which people gathered in the Confessing Church and which seemed to clarify the issues. Nor would it still attract and repel people today and, as the heritage from that time to ours, continue to have such a disturbing effect on the church and theology.

This insight requires us to examine more carefully what the slogan "natural theology" meant for people at the time of Barmen and what it means today. We particularly need to explore why it still evokes an emotional response. This slogan represents an unusually complex reality. One particularly important dimension of this reality is that the concept of "natural theology" provides a basic strategy for understanding how the Christian church exercises certain specific religious functions in a Christian society. These are the functions through which this society religiously legitimatizes its goals, structures, and moral systems. The German Christians were not the only ones who attempted to find a way for the church to exercise this function for Germany under the National Socialist government. Other theologians, such as Reinhold Seeberg, Werner Elert, and Paul Althaus—who were, at the very least, not organizationally affiliated with the German Christians—also tried to do this.[35]

This raises the question as to why any kind of "natural" theology was needed for this purpose. These theologians felt that it was necessary to have a religious interpretation of society, of its goals and of its values, that would be generally understandable. It could not be bound to the proclamation of Jesus Christ as Scripture bears witness to him. The reason why this was needed is clear. The Christian church and its theologians have almost never been so God-forsaken as to forget that not everyone believes the gospel—even when it has been proclaimed to them. Therefore it is not possible to make statements about a whole (Christian) society that will be generally applicable and apply to all members of society if such statements assume saving faith in the gospel of Jesus Christ. On the contrary, such statements must be based on insights that are in principle available to and able to convince every person.

This basis is provided by the natural knowledge of God, the obligation of the conscience to support God's will—Roman Catholic tradition calls this the "natural moral law"—and knowledge that the world as experienced is God's creation.

This means that the church has a dual responsibility. It needs to support and maintain this natural knowledge of God and especially of morality as the basis of a just and moral society. This is separate from its task of proclaiming the gospel of God's salvation in Jesus Christ. That was at least the church's understanding of its task through the centuries. Theologians described the church's task in this way; Lutheran theologians did this particularly in terms of the distinction between and the relationship of law and gospel. As a result the theological concept of the law became especially significant for Lutherans—particularly when the church had the opportunity and attempted to exercise its traditional function as part of the social structure.

Beginning with the Enlightenment and its accompanying pluralism, the church very slowly and gradually lost its traditional social function. Such processes extend over a long period of time and never proceed in a straight line. That fact is easily observed in this process. People were, and still are, used to thinking of the church as fulfilling certain functions in society and still expect it to do so. When the church withdraws and stops fulfilling these functions, it must always expect to lose influence, power, and its usual share of authority. At the same time, it is liberation. It sets the church free to serve the gospel. This is how the last thesis of the Theological Declaration of Barmen put it: "The Church's commission, upon which its freedom is founded, consists in delivering the message of the free grace of God to all people in Christ's stead, and therefore in the ministry of his own Word and work through sermon and sacrament."[36]

By reading the Barmen Declaration in the perspective of this sixth and last thesis, I have chosen to define the decision made at Barmen in a specific historical perspective. This goes beyond a simple rejection of modern Protestant theology as typified by Schleiermacher, Richard Rothe, and Ritschl. That definition was too simple and too limited. It was also not a simple rejection of "natural theology." That is a very complex phenomenon and deals with problems that still arise even for theologians who agree with the Barmen Declaration. Rather, the Barmen Declaration must be understood as the church's rejection of all of those legitimatizing functions in society that had been based on natural theology.

It was and still is very difficult for the church to make this decision. Power and influence are attractive and are easily legitimated on the basis of religion. After all, people need religious and moral leadership. If the church is socially recognized and influential, it will have even more possibilities of fulfilling its real task of proclaiming the gospel. On the other hand, this social function of the church presupposes not a modern society but a pre-Enlightenment society in which common acceptance of a closed world view can be taken for granted. This was a major reason why the German churches so enthusiastically greeted the Fascist takeover of the government in 1933. This enthusiasm appeared in varying degrees, of course. People hoped that they would once again live in a closed society—not an atheistic, anti-Christian Bolshevist society, but a society that had been shaped by the Christian tradition.

This is the dilemma: "Natural theology," understood as the basis of the church's function of legitimatizing society, is not the apex of a modern development. Rather, it is a relic of the closed societies that existed before the Enlightenment. This was illustrated by the First Vatican Council in terms of the Roman Catholic situation, when the council dogmatically rejected the complex of developments referred to as "modernism." Even though this kind of "natural theology" sometimes seems to enable us to move with the times, it is really not at all able to adequately respond to the challenge of the modern situation.

The Church's Obligation to Serve the Gospel

In retrospect, it is hardly possible to determine whether the National Socialist government would, at the beginning of its rule, have been prepared to permit an obedient church to fulfill the legitimatizing functions in society that are described above. In any case, the church proved to be far less obedient and compliant than the German Christians and their supporters wished. In spite of this, the fact is that many people in the church took this apparent opportunity to rise to positions of power and influence. This indicated how great the temptation was. This was more than the temptation that always accompanies any possibility of gaining power and influence. Rather, a special price was demanded in exchange for this power and influence. The gospel that the church administers would have been seriously affected. The church would have had to make—and sometimes did make—its concessions to the government's racist ideology. This was immediately demonstrated by the church's adoption of the Aryan paragraphs. These paragraphs, proclaimed as regulations for the church, specified that pastors should meet the same conditions as government officials did. Just as these officials could only be racially German, also called Aryans, so only Aryans could be pastors of the church.

This controversy should already have made it clear to everyone that something else than the distinction between law and gospel that had been developed in seventeenth-century Lutheran orthodoxy had survived in modern theology as the relationship between natural theology and the revelation of salvation. The government was now making demands that would change the church's definition of its task. This revealed the implicit decision that was latent in the explicit decision—a need to make a choice about the church's task that was present long before its presence was recognized by most people. Either the church had to decide to preserve its religious function and power in modern society; the price would be losing its real mission. This would take place by making tactical adjustments and selling out to the government's ideological and political position. Or the church had to be very unambiguous about preserving its mission of serving the gospel and focus solely on this task and on this gospel.

The Barmen Declaration made exactly this decision in 1934. That is why it is relevant to the present situation in ways that hardly anyone understands. In order to demonstrate this, I will briefly analyze the affirmations and rejections of Barmen's six theses.

Since Barmen was concerned about the task or mission of the church, it had to make the basis of this mission absolutely clear. It did so in its first thesis which refers to "Jesus Christ, as he is attested for us in Holy Scripture."[37] The accompanying rejection made it clear that it was not some theories of a general revelation, a natural knowledge of God, and an accompanying natural theology that are the issue. Rather, this thesis rejected any obligations that the church would have to accept were it to enter into an agreement to support the ideology of the people who were in power.

The second thesis underscored this. The law on which the church was attempting to develop a theological basis for its social function was a law that had been separated from the Holy Scripture. As a result, it was necessary for Barmen to assert that Jesus Christ is the only basis on which the church can either criticize or establish norms of action and behavior. This was not some kind of Antinomianism—an accusation that was directed against Barmen. Rather, Barmen established the biblical statement that Jesus Christ is the mediator through whom God had created the world as the primary factor in interpreting the biblical passages on the basis of which the church claimed to carry out God's will.

The third and fourth theses were the central theses of the Barmen Declaration—in terms of their content as well as of their position. These theses dealt with the doctrine of the church. They assert that the church has defined itself in terms of its mission of proclaiming the gospel. The church must therefore be described as an independent social entity. Only under this condition will the church be free to carry out its task.

This meant that the definition of the church in Article VII of the Augsburg Confession was no longer adequate. This definition of the church was formulated in terms of the pure teaching of the gospel and the proper administration of the sacraments. This is of course part of the church's structure and must be part of the church's self-definition. That emphasis was particularly necessary in the historical context of 1934. The state was reorganizing itself in terms of the principle that the leader *(Führer)* is personally the center of the state and the source of all authority. The German Christians were seeking to reorganize the Protestant church on the principle that this leader of the state was also the source of all authority in the church.

The fourth thesis explicitly asserted that the offices of the church were not based on dominion but on ministry. They thereby protect the church's structure from being conformed to the structure of a social order based on power. That would have clearly contradicted the church's character as servant. This decision has had implications for our churches which have hardly been understood in theory, to say nothing of having been realized in practice. Given this definition, it should no longer be possible to establish ecclesiastical organizations that have the necessary organizational structures to serve as part of the larger organization of society. On the contrary, it is now necessary for ecclesiastical organizations to discover their appropriate form and their own systems for justice—at least, if they desire to present themselves as organized to serve in a way appropriate to the gospel.

The fifth thesis of the Barmen Declaration set limits to the tasks of the state as well as of the church. It drew the necessary conclusions from the church's understanding of its own nature as limited by its ministry of the gospel. It clearly rejected the traditional alternative of the church assuming specific functions in society: "We reject the false doctrine, as though the Church, over and beyond its special commission, should and could appropriate the characteristics, the tasks, and the dignity of the State, thus itself becoming an organ of the State." The church at Barmen recognized that the state "has by divine appointment [Anordnung] the task of providing for justice and peace." It also has the task of reminding the state of the limitations of its authority. "It calls to mind the Kingdom of God, God's commandment and righteousness, and thereby the responsibility both of rulers and of the ruled." If the state were to establish itself as the order of salvation or no longer define itself on the basis of God's commandment and righteousness, then the church would have the responsibility of contradicting the state. The church "trusts and obeys the power of the Word by which God upholds all things." The church did not thereby shirk its political responsibility; on the contrary, this was precisely the way to exercise it. There was no clear indication of the way in which the church would "remind" the state of its true functions.[38]

The sixth thesis of the Barmen Declaration summarized: The church's freedom is based on its commission. Its freedom is also limited by this commission, and the church may not misuse its freedom by assuming tasks that are alien to the gospel. "We reject the false doctrine, as though the Church in human arrogance could place the Word and work of the Lord in the service of any arbitrarily chosen desires, purposes, and plans."[39]

Thus the Barmen Theological Declaration drew the necessary conclusions from the church's commitment to its proper mission of proclaiming the gospel. All kinds of objections can be raised. None of them is convincing as long as the gospel continues to be the basis of the church. Then, nothing except this gospel can be proposed as the basis for the nature and work of the church. This also means that the church cannot establish its legitimacy in the eyes of the world outside the church except on the basis of the gospel. It may very well be that the real problem in accepting the full consequences of subscribing to the Barmen Declaration lies precisely in the way in which all this appears to be taken for granted. The Barmen Declaration, however, continues to ask the church in our time where we stand on this issue.

Christian Confessing?

We can expect to find widespread agreement, at least verbal agreement, to the thesis that the church's mission is to proclaim the gospel. This present study of the theology of the Lutheran confessional writings presupposes such a consensus. This does not mean, however, that such a consensus about the gospel already existed. Nor does it mean that those who do think this way interpret this mission as strictly as the Barmen Theological Declaration intended. Are we to understand that the present theological and ecclesiastical situation is to be defined as a time to struggle on behalf of the gospel? This has often been asserted and there has been much talk about confessing and confession. This was especially true of the claim of the "Confessional Movement: No Other Gospel" which was organized in 1966.[40] This movement is understandable as a manifestation of the reaction to modern theology as well as to the historical criticism of the Bible, of the church's tradition, and especially of its confession that has appeared repeatedly during the past century. It must be granted there are difficult problems to be discussed. The criticism of theological scholarship, however, must validate itself by demonstrating its own agreement with the Scripture and the confession. It must express its own position clearly and unambiguously. Otherwise it will not improve the situaion but only add to the confusion.

It is therefore necessary to speak about the actual situation. The Confessional Movement has organized itself as a group that attempts to achieve its goals by gaining power and influence within the ecclesiastical organization. In so doing, its members do not call the ecclesiastical organizations and their power structure into question on the basis of the gospel. They only question the way in which the churches' leaders have attempted to maintain the unity of the churches in spite of the centrifugal forces at work in them. This movement objects to pluralism in the church. That became especially clear in the controversies during the 1970s in which it attacked the annual national gathering of Christians in Germany *(Kirchentag)* as fostering pluralism. When the leaders of this movement failed to reshape these conferences in terms of their own purposes they organized competitive conferences *(Gemeindetag)*. When these proved to be not very successful, they carried the controversy into other areas. Without attempting to decribe all that this movement has tried to do, I can only ask its members: In what you have done, you have repeatedly appealed to the authority of the Barmen Declaration. But did you really accept what it says and act upon it? This question must be asked especially about the central statements on the nature of the church. As long as this is not clearly the case, there is no basis for this movement's claim that the gospel is represented in our churches primarily through these confessing fellowships and assemblies of individual church members.

It is important to state very clearly what this "Confessional Movement: No Other Gospel" really represents. This movement's Düsseldorf Declaration of 1967 consciously imitated the form of the Barmen Theological Declaration.[41] The second thesis cited John 14:9 and Matt. 11:27 and then asserted: "We confess the gospel: The eternal Son of God became a human being [Mensch] in the historical Jesus of Nazareth and still remained God. We confess the gospel: The Son of God reveals his Father to us as our Creator and as our Father. We therefore reject this false doctrine: Jesus was merely a human being and we are able to know who God is and have fellowship with him even without faith in the Son of God." What does it mean to say that "the eternal Son of God became a human being [Mensch] in the historical Jesus of Nazareth and still remained God"? Remember the way in which the early church described the person of Christ.[42] The early church thought carefully about these matters and still did not arrive at any generally acceptable solution. The authors of the Düsseldorf Declaration did not go to any such trouble. Did they want to recapitulate the Nicene Creed? Then all they had to do was to say that the Son of God, of one being with the Father, was the subject of the incarnation. It would not even be necessary to say that this subject remained himself. The 1967 statement, however, gave the impression that the incarnation was not complete. If the intention was to say that the human being Jesus of Nazareth is also true God, however—and that seems to be the meaning of the very watered down rejection—and that Jesus was not simply a human being, then they should have said that. Of course, they would also have to add that they were using the traditional theological concept of the communication of attributes (communicatio idomatum)[43] in its first sense, as a way of speaking. Otherwise their statement would—if evaluated in terms of the traditional language of the church—be false, because the subject of the traditional christological statements is not humanity in and of itself as the human person of Jesus Nazareth but rather the divine-human person. No matter how anyone tries to twist and turn this statement of the Düsseldorf Declaration, it does not stand the test of conforming to the church's traditional way of describing and confessing the person of Christ. As long as it cannot even achieve that, we cannot possibly grant the claim of the "Confessional Movement: No Other Gospel" to be a clear confession of the gospel.

Nothing more needs to be said. No clear statement was offered that could be accepted or rejected. There was no proof of continuity with the church's confession and its formulations. Excited emotions alone are not enough to prove the claim of representing the church's confession.

Thus the question as to whether there is a Christian confession remains undecided. Such a confession may be made when the congregation gathers for worship and confesses its faith. The value of that continuity of confessing should not be underestimated. The decision, however, as to how and when such Confession should result in divisions and distinctions within the church must be left to the right time.

9

The Confession as Theological Criterion

It is, at present, simply not possible to see what a Christian confession would be like. This is related to the problematic situation of our territorial church in which membership is taken for granted *(Volkskirche)*. These churches are in a transitional situation. Nothing would be gained by insisting on decisive clarity as long as so many members of the church could not participate in the change. That situation can, however, change very rapidly. Although the confession remains problematic, the theological possibilities inherent in the confession are far from having been exhausted. It would be a fatal error to understand or, more likely, misunderstand the confessional tradition as though it could only be interpreted in a fundamentalistic way and to use it as the basis of all kinds of sentimental dreams about the past. Of course, the confessional tradition makes binding claims. Our obligation to this tradition, however, is also a help to us and frequently liberates us from other claims that make much more severe demands and offer much less help.

This last chapter will attempt to identify some critical points in the current theological discussion and to demonstrate how the confession might be helpful. Obviously, this will not help us solve all our problems or answer all our questions. It may, however, assist us to use the answers of the fathers as a resource in answering our questions. To the extent that we succeed in doing this, it is possible that the questions will be transformed. That may in turn enable us to find answers where the previous discussion has been going around in circles.

Certainly, it is possible to seek help from the confession in dealing with every theologically relevant question. The focus of this chapter, however, will

211

be on central issues that have been discussed for a long time and to show how the confession might give us some hints about possible solutions. One such issue is the complex of ideas commonly called "biblical theology." This is the point at which a broad range of questions associated with the historical approach to biblical interpretation manifest themselves in a wide variety of ways. Another issue is the "doctrine of the two kingdoms." This doctrine has frequently been used to exploit the confession for conservative political goals. This has been achieved by using this slogan to repress the claim of the gospel and convert it into a kind of "inner experience" and then to define the supposedly "real" task of the church as the care of souls *(Seelsorge)*. Finally I shall once again consider the possible significance of the confession for preaching, because the task of preaching requires us to speak about the gospel in a binding way. Preachers who try to speak about the gospel without accepting this obligatory claim to believe it themselves seek to exempt themselves from the demands that their sermons make on those who hear their sermons. The following suggestions for further work are intended to stimulate engagement with the confession itself. That will be a rewarding experience.

"BIBLICAL THEOLOGY" AS SYMPTOMATIC FOR THE PROBLEM OF SCHOLARLY INTERPRETATION OF THE BIBLE

Scholarly interpretation of the Bible currently uses a historical or, as most prefer to emphasize, a historical-critical method. Although that is presently usually taken for granted, it is still necessary to evaluate the results of this method of biblical interpretation. This method of scholarly scientific interpretation does work. The question is whether the results, measured in terms of their benefits to the church, justify the investment in time and effort. This is much more than a matter of calculating the cost-effectiveness and much more than some covert fundamentalist aversion to critical methods. The important question is whether this kind of exegesis actually helps us to preach the gospel—and that is the real task of the church—in a way that makes it more likely to be heard as a saving message. The question as to whether scientific exegesis has withdrawn itself from the struggle for the truth of the gospel was already raised in connection with the mention of a Protestant-Catholic commentary on the New Testament.[1] Such a joint commentary is probably possible because the Roman Catholic participants in this work have loosened the relationship between their loyalty to the Roman Catholic confessional position and the interpretation of Scripture. As a result, they are therefore able to use the historical method with less embarrassment. As much as such an obviously genuine common undertaking is to be approved, the question still must be raised as to what has happened to the still-unresolved controversies about the truth. At the time of the Reformation, these controversies were carried out in terms of the disputes about the interpretation of Scripture. Are we now to understand that the principle "that the prophetic and apostolic writings of the Old and New Testaments are the only rule and norm according to which all doctrines and teachers alike must be appraised and judged" has been set aside?[2] Or has this function of judging been transferred to another area of theology, perhaps to dogmatics? In that case, we would have to distinguish two kinds of scriptural interpretation. The one would be a scientific, scholarly, historical kind of interpretation that would stop at the level of describing what the Scripture had once meant; the other would be a evaluative, normative, judging kind of dogmatic interpretation, which would be less "scientific" in exchange for being more relevant to the life and work of the church. Obviously, many scientific exegetes would not approve of this distinction. The question, however, still remains to be answered: What are the implications of such a joint commentary for theological method?

This problem can be demonstrated by exploring its implications for "biblical theology." Without going into individual details, the basic question is, How can the interpretation of Scripture maintain what the church has always presupposed in its use of Scripture: The Bible, the entire Holy Scripture of the Old and New Testaments is a clear witness to divine truth? The church's proclamation has asserted this. Faith has established its certainty by referring to the Scripture. Neither this proclamation nor this basis of faith is a mere claim. The issue here is not some fundamentalistic dogma of verbal inspiration and an accompanying claim that the Scripture is infallible. Rather, the issue arises out of the experience of those who have reflected on and come to understand their own experience as having heard the saving gospel through the message of Scripture. Once again: How can this basic presupposition of the church's usage of Scripture be maintained by the scientific interpretation of Scripture? That can be done only by consistently understanding the Scripture as a clear witness to the saving gospel.

It is naturally possible to dismiss the question by referring to the way in which critical interpretation of Scripture developed.[3] This means, however, that exegesis is absolved of its responsibility to answer questions about how the message of Scripture has anything effective or redeeming to say to our contemporary situation. On the other hand, however, any attempt to answer this question seriously demonstrates that the historical-critical method—although apparently taken for granted as valid—is really a very questionable process. The following three sections will demonstrate this (1) by describing this question about method more fully, (2) then exposing some of the actual problems inherent in the compromises made by scholarly scientific interpretation of Scripture, and (3) indicating possible solutions that express the basic decisions of the confession.

The Presuppositions of
Historical-Critical Scholarship

Naturally, modern scientific scholarship, especially in the field of history, is a very complex phenomenon. This needs to be kept in mind—in spite of the fact that the issues will be oversimplified for the purposes of the following discussion. The significance of the question that has been raised can only be demonstrated by using a model of a process that in actual practice is always more complex. Modern scientific scholarship proceeds on the basis of a very strict presupposition: Every scientific process must be designed in such a way that any other qualified person could repeat it. The other person needs only be adequately informed about the situation, knowledgeable about the current state of the discipline, and have mastered the methods appropriate to the field of investigation. All other qualifications of this second person are totally irrelevant, for example, whether man or woman, Christian, Muslim, or Marxist, psychological condition on any given day, and whether motivated by love of money or by the joy of scholarship. This means that scientific study can be carried out by any qualified person. This is the necessary condition of scientific objectivity.[4] Such objectivity also requires that no value judgments be made, such as describing something as good or bad, beautiful or ugly, etc. Rather, every effort must be made to arrive at a description that is as objective as possible.

In historical studies, this takes the form of an objective reconstruction of the past. To the extent that such a reconstruction exactly corresponds to the reality of past history, it can be described as "true" in the sense of a scientific understanding of truth. (Remember that this is a skeleton model of the scientific process, not a description of its reality.) The people who lived in the past, however, were not abstract scholars. They were living people, with faith and hope, with emotions and passions, who made decisions on the basis of their own personal interests. The historian who attempts to reconstruct the past must use the materials that have been handed down—usually written documents—in order to draw conclusions about such living human beings. That is possible only through empathizing with their humanity. Such empathy with faith, hope, and love, with values and decisions that are made in the midst of life is, however, something quite different from the objective distance required by scientific investigation. This creates a dilemma that can be described in terms of the model: These abstract "historians" must be able to draw on their own individual personal experience of life in order to be able to empathize with the people they are studying. That, however, inevitably makes objectivity impossible.

For example, an atheist will have more difficulty in empathizing with a believing Christian than a scholar who is also a Christian. A man will have more difficulty empathizing with a woman than another woman would. If this supposition is valid, the universality and the objectivity of the reconstruction of history would suffer as a result of these limitations. This dilemma will not be explored as a problem of historical study in general but rather in terms of its significance for the claims to objectivity made by historical-critical interpretation of the Bible.

The methodology of scientific scriptural interpretation should follow the same pattern as the interpretation of other documents from the past. This assertion is made over and over again as a basic principle of historical-critical biblical interpretation. If that basic principle can actually be observed, it is immediately clear that the effort to write a Protestant-Catholic commentary is quite achievable. For it is also taken for granted that the abstract subjects who carry on historical study are neither Protestant nor Roman Catholic. In fact, however, this model of unlimited universality cannot be realized. This is due not only to the fact that historians must emphasize with people of the past and the present reality of historians' human nature plays a significant role in this process. On the contrary, exegetes will never be able to lay aside their personal identities as Protestants or Roman Catholics, nor should they want to. Their ongoing experiences as Christians in a specific ecclesiastical fellowship will influence their understanding the biblical texts—although they may not be aware that this is happening. None of that in any way changes the ideal of historical work, that is, the desire to be as objective as possible in describing what the past was like.

Wilhelm Wrede (1859–1906) was a good example of this. His programatic proposal defining the task of the method of New Testament theology asserted:

> Under the present circumstances, those who wish to engage in scientific research in New Testament theology must have the capacity to become interested in historical research. They must be driven by a pure unprejudiced interest in knowledge that permits them to pay attention to every insight that comes to their attention. They must be able to distinguish their own modern patterns of thought as alien to the past. No matter how much they value their own view of things, they must completely isolate them and suspend their own value judgments. For their intention is nothing more than to learn how things really were like then.[5]

This kind of historical positivism is very impressive—at least as long as we do not carefully ask what "dogmas" are presupposed. Yet it is not useful for interpreting Scripture for the church. For the church needs an interpretation of Scripture that is a resource in the search for the saving gospel in a form that can be received here and how. The strict method proposed by Wrede eliminates precisely this possibility. For listening to the gospel in this way is not something that can be done by the abstract subject of scientific research but only by the whole person as a unique individual living in the here and now. Heard in this way, the gospel addresses itself to our personal uniqueness.

215

Indeed the gospel is formed and shaped by this uniqueness. For this reason, the gospel cannot meet the demand for abstract universality made by modern scientific method.

This does not have to be spelled out in detail. It is enough to have made it clear that the basic demand of modern science for universality is not compatible with the manner in which the gospel addresses each of us in a way that matches our own unique individuality. The gospel is addressed to and seeks each person out individually in their own time and space. It is important that the problematical nature of this aspect of historical-critical interpretation of the Scripture be recognized before there is any discussion as to whether it is legitimate to step outside such interpretation in order to interpret the Scripture for the church.

The Actual Nature of the Scientific Interpretation of Scripture as a Compromise

Attention has been drawn to the basic dilemma of scientific scholarship in historical studies: Any historical reconstruction of past human experience only results from empathy with the past. Such empathy, however, demands the kind of close personal involvement that is possible only for a living individual human person. An abstract scientist, who ideally has no presuppositions and is not personally affected by the results of the study, cannot experience this. Thus, interpreters of biblical texts need to have a personal understanding of the subject matter of these texts—to describe it very generally, an understanding of the gospel and of faith. For this reason, interpreters can easily make the transition from empathy with lives now past, that were lived in faith in response to some past witness of the gospel, to their own experience of hearing the gospel and of being personally affected by the content of the biblical texts. Judged by the above-described model of scientific historical research, that is a breach of the scientific method. The knowledge that results from this approach is not universally available—as scientific knowledge must be. It is the very nature of the gospel to address the individual person at the point of uniqueness. It is not addressed to ideal scientific researchers who have abstracted themselves from their unique individual experiences. To say it from another perspective: The objective scientist cannot understand the gospel. It is by its very nature not available to modern scientific research. Since, however, the would-be scientific researcher may not be aware that the scientific method has been breached, it may be regarded as a possible accidental failure and therefore not a factor to be taken into account in describing the scientific methods of historical-critical biblical interpretation.

For the purposes of this discussion of method, however, this breach must be defined as clearly as possible. The topic is so delicate and controversial that discussion is almost impossible when these basic methodological issues have not been clearly defined. Thus, I presuppose that exegetes interpret Scripture in this transitional space between using the kind of empathy permitted by the scientific method and experiencing Scripture as addressed to them personally. That is right and proper—only thus can the interpretation of Scripture bear fruits useful in the church. For the church must be concerned about the ways in which the testimony of Scripture is experienced as gospel in the here and now. This is the question that the interpreter asks when personally addressed by the gospel. The interpreter who does not experience this personal address will not be able to give any useful answers to the church's question.

It is for this reason that scientific scriptural interpretation is compromised in terms of its method. The breach of the scientific method is accepted as necessary and fruitful. Only those who are not aware of this breach of the scientific method will disagree and claim that they practice purely scientific interpretation. Once that claim is made, the discussion becomes difficult. For the issue now is no longer the fact that the interpreters mediate between their scientific method and the concerns of the church but the issue of scientific method itself. That makes for bitter discussions. Once it is recognized, however, that the issue is the balance between more or less emphasis on scientific distance from the material on the one hand, and on the obligation to serve the church on the other hand, the discussion about method becomes more relaxed.

This raises the question as to whether the compromise that is being discussed can be more clearly described. The fascinating character of Rudolf Bultmann's method of interpretation is certainly due in part to the fact that he provides a method for making this compromise. Obviously his followers have not preserved his methodological discipline. Bultmann himself, however, described the distinction between the historical reconstruction of the situation in which the Scriptures were written and their interpretation for the present: "Either the writings of the New Testament can be interrogated as the 'sources' which the historian interprets in order to reconstruct a picture of primitive Christianity as a phenomenon of the historical past, or the reconstruction stands in the service of the interpretation of the New Testament writings under the presupposition that they have something to say to the present. The latter interest is the one for which historical labor is put to service in the presentation here offered."[6] This distinction seems to leave enough room in the reconstruction of the past through a strict scientific method for the gospel still to be able to address interpreters personally as is necessary for the kind of interpretation that the church needs. If the text is interpreted in order to arrive at a historical reconstruction, interpreters find that their personal relationship to the gospel is a resource in empathizing with people in the past. If, however, the historical reconstruction of the past is placed in the service of interpretation—as Bultmann claims it is in his *Theology of the New Testament*—then the interpreter's personal relationship to the gospel is transformed into being personally addressed by the subject matter of the biblical text.

Of course, Bultmann's view was not so simple that he abandoned the scientific method and its presupposition of the personally uninvolved scientist when he was discussing the interpretation of Scripture. This cannot be demonstrated here, since it would require an analysis of Bultmann's whole method of interpretation. What is important for our purposes is that Bultmann consciously asked a question that many interpreters of Scripture seem not to be aware of as an issue. I merely note that existential interpretation of Scripture attempts to interpret the fact that the interpreter is personally addressed by the gospel as the result of certain universal existential characteristics of all human beings. Thus Bultmann still saw the interpretation of the gospel in terms of the scientific method's claim to be a universally applicable process. Bultmann's own work followed this approach in a very disciplined way. His followers have not done so, however. Bultmann's claim that the existential interpretation of the New Testament could in principle be repeated by any scientific observer has given way to subjective explication of the text. What prevents such subjective explication from being arbitrary? Undoubtedly, the interpreters' healthy relationship to the church can protect them from the subjective excesses of their personal faith. That is, however, not a very reassuring answer to the question.

The Favorable Odds Resulting from Agreeing that the Gospel Heard in Scripture Will Be Interpreted as Filtered Through the Church's Confession

When the historical-critical method of biblical interpretation first appeared on the scene, it claimed that it would liberate biblical interpretation from the domination of the church's dogmas. It is another question as to how far this intention has agreed with the task of biblical interpretation. The whole range of problems that have currently manifested themselves in the controversy about the possibility of a "biblical theology" demonstrate that it is not only dogmaticians who need to come to terms with using Scripture for the church's purposes. That is also the task of those interpreters of Scripture who wish to be serious about their commitment to the church as well as to scientific method. Perhaps a better understanding of the task will provide the basis for reconciling the conflict between the interpretation of Scripture and dogmatics. For that conflict to be resolved, however, the discussion must work through the way in which the scientific interpretation of Scripture is always accompanied by the personal encounter between the interpreter and the gospel. Theologians—whether they are exegetes or dogmaticians—must describe the "what" (*fides, quae creditur*) and the "how" (*fides qua creditur*). If we follow the Reformation's list of priorities,[7] The goal of such discussions is always agreement about the gospel that is heard. At first, these seem to be only matters of form. They have more far-reaching significance, however, than definitions of method usually have.

The various possibilities are to be evaluated. It is not enough to simply say: This or that is how Paul proclaimed the gospel. If that is true in the sense of corresponding to reality, then it is true—at least, in the sense of the theory of truth which says that statements about history are true if they accurately describe the past. It is also necessary to say this is the gospel. This implicitly includes that this gospel should still be proclaimed in the way in which it has now been described. There is then no place in the church for anything that contradicts this gospel. For this gospel is the saving truth. Certainly, this truth can not be scientifically established. For the gospel cannot be "objectively" examined in the sense that all persons qualified to follow a specific method could discover the gospel for themselves. Human beings do not find the truth of the gospel. Rather, the truth of the gospel seeks out specific persons who are then able to confess that they have been encountered and to say: This is how I have heard the gospel.

Are there then any criteria at all for the truth of what claims to be a statement of the gospel? Of course, the Scripture is such a criterion. When there is doubt about the gospel, however, it is the interpretation and application itself that is the issue. Such disagreements must be resolved in some way.

The Fundamentalist position does not recognize this; for it, there is no difference between the biblical words and the process by which Fundamentalists understand the meaning of the biblical text. Fundamentalists identify their own understanding of the Word with the biblical text. This approach, however, leads to fruitless arguing. There must be a way of arriving at a common understanding when there is disagreement about the interpretation of Scripture.

We find, however, that the historical-critical method of interpretation has not been very useful in helping to resolve these controversies. This method has explicitly excluded the question of the truth of the gospel. Its practitioners may, therefore, not complain when they are not given any significant role in resolving the controversy.

In these controversies about the truth of the gospel the church's confession with its basic decisions has a significant role to play. The confession is not a statement of the gospel that can never be questioned because it is valid under all circumstances and only needs to be repeated. This would be a Fundamentalistic understanding, that is, a misunderstanding of the confession. There are other possibilities. The statements in the confessional writings are themselves formulas that were once adopted by consensus because they decided specific questions about the truth of the gospel in a particular situation. It is this act of consensus that becomes exemplary for later efforts to reach an agreement. Of course, the earlier statement of consensus will become a factor in arriving at the new consensus.

This is still a very preliminary consideration. The question about a "biblical theology" has not yet been answered. Any discussion of the content of such a theology must attempt to coordinate the exegetical issues with the basic decisions of the confession. One issue that will undoubtedly be discussed is that of the unity of the Old and the New Testaments. The issues will, however, be still deeper. For example, in what sense would such a biblical theology be "true"? We have already seen that this will have to be something different from the "truth" ascribed to scientific statements. For biblical theology requires the author to express a personal decision: This is the gospel witnessed to by the Scripture.

Such a decision must also make theological statements about God the Holy Spirit. For Scripture testifies that the Spirit works faith through the witness of Scripture. Since there is only one Holy Spirit who works faith, the claim of interpreters to understand the Scripture in this Holy Spirit must demonstrate itself in agreement among those who make this claim. Such spiritual understanding therefore is never a matter of subjective decisions whose truth can never be determined. Nor are they validated by the interpreters' "faith" that the Holy Spirit is in the Word, that is, by the assertion of literal verbal inspiration. For that assertion—more than anything else—leads directly to the equation of the interpreter's own thinking with the inspired Word of God. For verbal inspiration does not describe God as speaking to people but rather as dictating—because the believing author and the Holy Spirit seem to say one and the same thing. Nor does spiritual understanding occur because the exegetes (who in this case think of themselves as exercising critical understanding) at some point—even they do not know when—experience that biblical texts have become a message addressed to them personally that has convinced them of its truth. The end result is not essentially different than it was for the Fundamentalist opponent of historical-critical interpretation—with the exception that the Fundamentalist begins with the assumption that the entire Scripture is the Word of God even before understanding, whereas the critical exegete first understands the Scripture and then declares that it is God's Word.

The Holy Spirit creates agreement in the church. (If it seems necessary, this can be extended—although only by analogy—into a consensus theory of truth: The truth is whatever people have agreed to accept as true.) This agreement is not merely a decision about the interpretation of Scripture but is created in and by the process of interpreting and understanding the Word of Scripture. Thus the place in which understanding occurs is not some abstract process of scientific learning outside any specific context in which some universalized scientific subject, who could be replaced by any other competent researcher, deals with "objective" material. In contrast, the place in which the Scripture is understood is the living fellowship of the church, formed and shaped through God, the Holy Spirit. This is the living context in which understanding occurs and in which its results are commonly accepted, because they have demonstrated themselves to be true in the experience of this fellowship.

"Biblical theology" can be applied to life. If we are not clear about how it can be applied, we have not yet clearly understood it. Perhaps that sets too high a requirement for scientific work—both of the exegete and of the dogmatician. Ought and must it not be the purpose of theological scholarship, however, to join with the Augsburg Confession in saying: "Our churches teach with unanimity."[8]

DIVINE PROVIDENCE
AND THE CHRISTIAN'S CROSS

The title of this section combines topics that are usually discussed separately in handbooks of doctrine. Providence is usually discussed under the doctrine of creation. The cross is usually discussed as part of Christian life and experience. This already indicates the direction of this discussion. It is intended as a contribution to the much-discussed doctrine of the two kingdoms. In so doing, no effort will be made to provide historical insight into the development of the doctrine nor to summarize and clarify the totally confused discussion in theological literature.

The confessional writings make a number of varying references, and particularly assert the independence of the government and the political process from the church—which we today take for granted.[9] The primary concern of the Reformation was to assert that God defines what is good in the structures of secular life. Good works are those works that have to be done to make life possible. This is God's will. Obviously, these things are not done as they ought to be. Life in this world as we actually experience it is not simply God's good order but is always under the attack of Satan. Thus Luther spoke of

> our chief enemy, the devil, whose whole purpose and desire it is to take away or interfere with all we have received from God. He is not satisfied to obstruct and overthrow spiritual order, so that he may deceive men with his lies and bring them under his power, but he also prevents and hinders the establishment of any kind of government or honorable and peaceful relations on earth. This is why he causes so much contention, murder, sedition, and war, why he sends tempest and hail to destroy crops and cattle, why he poisons the air, etc. In short, it pains him that anyone receives a morsel of bread from God and eats in in peace. If it were in his power, and our prayer to God did not restrain him, surely we would not have a straw in the field, a penny in the house, or even our life for one hour—especially those of us who have the Word of God and would like to be Christians.[10]

The relationship of this activity of Satan to divine providence as well as the relationship of the salutary temptations (Anfechtung) that come from God and satanic temptations (Versuchung) cannot here be explored in detail. When described as the "cross," however, all of these events of life in this world have a positive meaning for Christians. Of course, there is more to this life than the "cross." Defining it as "cross," however, enables us to integrate negative as well as positive experiences into a life that is structured around faith. When we do this, we no longer separate what comes to us in the course of life from what comes to us from God as faith created by God's Word. In faith, our experience of the world is integrated with our experience of the Word in such a way that we come to understand our life in this world as following Jesus and bearing our cross.[11]

In this connection, it becomes clear that the contemporary controversies about the doctrine of the two kingdoms do not adequately reflect the full range of Christian experience. This is especially obvious when this experience is analyzed from the Reformation's God-centered perspective. This is the case regardless of whether participants in the controversy appeal to the Lutheran confession's doctrine of the two kingdoms as an authority or reject it as theologically wrong. It may be that the confession can give us a clearer understanding of this situation—even if it helps us see only that it is not so easy as it might seem to be to appeal to the confession in support of this or that opinion.

The Doctrine of the Two Kingdoms Is Not a Guide for Action

The complex body of material called "the doctrine of the two kingdoms" can be so oversimplified that it appears to provide a guide for action. Thus a handbook for lay members of church councils or vestries published by the Evangelical-Lutheran Church of Bavaria described the doctrine of the two kingdoms as a set of Luther's ideas that have become especially well known in this century.

> The doctrine of the two kingdoms is intended to help us understand the meaning of God's word for our life as citizens in the world of politics. . . . It tells us that God, or Christ, exercises lordship over everything the world in two spheres, the kingdom of the right hand and the kingdom of the left, one the proper sphere of God's work the other only figuratively, the one good and the other corrupt, the one the sphere of love and other the sphere of power. The kingdom which God wills and which serves the salvation of people is the former. It is realized among the justified *in the Christian congregation.* In this kingdom, neither coercive force nor power are needed, because the kind of life that develops in this kingdom is characterized by both of the kinds of love required by the commandments. The situation is different *in the sphere of the profane,* of the state, and of politics. This kingdom also stands under God's lordship, but this lordship now takes the form of order, power, and punishment in order to ward off the worst excesses of unrighteousness and wickedness. These two kingdoms are in severe tension, a tension which runs through every Christian. In so far as Christians act personally or in relation to other Christians, they are bound by the principles of love such as Jesus' instructions in the Sermon on the Mount. However, as soon as Christians

become politically active in any way, they assume responsibility for others and are then subject to the criteria of the government of the left hand.[12]

Reading this material makes us somewhat uncomfortable—completely ignoring the fact that it does not give any consistent role to the leaders of the church, who are, when they so choose and think it expedient, free to choose to act sometimes with love and at other times to use coercive force. Therefore, the author or some editor added the following explanation: "It cannot be denied that this doctrine is in danger of a double standard of morality, especially when these two kingdoms cannot be conceptually separated from each other. For this reason, the doctrine of the two kingdoms is controversial. Yet this doctrine can serve as a guide for action in questions of social ethics and politics. This presupposes not only the distinction between the two kingdoms but also that they are both subject to God."[13]

Of course, such a handbook for church council members should not be expected to provide an introduction to the teachings of the Lutheran church and certainly not to solve the very complex problem of the doctrine of the two kingdoms. It is, however, appropriate to expect basic information that is clear on at least two points: First, that this doctrine does not apply only to political, but rather to all human activity. Second, it must explain why the "kingdom of the left hand" needs coercive power and punishment. For the above description, this would mean totally eliminating the meaningless contrast of love and coercive force, that is, that God, or Christ, exercises lordship over the world in two spheres, the one the sphere of love and the other the sphere of power. All that could be said is that God's love responds to evil with coercive force and that acting in love and its realization in the kingdom of the left hand does not exclude but rather includes the use of coercive force.

In and of itself, the text of this handbook deserves no extensive analysis. It is, however, important because its intentional oversimplification of the doctrine of the two kingdoms falsifies this doctrine in two typical ways. First, it converts it into a tool for regulating the relationship between the church and political authorities. Second, it interprets the doctrine as a guide for action. As such a guide, it says, this doctrine tells us when and where the Christian is obliged to act in love and where he or she acts according to other criteria, those of the kingdom of the left hand, that is, "order, power, and punishment." That is only an apparent differentiation. Its practical effect, however, is to abandon not only political life, but life in every area of society, especially business, to its own autonomous self-regulation. Once it is granted that there is some other criterion of action than love, the goal of political action becomes power and the goal of economic life, profit. Actions that could possibly be useful as means are then made ends in themselves. The net result is the claim that the kingdom of the left hand is subjected to God, but there is no reality behind this claim. For who is the God to whom this kingdom is subject if not the God defined for us by the Jesus Christ to whom Scriptures witness? Probably this is not what the author intended; perhaps this was only a momentary slip in which he forgot the second thesis of the Theological Declaration of Barmen. This seems likely since this thesis is reprinted elsewhere in this handbook.[14] Such a lapse of memory will, however, really become noticeable in practical life. The author concedes the right of choosing their own criteria to the political authorities. And if the same approach prevails in the church, the actions of ecclesiastical authorities can easily be defined as in the "kingdom of the left hand" and decisions implemented with coercive force.

In contrast to the position taken by this handbook for church council members, we need to remember that the definition of the good work that a Christian might do in any specific situation will never be finally settled. Whatever good work the Christian undertakes, however, it cannot be done anywhere else than in the ongoing process of life. Where in all the world are we then going to find the kingdom of love which is supposedly "realized among the justified *in the Christian congregation"?* Where is the place where coercive force is never needed, because it can be taken for granted that life is lived in fulfillment of the double commandment of love? It is a fatal error to banish love to this never-never land so that we will not be troubled by the reminder that we should love one another. The truth is, however, that love is the task anywhere in the world where people live together and relate to one another. Those who relate to one another in love are not the "justified in the Christian congregation," but rather any and all who have anything to do with one another. The handbook interprets the doctrine of the two kingdoms as meaning that Christians are obligated to love only insofar as they act personally, on their own behalf, or in relation to other Christians. How then do I know whether I am playing the role of the righteous person, who has achieved new obedience, or the role of the sinner, who is under the control of sin?

Certainly the text of the handbook under discussion is full of thoughtless inconsistency. It would be so easy to criticize it—if that were my purpose. Instead I use its inconsistency to emphasize as sharply as possible what ought to be taken for granted: We always act in the world in which we live. And this world cannot be divided into a holy world and an unholy world, into the Christians and the others. This distinction does not exist in reality—any more than the distinction between pious and secular works. As obvious as this may seem, it still seems necessary to emphasize it. The theological distinction between the two kingdoms does not mean that we can say: Here is the autonomous kingdom of the left hand with its own rules and there is the kingdom of the right hand, the place where we ought to act in love. The good is always whatever must be done in any case—we might say, whatever is necessary to do support life. Supporting life is serving God, because God wants people to live. That does not solve any ethical question. It may, however, move us a little further along in understanding what it means that anything that God wills is the right thing to do.

Discerning the Times?

The value of asking when it is the right time to believe has already been demonstrated.[15] The time to believe is any time when we are not able to act—whenever we are tempted by God *(Anfechtung)* and experience the terrors of conscience. Whenever we become aware that we are in bondage, God grants the spontaneity of faith by making a place for us in the Word about Jesus Christ. The time to believe is any time when we experience God's saving work.

Any interpretation of the doctrine of the two kingdoms that sees it as a guide to action is always a misinterpretation. It distracts our attention from the time of faith because it says: Act like a politician here and like a Christian there. The question that such directions cannot answer is how this distinction can be made and who is able to make it? What is basically certain is that it is the time to hear and to receive only that in the kingdom of Christ; in the kingdom of the world it is the time to act and to give. Perhaps this distinction is too brief, however. Ought we not also ask when the time has come to act in one way or in another?

If we follow our confession and also Luther's lead, the question looks like this: When has the time come to love and when to suffer? Luther saw Christian behavior specifically as suffering injustice, as the Sermon on the Mount requires of us (Matt. 5:38–48). At the same time, however, the Christian intervenes on behalf of and attempts to obtain justice for the neighbor. "In this way the two propositions are brought into harmony with one another; at one and the same time you satisfy God's kingdom inwardly and the kingdom of the world outwardly. . . . In what concerns you and yours, you govern yourself by the gospel and suffer injustice toward yourself as a true Christian; in what concerns the person or property of others, you govern yourself according to love and tolerate no injustice toward your neighbor. The gospel does not forbid this in fact, in other places it actually commands it."[16]

The distinction that we are required to make in order to follow Luther's proposal is difficult. If I permit myself to be robbed and exploited, it may be that I have acted as a Christian and in conformity with the instruction of the gospel. As a result, however, my neighbors, for whom I am responsible, my family, my employer, etc., suffer damage. Distinguishing what I do as a Christian from what I do in my official capacity is a very problematical matter. This can easily be seen in those situations in which I, by enduring coercion and injustice, encourage the evil person to use coercive force and injustice in other situations.

It seems to me that not much is gained by making the distinction between these viewpoints. This also became clear from the handbook cited and analyzed above. Because I am also a living person in the world and need to act in the world, I always act in specific roles. I must do justice to these roles, such as, government official and father of a family. Perhaps I am even a pastor, a Christian by vocation. In this role, everyone expects all of my behavior to be specifically Christian. After all, pastors at their ordination promise to lead a God-pleasing life as an example to the people committed to their care. And ecclesiastical regulations make pastors at least pull themselves together in their external life and not step too far out of this role by threatening them with expulsion from the ministry.

It is probably useful to ask when the time has come for someone to step out of their role. This is not the kind of decision that one can make arbitrarily. Rather, it is laid upon us in such a way that we neither may nor can refuse. Melanchthon's arguments (based on Matt. 19:27) addressed to the defenders of a two-stage ethics for Christians are relevant here.[17] These people saw the religious life which demanded the renunciation of marriage and possessions as real discipleship. Melanchthon described this as useless service because it resulted from one's own decision and choice. He felt that a special vocation to this kind of life was necessary. He gave the example of the Christian who is faced with the inescapable alternative of denying Christ or of suffering. In other words, when the time for suffering has come we will clearly recognize it. It is not a matter of our own decision but rather is laid upon us. We may, at most, admonish one another to be prepared for this to be necessary and not to fail when our time comes. The discussions of the adiaphoristic controversies in the Formula of Concord demonstrated that it was possible to argue against confessing and against obeying the demand of love because that would be in conflict with one's official role.[18] That did not happen only during those controversies over the Interim. The indisputable fact that one was responsible for others has served many as an argument for failing to respond to the challenge. Many of us know from experience and yet none of us knows how we will respond when such a challenge comes to us.

This does not answer nearly all the questions that might be asked in this connection. This much should be clear, however: If we remain faithful to our confession, we cannot misuse the doctrine of the two kingdoms, even if we are unconscious of such misuse. This means that it can under no circumstances be used to discipline fellow Christians—here, there, or anywhere— who appeal to the commandment of love as their justification in combating the unjust use of force and thereby embarrass those who directly or indirectly cooperate in this misuse of coercive power.

It will also not take long to show how the doctrine of the two kingdoms can be used as comfortable strategy for avoiding conflict. This happens whenever the church or its pastors is admonished to focus on the real task of the care of souls and leave the business of political protest to others. Instead of following such advice, the church should always ask where justice and injustice are occurring and what kind of help the neighbor needs. Where there is need, there is no question of whether we are responsible or not. Jesus' parable of the Good Samaritan emphasized once and for all that the person closest to the situation is challenged to do what needs to be done. Luther in his personal confession of faith of 1528 discussed the three orders instituted by God, ordained ministry, marriage, and government, as the orders in which we serve God. He concluded: "Above these three institutions and orders is the common order of Christian love, in which one serves not only the three orders, but also serves every needy person in general with all kinds of benevolent deeds, such as feeding the hungry, giving drink to the thirsty, forgiving enemies, praying for all men on earth, suffering all kinds of evil on earth, etc."[19] The right time to love comes whenever we encounter the opportunity or the challenge to love; then it is the right time to do whatever needs to be done and to suffer whatever needs to be suffered.

God Determines the Times

The distinction between the two kingdoms, or two governments, is not intended to set limits for God's Word of promise and demand. This Word is never limited to the inwardness of religious salvation—as though other claims properly determine the nature of our external lives. Only under this presupposition can we possibly attempt to distinguish between God's working here and there, between people as being defined by God in this way here and in some other way there, and that the only question that can be asked here or there is whether people have properly responded to God's activity. We do justice to God's activity as long as we do what it is time to do and forget what cannot be done at this time. The only guidance that we need is whether it is time to act or not to act. For the devil, that is, human will seeking to define the form and shape of life and therefore also of the world for its own benefit, covers up what it is time to do and does what it is not time for.[20]

This only hints at something that will seem more and more strange as we examine it more closely. It seems to be a old-fashioned world view. Is it not really true that what we encounter in life is a complicated chain of cause and effect that we need to understand in order to control it as much as possible? The purposes for which we use it and control it are set by rational moral principles. The real purpose would then be to support people in doing what is reasonable. Faith and love would play a significant role only in relation to people's inner life with its complex motivation. This role would be that of effectively motivating people to do what is right and reasonable. Obviously that kind of theological thinking is far removed from the Reformation and especially far from the Reformation's confession. What else can we really expect? After all, the Reformation is separated from us by the breakthrough of the modern world, by the philosophy of Descartes and Kant, and by the triumph of modern science and technology. That triumph was only possible because we understood the world as defined in terms of human concepts and used for human purposes.

As incontrovertibly true as this is, it is simply not a valid theological argument. The issue here is not the very obvious fact that this understanding of humanity in terms of science and technology has reached its limit. It is indeed seriously doubtful that it will ever be possible to subject the very powerful modern technologies to the service of people. This question is not limited to the weapons systems that continue to develop with breathtaking speed. It has become a question about the very survival of the human race. As obvious as these questions are, the real issue is the common religious form of human life that these technologies make possible. It seems inevitable that this kind of life will finally see itself as generating its own religious possibilities. It certainly has the freedom to do so. That is a characteristic of this modern life. Does this self-produced modern religious life do anything more, however, than affect people's religious emotions? When people experience this reality, it does make sense to move beyond the realm of religious freedom to become involved in political activities. When that happens, religion no longer has a merely pacifying or edifying effect but becomes a disturbing factor in life. Then those who are in control of society and think of themselves as responsible for restoring peace and quiet will force religion back into its role of preserving peace and quiet. In so doing—note this very carefully—they use the doctrine of the two kingdoms to explain what the function of religion really is.

Modern life, especially religious life, has increasingly forgotten God as it has become more and more active. Judging by my own personal experience and assuming that it is typical, increasing engagement with Scripture and confession is only one fact among the many that make us increasingly aware of how prevalent this is. Religious life becomes increasingly active, not merely in terms of political activity but also in terms of efforts to increase the level of spirituality—a kind of exercise program for the inner life. All of this assumes that God's providence has been absorbed by the scientific laws that describe natural life in our world and that are now used by people to play the role of providence for themselves. When we play the role of providence, we either decide when it is time to act or refrain from acting or even permit ourselves to be manipulated by others who pretend to know what the times require. It does not finally matter whether this judgment is made on the basis of reason or theology. The ultimate effect is the same. The world forgets God and is God-forsaken. This seems to be the price we pay for our modern life and for the freedom of at least seeming to be able to define the possibilities of our own life.

God is still present with us in the modern world, however, present with his parental and providential care.[21] There is no doubt that we Lutherans believe and confess this. The confessional tradition teaches that clearly—from the early church's basic decision that God alone works our salvation through Barmen's rejection of natural theology. The question that now needs to be asked, however, is where we can experience this. This experience comes to us in the cross. As far as I can see, we cannot find this certainty in what we actively do. That would raise the old question of good works, certainly in a modified but still in a recognizable form. Good works, however, do not justify; they conceal God, hide the fact that God is close to us and active on our behalf. It really does not matter whether good works are done on the assumption that the two kingdoms are really only one and that religious activity is political activity or whether they are done by a really orthodox Lutheran who carefully distinguishes religious from political works. Anyone who tries to find certainty of salvation and of God's presence through doing good works effectively conceals God's will and God's goodness. God reveals this goodness by letting the good happen. This is what providence is really all about. Whether things happen with or without our involvement and approval, God orders life and works within it to make the good happen. We can become aware of that only if we are ready to accept everything that happens as coming from God.

That may sound fatalistic. Indeed it will be fatalistic for anyone who is busy trying to do good works and to create certainty about God. The very acceptable language of "the cross of the Christian" is chosen in order to prevent this misinterpretation; it does not suggest fatalism but rather submission.[22] The experience of the cross is the experience of the unity of the world and of salvation. This experience creates the certainty that this world, even with all of the evil that is present in it, is determined by God's goodness. Experiencing such suffering may also show us a new way of being human, that is, we find our life only at those places where we receive it as a gift. This new kind of person lives from what comes; this life is successful to the extent that it is aware of the richness of all that comes to it.

BINDING AND
LOOSING—HOMILETICAL NOTES

"The preaching of the Word of God is the Word of God" ("Praedicatio verbi Dei est verbum Dei"). This frequently quoted statement is not taken from one of the Lutheran confessional writings but from the Second Helvetic Confession (1566), *Confessio Helvetica posterior,* written by Heinrich Bullinger, who was Zwingli's successor as the leader of the Reformation in Zurich.[23] The claim that this statement makes for the sermon is still the subject of considerable controversy. Even those who recognize the validity of this claim distinguish God's Word from the preacher's word: The sermon is God's Word only if God uses this human word. That can, at best, be hoped and prayed for. That, however, seems to place the human activity of preaching in a remarkably ambiguous position. On the one hand, the highest possible claims are made for it; on the other hand, it seems to lose its significance as a human activity. For if God does not use this word and make it God's own Word, the preached word is nothing at all.

This makes it useful to try to define preaching in a different way and to instruct people to do it differently. If the preaching of God's Word is actually to become God's Word, the only standard of a good sermon is that it be scriptural. This would mean that the sermon should seek to understand and explain the text—only the text and what it intends to proclaim. This must become the basic rule of sermon studies and preparation.

Those methods, in contrast, that see preaching as a process of communication must be much more concerned about the hearer. What will the hearer understand when the message of the text is communicated? Given this perspective preaching can be understood as making a speech. It is then understood in terms of the methods and principles of speechmaking. If the purpose of the sermon is described in terms of the hearer learning something, then psychological learning theories determine the way in which the sermon is prepared and presented.

All of this is very true. It can also be taken as self-understood. When we look at what actually happens in the process of preaching and preparing to preach, however, we find that the emphases are somewhat different. The dialectical theologians understood preaching in terms of proclaiming God's Word. They also knew how to reach their hearers. The reverse is also true. Advocates of modern theories of preaching also knew that they only have something to say when they repeat the gospel to which the Scripture testifies.

The differences between these two viewpoints are not important for this discussion. The purpose is to draw attention to some guidelines that the confession provides for the work of preaching. These will be discussed in terms of the usual situation in which preaching takes place. There are obviously a large number of other forms of communication in which the gospel is transmitted—not limited to those which Luther listed in the Smalcald Articles.[24] The Sunday sermon will continue to be of such significance that it can serve as a useful paradigm for this discussion.

The External Word

The gospel that is administered in Word and Sacrament joins the objective element of Christ's person and work to the subjective work of the Spirit and combines them into God's saving work. This summary statement of the basic substance of the Reformation's doctrine of Word and Sacrament may, however, not be understood in a merely formal sense.[25] The gospel is the news of what has happened in Christ. In the gospel, Jesus Christ comes out to meet faith in such a way that this faith finds a place with Jesus Christ. To do this, he uses the external Word. As a result, faith is not simply absorbed into the inwardness of the believer. If that were the case, the believer would possibly have to preserve this faith as a precious possession. Since eternal salvation depends on faith, it really is precious, of course. That way of understanding the nature of faith would be a misunderstanding. This misunderstanding is incompatible with the Reformation's teaching and will certainly not lead to a God-pleasing life. For God is not pleased by a life that turns in upon itself in order to be together with God. Rather believers pay attention to the outer world because that is the place where they hear the external Word; it is also the place where the believer receives the opportunity to do whatever needs to be done at this particular time. Such action always takes place in the external world.

The sermon tries to announce the gospel in such a way that its Word offers such an external world. This offer is made through the Word which, of course, does not remain outside, but rather passes through the ear into the heart and the heart keeps it. Then is it really inside? If it is, then only because the sermon has failed. It has not properly expressed what it is that can be kept in the heart in such a way that it defines the person of the believer. What has happened, that is, the story of Jesus Christ for us to which the Scripture witnesses, is always outside us. It would not be appropriate to try to convert this history into a mere vehicle through which God's eternal Word could enter into our heart and remain there, enabling us to live a new life. Osiander proposed that, but the Formula of Concord rejected it.[26] It would be equally inappropriate to set too-narrow limits for this story. The witness to Jesus Christ is nothing less than the whole Scripture. No sermon that seeks to orient itself to the church's confession will deny itself the benefit of that full witness. For that reason, wherever the Word is preserved in someone's heart, this person's heart is to be shown the place in the external world where it belongs.

This is a very practical guideline, which can also be expressed in a very specific question. When the preacher has chosen a text, the question must be asked: Where do the preacher and the hearers appear in this text? The decision that this text can be adequately communicated in a sermon is the presupposition of its choice. This is no mere homiletical guideline, which advises preachers to apply the text to themselves first and then to their hearers. Rather, this gospel text comes from God. In it, we hear God's Word, his only Son, our salvation. He is the one Word of God, whom we are to hear, to trust in life and death, and to obey. When we find this point in the text, it is always the point where Jesus Christ is. Otherwise, it is not the gospel. The salvation that comes to us from outside ourselves then remains hidden. What gets through to our hearts is only the law. When the law sits in our hearts, we are really in trouble. It may take the form of pride or despair, or even of both at once. For the law is very effective at making people proud or creating despair. For the most part, the text is not at fault if preachers are not able to find their own personal place in the text and, as a result, also cannot find the point where their hearers are present. This is true even when it seems impossible

231

to preach on a specific text in a particular situation. When that happens, preachers should not desperately follow through on the decision, or even the assignment, to preach on a text; rather, they will do better to choose another text.

This may give rise to the objection: This is simply impossible. The text was written in a completely different world and historical epoch than that in which the hearers now live. It is dishonest to pretend that the hearers of sermons today can be found in these alien texts. This argument will be raised by advocates of those modern theories of homiletics that are oriented to the hearers. These theories have various descriptions for two basic elements that must be brought into a relationship with each one. The one is the message, the New Testament proclamation; the other is the modern person, living in the current historical situation. If we combine the Reformation confession's basic understanding of gospel with this model of preaching, the person of the preacher will be close to becoming an essential part of the gospel.

The gospel does indeed integrate the objective side of salvation, dealing with the person and work of Christ, and the subjective side, dealing with the work of the Holy Spirit, into a unified entity. In terms of this model, however, the preacher has the function of bringing the biblical message and the contemporary hearer together. The preacher brings this about as a result of preparing and delivering a sermon. This work of the preacher brings Christ and the hearer together. That never works out very well, no matter how often it is attempted. The preacher—or pastor, or teacher—is certainly never the gospel. Admittedly, we are tickled when people sometimes imply this—as though we had succeeded in helping, healing, and granting salvation by entering into fellowship with someone else. Forget that idea completely. At least, do not make it the basis of a theory of pastoral work.

The gospel comes to us and brings us salvation from outside ourselves. It is there that the heart finds its refuge. For that reason, the sermon must show the hearers the point at which they appear in the text. Sometimes this point is easily discovered. At other times the point is hidden and hard to find. Still, it must be found before the Word becomes the gospel that is able to lift the hearers out of themselves so that they will be able to find rest for their hearts in Jesus Christ, who is the Word of God. Preachers who want to follow the confession will work to discover this point, show the hearers where it is, and lead them to it as the place where they belong.

This does not need to be spelled out in detail. These basic elements are enough: Any understanding of ministry based on a model of correlation will make it difficult for preachers to find their way into the text and to preach it as gospel. This is why so many sermons are so legalistic. The preacher has attempted to force the Son and the Holy Spirit together—to use the Trinitarian terminology—and failed because they have always been together. Preachers who go about their work consciously become the first in the congregation to hear the message of the text and thereby discover that the people who will hear the sermon have already been received and accepted by the text. Once preachers discover this, they can hardly wait until it is time to preach and repeat this discovery.

The Right Time

Equating the preaching of God's Word with God's Word can be easily misunderstood as meaning that these two are identical. Such a misunderstanding assumes that God's Word is heard whenever the pastor stands in the pulpit and preaches. The fact is, however, that when I hear a sermon, I hear only the word of the preacher who more or less succeeds in delivering a sermon thought up by the preacher. It is not appropriate to assert dogmatically or, pseudo-dogmatically, that such a sermon really is God's Word. If preachers feel that this has to be the case, they try to make it happen and become very tense. Preachers may then tell the congregation that it is their duty to make it true that the sermon is God's Word: I preach the Word of God. Your duty is to believe it. This becomes a kind of sermon-centered Fundamentalism that is accompanied by other dogmatic short circuits, such as, the demand to believe that the sermon is God's Word. As long as people do not hear God's Word, however, but only hear the human word of the preacher, the best we can hope for is that has a friendly meaning. In any case, it does not do any good to demand that the congregation think it is hearing God's Word.

In interpreting the Reformation's understanding of faith, we have discussed the question of the right time.[27] It is useful to remember that it is God, and not people, who decides when the right time has come for them to believe. If the preacher demands that someone hears a particular sermon as God's Word, the preacher in effect demands that this person makes this time, for example, ten o'clock on Sunday morning, the time to believe. On what basis could we either make such a demand or expect to be able to respond to it?

None of us is God—we can therefore only pray and wait for this time to come. An untroubled person (homo otiosus) can imagine all kinds of things and assume that they are true. That is the kind of person that I usually am when I participate in worship—an untroubled person doing my duty by going to church. I just would not feel right about missing church on Sunday morning. If we follow the confession and its guidelines for understanding the gospel, however, we will be careful to avoid such a poorly considered identification of the sermon with God's Word. It presupposes that people have exactly those capacities that the confession denies that they have. It ascribes a capacity to the will, which God alone has. We are simply not as free as we think ourselves to be in going about our usual pattern of life.

This leads to an unconditional conclusion. In order to avoid the misunderstanding that the preached sermon can be equated with the Word of God—a rule accepted by many preachers as a law and passed on to their hearers—the sermon must distinguish the times. Even though the following two times are carefully distinguished, it may be that they occur simultaneously for one or the other hearer and, as God wills, sometimes for the whole congregation. That is a very rare exception, however, and will always be so. The time of the sermon and the time to believe must be distinguished. For that distinction to be made, the sermon must speak of the time to believe as some other time. An example of this would be Luther's well-known introduction to his Invocavit sermon of 1522: "The summons of death comes to us all, and no one can die for another. Every one must fight his own battle with death by himself, alone. We can shout into another's ears, but every one must himself be prepared for the time of death, for I will not be with you then, nor you with me."[28] Luther then went on to draw the conclusion that every one must know the chief points of faith. In order to know when the time to believe comes, we should use the present time as the right time to hear. The sermon preserves the distinction between this time and the right time by pointing to a future then and when as the time when faith will be needed.

There are many other ways that preachers can distinguish the right time to hear from the right time to believe. It is necessary, however, to learn to make this distinction. For that distinction must be made in order to preach the gospel in a way that distinguishes between what people do and what God does. If these times are confused, the human word of the sermon will be declared to be God's Word and people will believe that it is God's Word. The result will be a tragic time rather than the time of joy and freedom that the gospel brings.

It is still possible to ask: What claim may then be made for the sermon. Is the clear equation "the preaching of God's Word is God's Word" totally meaningless? Those questions can be answered by referring to the assertion of Article V of the Augsburg Confession that God works faith "when and where he pleases."[29] This forbids a simple identification of hearing and faith. Of course, the gospel that is believed is the same gospel that is heard; it is not some other mysterious inner word. This is what Luther said in a homily in Smalcald: "To summarize this sermon, we know and believe that we are Christians and redeemed. If anyone asks us, 'How do you know this?' we can answer, 'I know it because I have heard it in the word and sacrament and in the word of absolution. The Holy Spirit has also spoken to my heart and confirmed what I have heard with my ears."[30] We would, however, not think correctly about the God who is the triune God were we to separate the Word and the Spirit from the life in which we experience the changing times and conditions that God's care and providence ordains. The Spirit speaks in our hearts wherever this life confronts us with the challenge to believe. That is the acceptable time. Then the word of preaching that we have heard and kept in our heart becomes God's Word to us.

Decisive Preaching

This line of thought must be carried one step further. The terms "binding and loosing" echo Matt. 16:19. The sermon has the function of binding and loosing through the consolation of the gospel. Luther preached about this during the Leipzig Disputation on June 29, 1519. The sermon concluded: "Thus the power of the keys helps, not the priest as a priest, but only the sinful and abashed consciences, which receive grace through faith, and their hearts are set at peace and good confidence toward God. The result then is that all life and suffering is light, and a man, who otherwise never does any good because of the unrest of his heart, can serve his gracious God with joy. This means then the sweet burden of our Lord Jesus Christ [Matt. 11:30]."[31] The effective gospel binds and loosens. This is the most important thing to say. The preacher is nothing more than the servant of this effective gospel.

This leads to another conclusion about preaching. This presupposes what has just been said. Luther, for example, says this very pointedly in the sermon just referred to: It is not our faith, not our decision, that makes the Word true. "Flesh and blood," human nature with its will that is bound in sin, cannot generate faith in the gospel. This is the work of God. Only God creates real faith. This insight must find expression in the very structure of this sermon. Then the sermon speaks decisively. It has found the point in the text in which the hearers are present and points it out. It also knows how to speak of the right time when the hearer has or will come to faith. These are not suppositions but rather clear and decisive statements about what the situation really is. A proper sermon does not speak hypothetically. Of course, hypothetical grammatical constructions can be used—especially in those dialogical sections in which the sermon refers to the hearers' possible objections and thus expresses the hearers' own inner conversation.

The sermon, however, must clearly indicate where it begins to present the gospel itself. Then "if . . . when" statements are no longer appropriate. For example, "If you will surrender your life to Jesus, then you will be happy." Anyone who preaches like that, no matter how smoothly and how modern the formulation, is still preaching works and not faith. Perhaps it is difficult for us to take that seriously. Is not the confessional writings' talk of the bondage of the will really a strange, old-fashioned, medieval idea? After all, we are modern people and our freedom is our most valuable possession—personal, political, economic, moral, and religious freedom. It is we who personally choose our life style, decide which political party to support, select a career, decide how to spend our money, whether to follow traditional moral standards or not, whether we want to be religious and/or join the church—and we can choose one without the other. Preaching that confirms this self-understanding of "I make my own choices" is already outside the limits of the proper decisive and assertive preaching that Luther described at the beginning of *The Bondage of the Will*.[32] Either preachers fulfill their task of speaking decisively or they assume that the will is really as free to decide for itself as it sometimes seems to be.

Preaching that does not address the hearers decisively leaves the hearers free to make their own decisions. Under some circumstances, they are all too pleased to accept this opportunity. For this corresponds to people's prevalent opinion that they themselves make the decision. Some will not be pleased by this opportunity. These people have tasted the gospel and are glad to be what they are, people who live with Christ in the gospel and no longer need to make bad decisions that result in their missing out on life itself. However that may be, indecisive preaching leaves the decision up to the hearer.

There are two forms of such indecisive preaching. One obviously presses for a decision, the other is more restrained. The style that presses for a decision appeals to the hearer's freedom and tries to influence the decision. With threats and promises, it attempts to lead the hearer to make a decision for faith, for God, or for Jesus. It is sometimes not clear what that decision would really be. But it is not necessary to be clear. It is basically satisfied as long as those who make a positive decision are confirmed in their good feeling about the decision, while those who have not made a decision—possibly because they really do not know what a positive decision might be—feel badly about not making one.

There is a second kind of indecisive preaching in addition to the form that tries to extract a decision from the hearer. This second form has become more common in recent years. It gives the preacher's personality a significant role in the pulpit—perhaps in reaction to a previous unfair condemnation of the use of the preacher's own personal experience. In this second kind of indecisive preaching, preachers speak about themselves, their own understanding of the text, their own random thoughts about it, and whatever conclusions they draw for their own personal lives. These preachers, however, do not want to invade their hearers' privacy. They wish to respect their freedom. As a result, they limit themselves to very indirectly challenging the hearers to follow their example, to understand the text as they understand it, and to draw similar conclusions.

This model of indecisive preaching is familiar to everyone. It is easy for any of us to fall into this kind of speaking. It is part of the common ecclesiastical style and is the constant background noise in the ears of those who pursue their vocation in the church.

It is good to have the confession call us to order at this point. As certainly as the gospel calls to faith and cannot be properly understood without this faith, it is equally certain that faith makes the gospel true. This also happens when faith is understood as a person's free decision. The confession does not leave the decision to the hearer and put the hearer off with hypothetical statements and imperatives. It does not suggest that the hearer should realize the meaning of what has been heard in "everyday life" *(Alltag)*—a typical term of debased preaching language.

Decisive preaching calls sin by its name and speaks clearly about things in general. It speaks especially clearly about the time of the gospel and puts what it says about the hearer into the context of these statements about the time of the gospel. That kind of preaching both binds and loosens. Of course, it is sometimes easier to say something and then take it back. It seems more cultured and generates less resistance than describing our own experiences in responding to the text. It is probably also simpler—in terms of exegesis, systematics, and homiletics—to speak indecisively. Preachers, however, who restrict their preaching to the indecisive never speak the message, of which—when spoken at the right time—we can truly say: The preaching of God's Word is God's Word.

Abbreviations

AC	Augsburg Confession
Ap.	Apology of the Augsburg Confession
BC	*The Book of Concord: The Confessions of the Evangelical Lutheran Church,* trans. and ed. Theodore G. Tappert et al. Philadelphia: Fortress Press, 1959; reprinted, 1983.
Cl.	Clemen edition of Luther's works, ed. Otto Clemen. 8 vols. 1st ed., 1912–33.
Con.	Conclusion (to the Augsburg Confession)
Ep.	Epitome (of the Formula of Concord)
Ep. Comp. Sum.	Comprehensive Summary of the Epitome
FC	Formula of Concord
LBW	*Lutheran Book of Worship*
LC	Large Catechism
LCC	Library of Christian Classics
LW	*Luther's Works,* ed. Jaroslav Pelikan, Hilton C. Oswald, Helmut T. Lehmann. Vols. 1–30, St. Louis: Concordia Publishing House, 1955–; vols. 31–55, Philadelphia: Fortress Press, 1957–86.
NPNF	Nicene and Post-Nicene Library of the Fathers
Pref.	Preface (to the Large and Small Catechisms)
SA	Smalcald Articles
SC	Small Catechism
SD	Solid Declaration (of the Formula of Concord)
TOC	*The Teaching of the Catholic Church as Contained in Her Documents,* Eng. trans.: ed. Karl Rahmer; trans. Geoffrey Stevens. Staten Island, N.Y.: Alba House, 1967.
Tr.	Treatise on the Power and Primacy of the Pope

Notes

TRANSLATOR'S NOTE

1. Theodore G. Tappert, et al., trans. and eds., *The Book of Concord: The Confessions of the Evangelical Lutheran Church* (Philadelphia: Fortress Press, 1959; reprinted 1983). Hereafter cited as BC.
2. *Die Bekenntnisschriften der evangelisch-lutherischen Kirche. Herausgegeben im Gedenkjahr der Augsburgischen Konfession 1930* (Göttingen: Vandenhoeck & Ruprecht, 1930; 2d corrected ed., 1952). Recent editions are reprints of the second edition.
3. The common German abbreviation is CA (for its Latin title *Confessio Augustana*) and it is sometimes referred to as the Augustana. Older English works often refer to the CA, although the modern custom is to refer to AC.
4. Friedrich Mildenberger, *Theologie der Lutherischen Bekenntnisschriften* (Stuttgart: Kohlhammer, 1983), 11.
5. The rapid development of bibliographical data bases meets the need for references to the broader literature. For a printout of selected recent references, see *Luther and Lutheranism: A Bibliography Selected from the American Theological Library Association Religion Databases* (Chicago: ATLA, 1985).
6. Mildenberger, *Theologie der Lutherischen Bekenntnisschriften*, 200–211.

INTRODUCTION

1. Church Constitution of the Evangelical Church in Bavaria, Article 72.
2. AC, V:3, in BC, 31 (German).
3. See chap. 1, under "The Augsburg Confession as the Evangelical-Lutheran Symbolic Creed."
4. See Friedrich Mildenberger, *Grundwissen der Dogmatik* (Stuttgart: Kohlhammer, 1982), 1.1, 23–25.
5. Karl Barth, *The Doctrine of the Word of God*, trans. G. W. Bromiley, vol. I, 1

of *Church Dogmatics,* ed. G. W. Bromiley and T. F. Torrance (Edinburgh: T & T Clark, 1975), 275–76.

6. Leonard Hutter, *Compendium Locorum Theologicorum,* first published in 1610. *Compendium of Lutheran Theology: A Summary of Christian Doctrine, Derived from the Word of God and the Symbolic Books of the Evangelical Lutheran Church,* trans. H. E. Jacobs and G. F. Spieker (Philadelphia: Lutheran Book Store, 1868).

7. Philip Melanchthon, *Melanchthon on Christian Doctrine: Loci Communes, 1555,* trans. and ed. Clyde L. Manschreck (New York: Oxford University Press, 1965).

8. Friedrich Brunstäd, *Theologie der lutherischen Bekenntnisschriften* (Gütersloh: Bertelsmann, 1951), 17.

9. Edmund Schlink, *Theology of the Lutheran Confessions,* trans. Paul F. Koehneke and Herbert J. A. Bouman (Philadelphia: Fortress Press, 1961), 32.

10. Holsten Fagerberg, *New Look at the Lutheran Confessions (1529–1537),* trans. Gene J. Lund (St. Louis: Concordia Publishing House, 1972).

CHAPTER 1

1. Since the nineteenth century, the German term *Konfession,* which is here translated as "confessional church," has been used to designate the main branches of Christianity that developed as a result of the Reformation. A confessional church therefore is broader and more inclusive than a denomination. [The reader who is familiar with Germany may find it helpful to remember that the German term for "confession" is *Bekenntnis.* This term also refers to the confessional document itself, although the term *Bekenntnisschrift* is also used and more specifically refers to the written document.—Trans.]

2. [The legal basis of the German Empire presupposed that all citizens would share a common religion. This treaty permitted princes who so wished to recognize the Augsburg Confession in their territories; for the text, see B. J. Kidd, ed., *Documents Illustrative of the Continental Reformation* (Oxford: Clarendon Press, 1911), 363–64—Trans.]

3. This document is the agreement reached by the Swiss churches, especially Zurich and Geneva, on the Lord's Supper. It became the basis of other Calvinist confessions. English translations are not common. Selections appear in G. R. Potter and M. Greengrass, *John Calvin* (New York: St. Martin's Press, 1983), 128–30. The full text is John Calvin, "Mutual Consent in Regard to the Sacraments Between the Ministers of the Church of Zurich and John Calvin, Minister of the Church of Geneva. Now Published by Those Who Framed It. MDLIV," in *Tracts Relating to the Reformation,* trans. H. Beveridge (Grand Rapids: Wm. B. Eerdmans, 1958), 2:199–244. The actual text of the agreement: 2:212–20.

4. For a discussion of the problematic nature of the FC, see below, chap. 7.

5. This is usually the revised text of the AC that is meant by the title *Variata.* Selections are given by Johann Michael Reu, *The Augsburg Confession: A Collection of Sources with an Historical Introduction* (Chicago: Wartburg Publishing House, 1930), *398–*411. This will be referred to as Reu, *Sources.* The asterisks associated with the page numbers were Reu's convention for indicating that these pages are part of the second section of the book containing the sources. For the full text, see Henry E. Jacobs, ed., *The Book of Concord; or the Symbolical Books of the Evangelical Lutheran Church, with Historical Introduction, Notes, Appendices, and Indexes,* 2 vols. (Philadelphia: G. W. Frederick, 1883), 2:103–47. This will be referred to as Jacobs, *Historical Introduction.* Jacobs, 147–58, provides the significant variations in the altered text of 1542.

6. [The German word translated "papal" here and elsewhere in this book is *Altgläubigen*. It refers to those Christians who did not support the Reformation. When the emphasis is on this group as it existed before the Council of Trent (1545–63), I have used the word "papal" because their varying degrees of support of the papacy were a common element not shared by the Reformers. After the Council of Trent, I have referred to them as "Roman Catholics."–Trans.]

7. Compare the confessional paragraphs quoted in the Introduction, under "The Binding Character of the Confession."

8. The Heidelberg Catechism presented a Calvinist version of Reformation theology.

9. BC, 11–12. BC prints this as the introduction to the Book of Concord. *Bekenntnisschriften* prints it as part of the FC, 755–57.

10. BC, 12.

11. ". . . Further, all those things are to be believed with divine and Catholic faith which are contained in the word of God, written or handed down, and which the Church, either by a solemn judgment, or by her ordinary and universal magisterium, proposes for belief as having been divinely revealed," Henricus Denzinger, *Enchiridion Symbolorum Definitionum et Declarationum de Rebus Fidei et Morum*, ed. Carolus Rahner et al., 34th ed. (Freiburg im Breisgau: Herder, 1967), 3011. This is referred to as Denzinger. The numbers following do not refer to pages, but rather to Denzinger's marginal numbering of paragraphs. See also *The Teaching of the Catholic Church as Contained in Her Documents*, English trans.: ed. Karl Rahner, trans. Geoffrey Stevens (Staten Island, N.Y.: Alba House, 1967), 63, 90. In the following, this is referred to as *TOC.*

12. Philip Melanchthon, "Examen ordinandorum" (1552) in *Bekenntnisse und Kleine Lehrschriften*, vol. 6 of *Werke in Auswahl. Eine Studienausgabe*, ed. Robert Stupperich et al. (Gütersloh: Bertelsmann, 1955), 17.

13. Ibid., 174–75. Luther's "personal confession of faith" is the third part of his *Confession Concerning Christ's Supper*, LW 37:360–72. Written by Luther in 1528 in anticipation of his death, it became one of the sources of the AC.

14. Ernst Sehling, *Die evangelischen Kirchenordnungen des XVI. Jahrhunderts*, ed. Institut für evangelisches Kirchenrecht der Evangelischen Kirch im Deutschland (Tübingen: J. C. B. Mohr [Paul Siebeck], 1955), 6:91–92.

15. Ibid.

16. BC, 503.

17. BC, 503n. Not to be confused with the Torgau Articles of 1530, one of the source documents for the AC.

18. See the Ep. of the FC, in BC, 465, 8.

19. FC, SD, 2, in BC, 504.

20. FC, SD, 17–20, in BC, 507–8.

21. See in the Introduction, under "The Binding Character of the Confession."

22. The proceedings of this trial have been published: *Nachdruck der Niederschrift über das Feststellungsverfahren* (Hamburg: Lutherisches Kirchenamt Hannover, 1979), 93ff.

23. FC, SD, 5, in BC, 504.

24. See chap. 7, under "Freedom in Church Order," and chap. 8, under "Was Barmen a New Basic Decision?"

25. Wilhelm Dantine, in *Bekennendes Bekenntnis*, ed. Erich Hultsch and Kurt Lüthi (Gütersloh: Gerd Mohn, 1982), 60.

26. Although ranked by the Book of Concord with these two creeds, the Athanasian Creed was first used somewhat later, probably after A.D. 500.

27. Regin Prenter, *Creation and Redemption*, trans. Theodore I. Jensen (Philadelphia: Fortress Press, 1967), 115.
28. Ibid., 137.
29. See below, chap. 3.
30. Dantine, in *Bekennendes Bekenntnis*, 52.
31. BC, 23.
32. "The Protestation of the Evangelical Minority at Speyer, April 19, 1529," in Reu, *Sources*, *487–*98. See also "The Resolution of the Majority at Speyer, April 7, 1529," in Reu, *sources*, *33–*34.
33. "The Secret Agreement of Speyer, April 22, 1529," in Reu, *Sources*, *34–*37.
34. AC (untitled section after Article 21), 1, in BC, 47 (German).
35. Ibid., 48, 2 (German).
36. See below, chap. 5.
37. "Dr. Eck's 404 Articles, March, 1530," in Reu, *Sources*, *97–*121.
38. AC, Con., 7, in BC, 96 (Latin).
39. BC, 24–27.
40. BC, 25, 8.
41. BC, 25, 10.
42. See the opening statements of each of the first three articles of the AC, I–III, in BC, 27–29 (Latin).
43. See the introductory paragraphs to this chapter.
44. "Schwabach Articles, Summer, 1529," in Reu, *Sources*, *40–*44. See also in Jacobs, *Historical Introduction*, 69–74.
45. Jacobs, *Historical Introduction*, 253–60.

CHAPTER 2
1. See the introduction, under "The Binding Character of the Confession."
2. For an example of this approach, see Paul C. Empie et al., eds., *Lutherans and Catholics in Dialogue* (Minneapolis: Augsburg Publishing House, 1965–80), and Joseph Burgess et al., eds., *The Role of the Augsburg Confession: Catholic and Lutheran Views* (Philadelphia: Fortress Press, 1980).
3. "Facienti quod in se est Deus non denegat gratiam," literally, "God does not refuse his grace to anyone who does what is possible."
4. Decree of the General Conference of Florence, 1439, in Denzinger, 1323; *TOC*, 307–8, 542.
5. AC, XX:3–7, in BC, 41–42 (German).
6. For the text, see *TOC*, 383–402.
7. Denzinger, 1522; *TOC*, 384–85, 711.
8. Denzinger, 1521; *TOC*, 384, 710.
9. Denzinger, 1526; *TOC*, 386–97, 715.
10. Denzinger, 1525; *TOC*, 386, 714.
11. Denzinger, 1528; *TOC*, 387, 717.
12. Denzinger, 1582; *TOC*, 402, 769.
13. Denzinger, 1582; *TOC*, 402, 769.
14. Johann Adam Möhler, *Symbolism: or, Exposition of the Doctrinal Differences between Catholics and Protestants, as Evidenced by their Symbolical Writings*, trans. James Burton Robertson (New York: Edward Dunigan, 1844), 262.
15. Ibid., 270.
16. The Latin is "articulus stantis et cadentis ecclesiae." For a history of the development of this traditional designation, see Friedrich Loofs, "Der articulus stantis et cadentis ecclesiae," *Theologische Studien und Kritiken* 90 (1917): 324–420.

17. SA, II, I:5, in BC, 292.
18. SA, II, I:4, in BC, 292.
19. SC, II, III:6, in BC, 345.
20. AC, V:2, in BC, 31.
21. See chap. 7, under "Predestination."
22. See chap. 7, under "Anthropological Definitions."
23. See chap. 2, under "The Relationship Between the Roman Catholic Doctrinal Form and Its Contradiction by the Reformation."
24. AC, V:2, in BC, 31.
25. See Wilfried Joest, *Ontologie der Person bei Luther* (Göttingen: Vandenhoeck & Ruprecht, 1967), 232–353.
26. AC, XX:15, 17, in BC, 43 (Latin).
27. AC, XX:18, in BC, 43 (Latin).
28. AC, XX:24, in BC, 44 (German).
29. AC, V:4, in BC, 31 (German).
30. See in chap. 4, under "Faith as God's Own Determination of the Person."
31. AC, IV:2, in BC, 30 (German).
32. AC, V:1-3, in BC, 31 (German).
33. See chap. 7, under "Christ as the Righteousness of Faith."
34. See chap. 5, under "The Office of the Ministry."
35. SA, III, IV, in BC, 310.

CHAPTER 3

1. The reader who has little familiarity with the historical development of the creeds will find J. N. D. Kelly, *Early Christian Creeds* (New York: Longmans, Green & Co., 1950), a useful introductory guide.
2. See chap. 2, under "Confessing as a Communal Act and the Theological Defense of the Confession and Its Doctrines."
3. Modern examples are Joseph Ratzinger, *Introduction to Christianity*, trans. J. R. Foster (New York: Herder & Herder, 1970), and Wolfhart Pannenberg, *The Apostles' Creed in the Light of Today's Questions*, trans. Margaret Kohl (Philadelphia: Westminster Press, 1972).
4. Quoted from a Valentinian tract, in Kurt Rudolph, *Gnosis: The Nature and History of Gnosticism*, trans. Robert McLachlan Wilson (San Francisco: Harper & Row, 1983), 62.
5. Karlman Beyschlag, *Gott und Welt*, vol. 1 of *Grundriss der Dogmengeschichte* (1982), 157.
6. My brief summary of this decision refers to "biblical history." (See chap. 2, under "Confessing as a Communal Act and the Theological Defense of the Confession and Its Decision," and the title of this chap. [3].) The expression is an awkward one. But I would generate still more misunderstanding were I to use the technical term "salvation history."
7. See chap. 9, under "God Determines the Times."
8. "An Anonymous Sermon, Commonly Called Clement's Second Letter to the Corinthians," in *Early Christian Fathers*, trans. and ed. Cyril C. Richardson, LCC 1 (Philadelphia: Westminster Press, 1953), 193.
9. This is an ontological term that describes an independent being. In Latin, it would be translated *substantia* or *concretum*—although these are not always adequate equivalents. In the doctrine of the Trinity, *hypostasis* refers to the individual persons; in Christology, the term describes the identity of the person who is both God and human.

10. Arianism was named after the—later defined as heretical—position represented by the Alexandrian priest Arius. He was neither its most important nor its spiritually most significant representative, however.

11. *TOC*, 424–25, 829–31.

12. See this chap., under "The Holy Threesome."

13. [The translation is based on *TOC*, 424, 829. I have revised it by translating *ousia* as "being" rather than "substance." In Latin versions of the creeds, *substantia* replaced the original Greek term. See this chap., under "The Holy Threesome." The term *homousios* is used in the creed of 381 (see n. 14) but not in this creed—Trans.]

14. *LBW*, 64. The ecumenical text of this Creed currently used in the liturgies of the German churches reads "Aus dem Vater geboren vor aller Zeit . . . gezeugt, nicht geschaffen. . . ." The expressions *geboren* and *gezeugt* are both translations of the same Greek term *gennethenta*. [The translation in BC (p. 18) follows the Latin tradition. The Greek text of 381—for the text of which there is no firm evidence until 451—is reprinted in *Bekenntnisschriften*, 26. The Latin text of the Book of Concord follows *natum* and *genitum*. The German text of this Creed in the Book of Concord uses *geboren* and *geborn*. The translation in BC follows the German text in using the same term in both instances but chooses "begotten" rather than "born." The custom of using two terms corresponding to "born" and "begotten" seems to have been set by variations in the Latin liturgical text and was not intended as a variation in meaning. See Hans Lietzmann, *Symbole der Alten Kirche*, 6th ed. (Berlin: Walter de Gruyter, 1968), 39—Trans.]

15. See this chap., under "God's Presence in the World."

16. See ibid.

17. The words "and from the Son" in our present liturgical creed are a later addition of the Western church.

18. This is the current ecumenical text of this Creed in English as used in *Lutheran Book of Worship* (Minneapolis: Augsburg Publishing House; Philadelphia: Board of Publication, Lutheran Church in America, 1978), 54. For another translation, see BC, 20, 20–22.

The Athanasian Creed follows the Western Augustinian pattern of describing the Spirit as proceeding from the Father *and the Son*. This also expressed itself in the Western church's addition of this phrase to the text of the Nicene-Constantinopolitan Creed. This resulted in the so-called *filioque* (Latin for "and the Son") controversy.

19. The term "economic" here translates—and also transliterates—a Greek word that appears in this sense, for example, in Eph. 1:10 and 3:9. In these cases, the RSV translates it as "plan."

20. See this chap., under "God's Presence in the World."

21. Basil the Great, *On the Holy Spirit*, xvi. 38, NPNF 2d series, 8, 23b. [This translation is from *Basil the Great, Archbishop of Caesarea in Cappadocia, on the Holy Spirit*, trans. and ed. George Lewis, new rev. ed. (Picadilly: Religious Tract Society, n.d.), 77.—Trans.].

22. See this chap., under "The Trinitarian Development of the Basic Decision of the Early Church."

23. "The Anathemas of the Second Council of Constantinople (Fifth Ecumenical)," in *Christology of the Later Fathers*, ed. E. R. Hardy, LCC 3 (Philadelphia: Westminster Press, 1954), 378–81.

24. SC, II:4, in BC, 345.

25. See this chap., under "God's Presence in the World."

26. *LBW*, 54; BC, 20, 27. [Quotations from the Athanasian Creed are ordinarily from the current ecumenical liturgical text. A reference to the translation in BC is also provided.—Trans.]

27. *LBW*, 54–55; BC, 20, 28–35.

28. Denzinger, 301–2; *TOC*, 153–54, 252.

29. *Bekenntnisschriften*, 29–30, 29–34. The liturgical text quoted above does the same. The translation in BC is based on the Latin text and translates *substantia* as "substance."

30. *TOC*, 424, 829–30.

31. *LBW*, 64; BC, 18–19.

32. *LBW*, 54; BC, 20, 35.

33. Second Letter to Nestorius, Denzinger, 246; *TOC*, 150, 246. *Cyril of Alexandria: Select Letters*, ed. and trans. Lionel R. Wickham (Oxford: Clarendon Press, 1983), 2–11. See also xxv–xli. This position was approved by the Council of Ephesus in 431.

34. Denzinger, 421; *TOC*, 154, 302.

35. Denzinger, 294; *TOC*, 153, 251; The full text of Leo's *Tome* is in *Christology of the Later Fathers*, LCC 3:360–70.

36. Denzinger, 556–57; *TOC*, 169–70, 295–96; *Christology of the Later Fathers*, LCC 3:383–85.

37. For example, see Luther's hymn, "Dear Christians, Let Us Now Rejoice," in *LW* 53:219–20. Verses 5 and 6 describe the work of salvation.

38. See chap. 7, under "Christ as the Righteousness of Faith." Whatever weaknesses there may be in Article III of the FC, they are not caused by its Christology.

39. FC, SD, III:55, in BC, 549.

CHAPTER 4

1. SA, I, in BC, 292.

2. *Bekenntnisschriften*, 415n.

3. See chap. 2, under "Freedom: We Are Responsible for Accepting or Rejecting God's Grace."

4. Denzinger, 806; *TOC*, 99, 156. The quotation is from the Fourth Lateran Council's condemnation of the errors of Joachim of Flora.

5. See chap. 7, under "Anthropological Definition."

6. See chap. 7, under "Decisions About the Savior and Salvation."

7. See chap. 3, under "The Hellenistic Concept of the Logos as a Handicap for Theological Reflection."

8. AC, V:1–2, in BC, 31 (German).

9. LC, II, III:36, in BC, 415.

10. LC, II, III:37, in BC, 415.

11. AC, 1:5–6, in BC, 28 (German).

12. AC, IV:1, in BC, 30.

13. SA, III, VIII:5–6, in BC, 312.

14. See chap. 5, under "Word and Sacrament."

15. AC, III:4–5, in BC, 30 (German).

16. *Loci Communes Theologici*, trans. Lowell J. Satre, in *Melanchthon and Bucer*, ed. Wilhelm Pauck, LCC 19 (Philadelphia: Westminster Press, 1969), 21–22.

17. AC, XX:9–10, in BC, 42 (German).

18. [For the most recent critical edition of the Roman Confutation, see Herbert Immenkötter, ed., *Die Confutatio der Confessio Augustana vom 3. August 1530*, Corpus Catholicorum, vol. 33 (Münster/Westfalen: Aschendorff, 1979). Immenkötter has translated the Roman Confutation into modern German: *Der Reichstag zu Augsburg und die Confutatio. Historische Einführung und neuhochdeutsche Übertragung*. (Münster/Westfalen: Aschendorff, 1979). A complete English translation of a text that

is now somewhat in need of re-editing is available: "Confutatio Pontificia, August 3, 1530," in Reu, *Sources*, *348–*83. See also Jacobs, *Historical Introduction*, 209–41. The above quotation is from Reu, *Sources*, *359.—Trans.]

19. See chap. 7, under "Christ as the Righteousness of Faith."

20. See Mildenberger, *Grundwissen der Dogmatik*, 103–11.

21. SC, II:2, in BC, 345.

22. The most important statements have been collected in the report, *Gesetz und Evangelium, Beiträge zur gegenwärtigen theologischen Diskussion*, ed. Ernst Kinder und Klaus Haendler, Wege der Forschung 142 (Darmstadt: Wissenschaftliche Buchgesellschaft, 1968).

23. Ap., IV:8, in BC, 108.

24. SC, I:2, in BC, 342.

25. This is the summary statement to Section 46, in Friedrich Schleiermacher, *The Christian Faith*, ed. H. R. Mackintosh and J. S. Stewart (Philadelphia: Fortress Press, 1976), 170.

26. Ap., IV:9, in BC, 108.

27. See the discussion in chap. 2, under "The Time and Place of Faith."

28. Ap., IV:9, in BC, 108.

29. Ap., IV:37, in BC, 112.

30. Ap., IV:38, in BC, 112.

31. AC, XX:24, in BC, 44 (German).

32. AC, V:2, in BC, 31 (Latin).

33. Ap., IV:167, in BC, 130.

34. *The Disputation Concerning Man* (1536), Thesis 32, LW 34:139.

35. *The Disputation Concerning Man*, Thesis 35, LW 34:139. The Latin is: "Quare homo huius vitae est pura materia Dei ad futurae formae suae vitam," WA 39^1:177.

36. Denzinger, 1510–16; *TOC*, 137–40, 220–26.

37. Kidd, *Documents*, 75–79.

38. *LW* 31:48. Denzinger, 1486; *TOC*, 382, 708.

39. Denzinger, 1555; *TOC*, 398, 742.

40. AC, II:1, in BC, 29 (Latin). The Latin term for original sin was *peccatum originis*. It was translated into German as *Erb-* or *Ursünde*, literally "inherited" or "primal" sin.

41. AC, II:2, in BC, 29 (Latin).

42. BC, 100 n. 2; Reu, *Sources*, *349–*50.

43. Ap., II:3, in BC, 101.

44. Ibid.

45. AC, XVIII, in BC, 39–40.

46. Reu, *Sources*, *328. Reu provides a translation of part of this "First Draft of the Confutation, July 8, 1530," *Sources*, *326–*43. See also n. 18 above.

47. Johannes Ficker, *Die Konfutation des Augsburgischen Bekenntnisses. Ihre erste Gestalt und ihre Geschichte* (Leipzig, 1891), 61. The last sentence of the quotation seems to be a summary of the rest of Melanchthon's paragraph. See *Loci Communes Theologici*, in LCC 19:24.

48. *Cl* 3:127; *WA* 18:636; *LW* 3:68.

49. *Loci Communes Theologici*, in LCC 19:30.

50. However, see chap. 5, under "The Holiness of Secular Life."

51. For a more extended discussion, see chap. 7, under "The Experience of the Self and the Theological Interpretation of the Freedom of the Will."

52. *LW* 33.

53. Ap., XVIII:9, in BC, 226.

54. See the Council of Trent's interpretation of Rom. 3:22: "We are therefore said

to be justified by faith because faith is the beginning of human salvation." Denzinger, 1532; *TOC,* 389, 722.

55. Ap., IV:144, in BC, 127.
56. Denzinger, 1578; *TOC,* 401, 765.
57. See chap. 2, under "The Time and Place of Faith."
58. Ap., IV:48, in BC, 114.
59. For example, Ap., IV:142, in BC, 126.
60. Ap., IV:56, in BC, 114.
61. Ap., IV:228, in BC, 139.
62. Ap., IV:308, in BC, 114.
63. Ap., IV:86, in BC, 119.
64. Ap., IV:67, in BC, 116.
65. AC, VI:1, in BC, 31–32.
66. *Bekenntnisschriften,* 60. Reu, *Sources,* *42, *46.
67. AC, XX:28–29, in BC, 45 (Latin).
68. AC, XX:36–37, in BC, 46 (German).
69. See AC, VI.
70. AC, VI:1, in BC, 31–32.
71. AC, XX:3, in BC, 41 (German).
72. See the extensive discussion of this factor in chap. 5, under "The Holiness of Secular Life."
73. See, for example, LC, I:145–49, in BC, 385.
74. Ap., IV:170–71, in BC, 130.

CHAPTER 5

1. See chap. 1, under "The Augsburg Confession as the Evangelical-Lutheran Symbolic Creed."
2. Reu, *Sources,* *40–*47.
3. AC, Conclusion to Part I (following Article XX), 2, in BC, 47.
4. See chap. 4, under "The Gospel of Jèsus Christ," and n. 18.
5. BC, 286–318.
6. BC, 320–35.
7. See chap. 6, "The Development and the Nature of the Smalcald Articles."
8. SA, II, II, 10, in BC, 295.
9. See chap. 6, under "The Smalcald Articles."
10. [This usage survives in the English term "Evangelical-Lutheran."–Trans.]
11. [In the Federal Republic of Germany, a fixed percentage of the income tax is assessed and collected by the government's tax office and forwarded to the church. Exemption from this "church tax" is gained by filing a declaration abrogating church membership.–Trans.]
12. *Cl* 1:7; *WA* 1:23; *LW* 31:31.
13. Denzinger, 1753; *TOC,* 300, 523.
14. AC, XXIV:12–13, in BC, 57 (German).
15. AC, XXIV:21, in BC, 58.
16. Reu, *Sources,* *370.
17. AC, XXIV:22, in BC, 58 (Latin text).
18. See AC, XXIV:23, in BC, 58.
19. *The Documents of Vatican II,* ed. Walter M. Abbott, trans. Joseph Gallagher (New York: Guild Press, 1966), 137–78.
20. Quoted in this chap., under "The Gospel in Word and Sacrament," Denzinger, 1753; *TOC,* 300, 523.

21. AC, XXIV:5, in BC, 60.

22. Reu, *Sources,* *373.

23. Ap., XIII:5, in BC, 209–10.

24. AC, XIII:1, in BC, 35 (Latin).

25. AC, XIII:3, in BC, 36 (Latin).

26. See Paul C. Empie and James I. McCord, eds., Marburg Revisited: A Reexamination of Lutheran and Reformed Tradition (Minneapolis: Augsburg Publishing House, 1966), 39–104.

27. [The German term is *Busse,* the Latin *poenitentia.* The technical term for the Roman Catholic sacrament is "penance." *BC* differentiates the Lutheran rite by calling it "the sacrament of penitence." I shall therefore refer to its Lutheran form in the same way.—Trans.]

28. Ap., XIII:4, in BC, 211.

29. AC, XXV:1, in BC, 61 (Latin).

30. AC, XXV:8–9, in BC, 62–63 (German).

31. See Ernst Bezzel, "Die Privatbeichte in der lutherischen Orthodoxie. Eine pastoraltheologische Untersuchung" (Dissertation, Theological Faculty, University of Erlangen, 1975).

32. *LW* 31:25.

33. See the central section of the discussion of penitence, Ap., XII:28–43, in BC, 185–87.

34. Ap., XII:29, in BC, 185.

35. Ap., XII:36, in BC, 186.

36. Ibid.

37. Ap., XII:42, in BC, 187.

38. Ap., XIII:11, in BC, 212.

39. See in this chap., under "The Office of the Ministry."

40. Werner Elert, *Der christliche Glaube. Grundlinien der lutherischen Dogmatik,* 3d ed. (Hamburg: Furche, 1956), 452.

41. See in this chap., under "The Gospel in Word and Sacrament."

42. AC, IX:3, in BC, 33.

43. See in this chap., under "Word and Sacrament."

44. Ap., IX:2, in BC, 178.

45. LC, IV:56, in BC, 443–44.

46. Paul Althaus, *Die christliche Wahrheit. Lehrbuch der Dogmatik,* 8th ed. (Gütersloh: Bertelsmann, 1969), 555–56.

47. AC, XXVI:2–3, in BC, 62 (German).

48. AC, XXVI:10, in BC, 65 (German).

49. Johannes Ficker, *Die Konfutation des Augsburgischen Bekenntnisses. Ihre erste Gestalt und ihre Geschichte* (Leipzig, 1891), 111. See also Immenkötter, *Die Confutatio der Confessio Augustana,* 180; Reu, *Souces,* *376.

50. Imemenkötter, *Die Confutatio der Confessio Augustana,* 178–80; Reu, *Sources,* *375.

51. AC, XXVI:15, in BC, 66 (German text).

52. AC, XXVI:29, in BC, 68 (German text).

53. AC, XXVI:31–32, in BC, 68 (German text). See in this chap., under "The Active Life," for a discussion of some questions related to the intentionality and actual shape of the Christian life.

54. AC, XXVI:33–38, in BC, 69.

55. For a discussion of prayer and Bible reading, see in this chap., under "The Holiness of Secular Life."

56. AC, XXVIII:12–13, in BC, 83 (German).
57. See AC, XXVIII:19–20, in BC, 83–84.
58. AC, XXVIII:29, in BC, 85 (German).
59. See Wilhelm Maurer, *Historical Commentary on the Augsburg Confession,* trans. H. G. Anderson (Philadelphia: Fortress Press, 1986), part I, chap. 9.
60. BC, 320–35.
61. AC, XIV, in BC, 36 (German).
62. *To the Christian Nobility of the German Nation Concerning the Reform of the Christian Estate,* in *LW* 44:127.
63. See Tr., 61, in BC, 330.
64. AC, XXVIII:20–21, in BC, 84 (German).
65. AC, XXVIII:22, in BC, 84 (German).
66. AC, XXVIII:23, in BC, 84 (Latin).
67. Ap. XXVIII:18–19, in BC, 284.
68. Tr., 66–67, in BC, 331.
69. Tr., 79–82, in BC, 333–34.
70. Tr., 54, in BC, 329. The original context of this quote is not a discussion of the reorganization of the church but rather of the defense of the church against papal tyranny.
71. Tr., 54, in BC, 329.
72. The National Socialist Government of Adolf Hitler tried to assume control of the churches and to use them in support of its political philosophy and its political goals. This political philosophy contained explicit religious presuppositions. This government—more explicitly than many others—described itself in messianic and millenial terms. The struggle of the churches to retain their independence and integrity and to work more effectively to oppose and change the government's policies is called the *Kirchenkampf.* One of the great difficulties in organizing the church for action was the general assumption among Protestants that the government historically had and would continue to influence strongly the teaching and life of the church. See chap. 8.
73. Some of these topics have been briefly described in chap. 4, under "The Active Life," and in this chap., under "The Church's Rules of Religious Life."
74. AC, XXIII:26, in BC, 55–56 (German).
75. AC, XXVII:11, in BC, 72 (German).
76. *Documents of Vatican II,* chap. 6, 75.
77. AC, XXVII:49, in BC, 78–79 (German).
78. Immenkötter, *Die Confutatio der Confessio Augustana,* 194; Reu, *Sources,* *380.
79. Ap., XXVII:37, in BC, 275.
80. Immenkötter, *Die Confutatio der Confessio Augustant,* 190; Reu, *Sources,* *378–*79.
81. Ap., XXVII:41–42, in BC, 276.
82. AC, XXVII:19, in BC, 74 (Latin).
83. AC, XXVII:59, in BC, 80 (Latin).
84. Ap., XV:25, in BC, 219.
85. AC, XXVII:51–55, in BC, 79 (German).
86. AC, XXVII:49–50, in BC, 78–79 (German).
87. AC, XVI:7, in BC, 38 (German).
88. AC, XVI:4–5, in BC, 37–38 (Latin).
89. AC XVI:4–5, in BC, 38 (German).
90. Ap., XVI:6, in BC, 223.
91. See chap. 9, under "The Doctrine of the Kingdom Is Not a Guide for Action."

92. AC, XVI:5, in BC, 38 (German).

93. See Luther's explanation of the First Commandment in the LC, I:26–27, in BC, 368.

94. Ap., XVI:13, in BC, 224.

95. See in this chap., under "Divine Guidance in Worldly Life."

96. See in this chap., under "The Church's Rules of Religious Life."

97. Ap., XV:45, in BC, 221.

CHAPTER 6

1. See chap. 5, under "An Introductory Note on the Interpretation of the Augsburg Confession."

2. Jacobs, *Historical Introduction,* 2:254–60. See chap. 1, under "The Religious-Political Significance of the Augsburg Confession."

3. SA, Preface of Dr. Martin Luther, in BC, 288–91.

4. SA, Preface of Dr. Martin Luther, 15, in BC, 291.

5. SA, II, IV:16, in BC, 301.

6. SA, II, II:10, in BC, 294.

7. SA, III, XV:3, in BC, 316.

8. SA, I, in BC, 291.

9. SA, II, in BC, 292.

10. See chap. 2, under "The Doctrine by Which the Church Stands and Falls."

11. SA, III, Signatories, in BC, 316.

12. SA, III, in BC, 302.

13. SA, III, III:10–45, in BC, 304–10.

14. SA, III, VIII:3–13, in BC, 312–13.

15. SA, III, XIV, and XV, in BC, 315–16.

16. SA, III, XV:4–5, in BC, 316.

17. *Bekenntnisschriften,* 415.

18. SA, II, in BC, 292.

19. See chap. 2, under "God's Grace and Human Freedom—the Roman Catholic Doctrinal Form."

20. SA, II, II:1, in BC, 293.

21. See chap. 5, under "The Reform of the Mass."

22. SA, II, II:11, in BC, 294.

23. Brotherhoods were fraternal societies organized to finance the celebration of masses for their deceased members. See chap. 5, under "The Reform of the Mass."

24. SA, II, II:24, in BC, 296.

25. SA, II, III:2, in BC, 298.

26. SA, III, XIV:1, in BC, 315–16.

27. SA, II, III:2, in BC, 298.

28. SA, II, IV:1, in BC, 298.

29. SA, II, IV:3, in BC, 298.

30. SA, II, IV:14, in BC, 301.

31. SA, II, IV:9, in BC, 300.

32. SA, III, VIII:3–6, in BC, 312–13.

33. SA, III, XV:3, in BC, 316.

34. SA, III, in BC, 302.

35. FC, SD, 8, in BC, 505.

36. SC, Pref., 2–6, in BC, 338.

37. LC, Shorter Pref., 18, in BC, 363.

38. FC, Ep. Comp. Sum., 5, in BC, 465.
39. LC, Martin Luther's Pref., 7, in BC, 359.
40. SC, Pref., 7, in BC, 338–39.
41. LC, Shorter Pref., 26, in BC, 364.
42. SC, Pref., 141–16, in BC, 339–40.
43. SC, Pref., 17, in BC, 340.
44. LC, I:2, in BC, 365.
45. Ludwig Feuerbach, *The Essence of Faith According to Luther,* trans. Martin Cherno (New York: Harper & Row, 1967).
46. LC, I:4, in BC, 365.
47. LC, I:5, in BC, 365.
48. LC, I:10, in BC, 366.
49. LC, I:18, in BC, 367.
50. LC, I:22–23, in BC, 367.
51. See chap. 4, under "The Active Life."
52. LC, I:21, in BC, 367.
53. LC, I:13–14, in BC, 366.
54. LC, I:42, in BC, 370.
55. LC, I:91, in BC, 377.
56. LC, I:99, in BC, 378.
57. LC, I:101, in BC, 379.
58. LC, I:105–6, in BC, 379.
59. LC, I:108, in BC, 379.
60. LC, I:141, in BC, 384.
61. LC, I:158, in BC, 387.
62. See chap. 5, under "Divine Guidance in Worldly Life."
63. LC, I:155–56, in BC, 386.
64. LC, I:165, in BC, 387.
65. LC, I:310, in BC, 407.
66. LC, I:313, in BC, 407.
67. LC, I:329, in BC, 410.
68. An earlier discussion of the doctrines of the Creed in the Lutheran confessional writings was based on Melanchthon's Apology of the Augsburg Confession. It did not follow the order of the Creed but rather began with the doctrine of the Spirit. See chap. 4, under "The Triune God Acts to Save Human Beings."
69. LC, II:63–65, in BC, 419. Luther has stated this even more clearly than in the LC in the summary of his Trinitarian faith at the end of *Confession Concerning Christ's Supper* (1528), *LW* 37:365–66.
70. LC, II:7, in BC, 411.
71. See chap. 4, under "The Granting of Salvation as the Work of the Holy Spirit."
72. LC, II:64, in BC, 419.
73. LC, II:67, in BC, 419.
74. LC, II:69, in BC, 420.
75. LC, III:1–21, in BC, 420–23.
76. LC, III:22, in BC, 423.
77. LC, III:68, in BC, 429.
78. LC, III:47, in BC, 426.
79. LC, III:53, in BC, 427.
80. LC, III:65, in BC, 429.
81. LC, III:90, in BC, 432.
82. LC, III:96, in BC, 433.

NOTES

83. LC, III:107, in BC, 434.
84. LC, III:108, in BC, 434–35.
85. LC, III:113, in BC, 435.

CHAPTER 7

1. See chap. 1, under "The Historical Necessity of the Development of a Lutheran Confessional Church."
2. See FC, Ep. Comp. Sum., 1, 7. in BC, 464–65.
3. See chap. 4, under "We Are Dependent on God's Work to Be Really Human."
4. FC, Ep., I:8, and SD, I:1, in BC, 467, 508. The opening line of the hymn is "Through Adam's fall, man's nature and essense are all corrupt" ("Durch Adams Fall ist ganz verderbt menschlich Natur und Wesen"). A free translation "All Mankind Fell in Adam's Fall" appeared in *The Lutheran Hymnal* (St. Louis: Concordia Publishing House, 1941), nr. 369.
5. FC, SD, I:3–4, in BC, 510. The Pelagians were named after Pelagius, who died in 418—although their position was widely held in the early church before this time. They asserted that, even after the Fall into sin, the human person had full freedom of the will to turn to God.
6. The Manichaeans were a Gnostic group that had been known since the third century. They held a dualistic view of human being and asserted that only part of the human person could be saved.
7. FC, SD, I:33, in BC, 514.
8. FC, SD, I:51–52, in BC, 517.
9. FC, SD, I:57, in BC, 518.
10. FC, SD, I:60, in BC, 519.
11. FC, SD, I:61, in BC, 519.
12. Emil Brunner and Karl Barth, *Natural Theology; Comprising Nature and Grace by Emil Brunner and the Reply No! by Karl Barth,* trans. Peter Fraenkel (London: Geoffrey Bles, 1946).
13. Ibid., 31.
14. Ibid., 200.
15. Philip Melanchthon, *Melanchthons Werke in Auswahl,* ed. Robert Stupperich (Gütersloh: Bertelsmann, 1952), II, 1, p. 243. [It is instructive to compare this clear statement of synergism with the still-restrained hints of this position in the 1955 edition of the *Loci,* which is available in an English translation. See Manschreck, trans. and ed., *Melanchthon on Christian Doctrine,* 56–60.—Trans.]
16. See chap. 4, under "God the Creator."
17. FC, SD, II:3, in BC, 520.
18. FC, SD, II:7, in BC, 521.
19. FC, Ep., II:1, in BC, 469; compare FC, SD, II:2, in BC, 520.
20. See in this chap., under "Christ as the Righteousness of Faith."
21. FC, SD, II:46–47, in BC, 530.
22. FC, SD, II:53, in BC, 531.
23. As the FC attempted to do; see SD, II:76, in BC, 536.
24. FC, SD, II:56, in BC, 532.
25. See in this chap., under "Freedom in Church Order."
26. FC, SD, III:2–4, in BC, 539–40.
27. FC, SD, III:15, in BC, 541.
28. FC, SD, III:32, in BC, 544–45.
29. Ap., IV:161, in BC, 129.
30. FC, SD, III:32, in BC, 545.

NOTES

31. See in this chap., under "The Experience of the Self and the Theological Interpretation of the Freedom of the Will."

32. FC, SD, III:41, in BC, 546.

33. FC, SD, III:57, in BC, 549.

34. AC, XX:27, in BC, 45.

35. FC, SD, IV:4, in BC, 551.

36. The Latin for "free will" is *liberum arbitrium*. Since the issue at this point in the FC was the good works of the regenerate, we need to think in terms of *liberatum arbitrium*, that is, as above, "liberated" or "freed will."

37. FC, SD, IV:16, in BC, 554.

38. LC, I:26, in BC, 368.

39. FC, Ep., IV:18, in BC, 477.

40. FC, SD, V:12, in BC, 560.

41. See the discussion of Luther's explanation of the First Commandment in chap. 6 under "The Interpretation of the Decalogue."

42. FC, SD, V:1, in BC, 558.

43. FC, SD, V:10, in BC, 559-60.

44. FC, SD, V:11, in BC, 560.

45. FC, SD, V:17, in BC, 561.

46. Ibid.

47. FC, SD, V:21, in BC, 561-62.

48. [Older translations of the Book of Concord translated *usus* as "use. BC introduced the translation of "function" as a better translation for this time. Thus Article VI is titled "The Third Function of the Law." The translation in terms of the "third use" survives in the titles at the head of each page in this article.—Trans.]

49. FC, SD, VI:3, in BC, 564.

50. FC, SD, VI:24, in BC, 568.

51. FC, Ep., VI:7, in BC, 481.

52. FC, Ep., VII:3-4, in BC, 482.

53. For a translation, see Jacobs, *Historical Introduction,* 2:253-60.

54. FC, SD, VII:12-16, in BC, 571-72.

55. FC, SD, VII:18, in BC, 572.

56. FC, SD, VII:19, in BC, 572. See SA, III, VI:1, in BC, 311.

57. FC, SD, VII:41, in BC, 576.

58. Ibid.

59. John Calvin, *Institutes of the Christian Religion,* IV, XII:5, ed. John T. McNeill, LCC 21:1364.

60. FC, SD, VII:61, in BC, 580-81.

61. FC, SD, VII:63, in BC, 581.

62. FC, SD, VV:64-65, in BC, 581.

63. *Confession Concerning Christ's Supper, LW,* 37:161-372.

64. Ap., XXIV:72, in BC, 262.

65. Ap., X:4, in BC, 179-80.

66. FC, SD, VII:18, in BC, 572.

67. FC, Ep., VII:16-17, in BC, 483-84.

68. *The Heidelberg Catechism with Commentary,* trans. Allen O. Miller and M. Eugene Osterhaven (Philadelphia: United Church Press, 1962), 91.

69. See in this chap., under "The Doctrine of the Lord's Supper."

70. FC, SD, VIII:92, in BC, 609.

71. FC, SD, VIII:87, in BC, 608.

72. FS, Ep., VIII:16, in BC, 489.

73. FC, SD, VIII:44-52, in BC, 599-600.

74. FC, SD, VIII:46–47, in BC, 600.
75. See chap. 3, "The One Lord Jesus Christ."
76. FC, SD, VIII:49–52, in BC, 600–601.
77. FC, SD, VIII:26, in BC, 596.
78. FC, SD, XI:6, in BC, 617.
79. FC, SD, XI:8, in BC, 617.
80. FC, SD, XI:12, 91, in BC, 618, 631–32.
81. FC, SD, XI:29, in BC, 621.
82. FC, SD, XI:35, in BC, 622.
83. FC, SD, XI:37, in BC, 622.
84. FC, SD, XI:40–41, in BC, 623.
85. FC, SD, XI:43–50, in BC, 623–24.
86. FC, SD, XI:89–90, in BC, 631.
87. FC, SD, XI:12 (cf. 91), in BC, 618. (cf. 631–32).
88. "Quando ipsa electio nisi reprobatione opposita non staret," in *Institutes* III, XXIII:1, LCC 21:947.
89. See chap. 2, under "The Doctrine by Which the Church Stands and Falls," and chap. 4, under "The Theocentric Understanding of Our Relationship to God as the Point of Departure for Interpretation."
90. See chap. 5, under "The Freedom to Believe as the Basic Characteristic of the Church."
91. See chap. 5, under "The Office of the Ministry."
92. The Latin text is found in Kidd, *Documents,* 359–62; see also Joachim Mehlhausen, ed., *Das Augsburger Interim von 1548* (Neukirchen-Vluyn: Neukirchener Verlag, 1970).
93. "The Leipzig Interim," in Jacobs, *Historical Introduction,* 2:260–72.
94. FC, SD, X:5, in BC, 611.
95. FC, SD, X:10, in BC, 612.
96. Kidd, *Documents,* 363–64.

CHAPTER 8

1. See chap. 1, under "The Lutheran Confessional Writings as a *Corpus Doctrinae.*"
2. *Evangelisch-Katholischer Kommentar zum Neuen Testament,* ed. Josef Blank, Rudolf Schnackenburger, Eduard Schweizer, and Ulrich Wilckens (Neukirchen-Vluyn: Neukirchener; Zurich: Benzinger, 1970-).
3. See chap. 9, under "'Biblical Theology' as Symptomatic for the Problem of Scholarly Interpretation of the Bible."
4. See Arthur C. Cochrane, *The Church's Confession under Hitler* (Philadelphia: Westminster Press, 1962); Ernst Christian Helmreich, *The German Churches under Hitler* (Detroit: Wayne State University Press, 1979).
5. [The documents adopted by the Barmen Synod are in Cochrane, *The Church's Confession under Hitler,* 237–47. The Theological Declaration in on 238–42. Another translation of the Theological Declaration is frequently quoted and is reprinted in John H. Leith, ed., *Creeds of the Churches: A Reader in Christian Doctrine from the Bible to the Present* (Garden City, N.Y.: Doubleday Anchor Books, 1963), 518–22.—Trans.]
6. In addition to the reference in Leith, see Jack Rogers *Presbyterian Creeds: A Guide to the Book of Confessions* (Philadelphia: Westminster Press, 1985). The Barmen Declaration has been received by The United Presbyterian Church U.S.A. and by the United Church of Christ.
7. [Jürgen Roloff, "The Questions to the Church Are Getting Louder—On the For-

mation of the 'Confessional Movement: No Other Gospel,'" *Lutheran World* 13, no. 3 (1966): 319–22.—Trans.]

8. See chap. 9, under "The Favorable Odds Resulting from Agreeing that the Gospel Heard in Scripture Will Be Interpreted as Filtered Through the Church's Confession."

9. See chap. 7, under "Freedom in Church Order."

10. This name was chosen because the churches to be united were Evangelical Lutheran and Evangelical Reformed.

11. Friedrich Wilhelm III, "Allerhöchste Königliche Cabinets Order die Vereinigung der lutherischen and reformierten Kirche, vom 27 sten September 1817," in Walter Geppert, *Das Wesen der preussischen Union: Eine kirchengeschichtliche und konfessionskundliche Untersuchung* (Breslau: Diesdorf, 1939), 463–64. Quoted by Robert C. Schultz, "The European Background," in *Moving Frontiers: Readings in the History of the Lutheran Church—Missouri Synod*, ed. Carl S. Meyer (St. Louis: Concordia Publishing House, 1964), 58b–59a.

12. Gottfried Thomasius, *Das Wiedererwachen des evangelischen Lebens in der lutherischen Kirche Bayerns: ein Stück süddeutscher Kirchengeschichte (1800–1840)* (Erlangen: Andreas Deichert, 1867), 244–45. Quoted by Schultz, *Moving Frontiers*, 72. Italics are in the original German text.

13. *Bekenntnisschriften*, I.

14. Kurt Dietrich Schmidt, *Die Bekenntnisse und grundsätzlichen Aüsserungen zur Kirchenfrage des Jahres 1933;* vol. 2: *Das Jahr 1934;* vol. 3: *Das Jahr 1935* (Göttingen: Vandenhoeck & Ruprecht, 1934–36).

15. *Das Bekenntnis der Väter und die bekennende Gemeinde* (Munich: Chr. Kaiser, 1934). Reprinted in Schmidt, *Die Bekenntnisse und grundsätzlichen Äusserungen des Jahres 1933*, 105–31.

16. See Eberhard Bethge, *Dietrich Bonhoeffer: Theologian—Christian—Contemporary*, ed. Edwin Robertson (London: William Collins Sons, 1970), 231–34.

17. "The Constitution of the German Evangelical Church, July 14, 1933," in Cochrane. *The Church's Confession under Hitler*, 224–28. The quotations are on 224.

18. "The Guiding Principles of the Faith Movement of the 'German Christians,' June 6, 1932," in Cochrane, *The Church's Confession under Hitler*, 222.

19. Cochrane, *The Church's Confession under Hitler*, 238–39.

20. Ibid., 252–53. The text of the entire address appears on 248–63.

21. Dietrich Bonhoeffer, *Zur Frage der Kirchengemeinschaft*, in *Gesammelte Schriften*, ed. Eberhard Bethge, 4 vols. (Munich: Chr. Kaiser, 1958–61), 2:238–39. See Ebernhard Bethge, *Dietrich Bonhoeffer*, 430–40.

22. "Leuenberg Agreement," (2), in *Lutheran World*, 20, no. 4 (1973): 349b. The numbers in parentheses refer to the numbered paragraphs of the agreement.

23. "Leuenberg Agreement," (5), in *Lutheran World*, 350a.

24. "Leuenberg Agreement," in *Lutheran World*, 350a–52a.

25. "Leuenberg Agreement," (13), in *Lutheran World*, 351a.

26. "Leuenberg Agreement," (27), in *Lutheran World*, 352a.

27. "Leuenberg Agreement," (29), in *Lutheran World*, 352a.

28. "Leuenberg Agreement," (33), in *Lutheran World*, 352a.

29. For a detailed analysis, see Ernst Wolf, *Barmen. Kirche zwischen Versuchung und Gnade*, 3d ed. (Munich: Chr. Kaiser, 1934); also, Friedrich Mildenberger, *Geschichte der deutschen evangelischen Theologie im 19. und 20. Jahrhundert* (Stuttgart: Kohlhammer, 1981).

30. Karl Barth, *The Doctrine of God*, trans T. H. L. Parker et al., vol. II, 1 of *Church Dogmatics*, ed. G. W. Bromiley and T. F. Torrance (Edinburgh: T & T Clark, 1957), 177.

31. Cochrane, *The Church's Confession under Hitler*, 239.
32. Ibid., 254–55.
33. Barth, *Doctrine of God*, 174-75.
34. Cochrane, *The Church's Confession under Hitler*, 255.
35. See Mildenberger, *Geschichte der deutschen evangelischen Theologie*, 155–58, 217–22.
36. Cochrane, *The Church's Confession under Hitler*, 242.
37. Ibid., 239.
38. Ibid., 241.
39. Ibid., 242.
40. See the introductory paragraphs to this chapter. It is not my intention to come to terms personally with this movement through this discussion.
41. See Jan J. van Capelleveen, "Germany: Theses and Protests," *Christianity Today* 9, no. 6 (December 22, 1967): 315–16, for a summary of this statement.
42. See chap. 3, under "The Implications of the Doctrine of the Trinity for Christology."
43. See chap. 7, under "Christology."

CHAPTER 9

1. See the introductory paragraphs to chap. 8. [The terms translated as "science" and "scientific" in this chapter are *Wissenschaft* and *wissenschaftlich*. These terms could also be translated as "scholarship" and "scholarly." This choice was made because of the emphasis on "scientific objectivity" in the discussion of the historical-critical method. The translations chosen, however, carry more associations with the natural sciences in English than they do in German. The reader may find it helpful to keep this in mind. —Trans.]
2. FC, Ep. Comp. Sum., 1, in BC, 464.
3. This is the response of Georg Strecker, " 'Biblische Theologie?', Kritische Bemerkungen zu den Entwürfen von Hartmut Gese und Peter Stuhlmacher," in *Kirche: Festschrift Günther Bornkamm zum 75. Geburtstag*, ed. Dieter Lührmann and George Strecker (Tübingen: J. C. B. Mohr [Paul Siebeck], 1980), 424–25.
4. Mildenberger, *Grundwissen der Dogmatik*, 50.
5. Wilhelm Wrede, *Über Aufgabe und Methode der sogenannten neutestamentlichen Theologie* (Göttingen: Vandenhoeck & Ruprecht, 1897); reprinted in George Strecker, *Das Problem der Theologie des Neuen Testaments*, in Wege der Forschung 367 (Darmstadt: Wissenschaftliche Buchgesellschaft, 1975), 85.
6. Rudolf Butlmann, *Theology of the New Testament*, trans. Kendrick Grobel, 2 vols. (New York: Charles Scribner's Sons, 1955), 2:251.
7. See chap. 4, under "Faith as God's Own Determination of the Person."
8. AC, I:1, in BC, 27.
9. See chap. 5, under "The Legal Authority of the Church and the State."
10. LC, IV:80–81, in BC, 431.
11. See chap. 5, under "The Confident Life."
12. *Handbuch für Kirchenvorsteher*, Bavarian ed. (Munich: Evangelischer-Lutherischer Landeskirchenrat, 1977), 20–21.
13. Ibid.
14. See ibid., special section. See chap. 8, under "The Church's Obligation to Serve the Gospel."
15. See chap. 2, under "The Time and Place of Faith," and chap. 4, under "God the Creator."

16. *Temporal Authority: To What Extent It Should Be Obeyed* (1523) *LW* 45:96.
17. See chap. 5, under "Divine Guidance in Worldly Life."
18. See chap. 7, under "Freedom in Church Order."
19. *Confession Concerning Christ's Supper, LW* 37:365.
20. Compare Luther's explanation of the First Commandment, LC, I. See chap. 6, under "The Interpretation of the Decalogue."
21. AC, XX:24, in BC, 44.
22. See the discussion of the "cross" in Melanchthon's confessional writings, chap. 5, under "The Confident Life."
23. [This is the heading of I, 4. It was apparently added to the printed text of the confession. Philip Schaff, *Creeds of Christendom,* omits it completely (4th ed. [New York: Harper & Brothers, 1877], III, 237 and 832). John H. Leith, *Creeds of the Churches,* 133, therefore puts the statement in parentheses. The text of the confessional statements reads: "Wherefore when this Word of God is now preached in the church by preachers lawfully called, we believe that the very Word of God is preached and received of the faithful."—Trans.]
24. SA. III, IV, in BC, 310.
25. [See chap. 4, under "The Granting of Salvation as the Work of the Holy Spirit."—Trans.]
26. See chap. 7, under "Christ as the Righteousness of Faith."
27. See chap. 2, under "The Time and Place of Faith," and chap. 4, under "God the Creator."
28. *The First Sermon, March 9, 1522, Invocavit Sunday, LW* 51:70.
29. AC, V:2, in BC, 31 (German).
30. *WA,* 45:24.
31. *LW,* 51:60.
32. *LW,* 33:19–24.